Edward J Weldon

3/III/46

Dunollie
86, Warwick Park
Tunbridge Wells

OLIVER CROMWELL
THE CONSERVATIVE DICTATOR

ACADEMY BOOKS

Uniform
with this volume

OLIVER CROMWELL
An unfinished miniature by Samuel Cooper

OLIVER CROMWELL
THE CONSERVATIVE DICTATOR

by

MAURICE ASHLEY

JONATHAN CAPE
THIRTY BEDFORD SQUARE
LONDON

FIRST PUBLISHED 1937

RE-ISSUED IN
ACADEMY BOOKS
1940

JONATHAN CAPE LTD.   30 BEDFORD SQUARE, LONDON
AND 91 WELLINGTON STREET WEST, TORONTO

PRINTED IN GREAT BRITAIN IN THE CITY OF OXFORD
AT THE ALDEN PRESS
PAPER MADE BY JOHN DICKINSON & CO. LTD.
BOUND BY A. W. BAIN & CO. LTD.

CONTENTS

ILLUSTRATIONS

MAPS

INTRODUCTION

ACCORDING to Benedetto Croce 'all true history is contemporary history', and if there is truth in his saying every generation needs to re-interpret its great historical figures. Until Mr. John Buchan (since created Lord Tweedsmuir) published his biography of Oliver Cromwell in 1934 a modern English interpretation of the Puritan ruler, based on a serious study of the sources, was completely lacking. The important biographies by Gardiner, Firth and Lord Morley were all written at the turn of the century. The present book is written by one of a different generation and entirely different point of view from Lord Tweedsmuir, and is an attempt to explain Cromwell's political and economic ideas through the medium of biography to an age which is perforce only too interested in the thoughts of dictators.

Lord Morley wisely said that 'any such career and character as Cromwell's, like one of the great stock arguments of old-world drama, must still be capable of an almost endless range of presentment and interpretation'. My interpretation of Cromwell as a conservative dictator is illustrated largely from his career as Lord Protector of England, Scotland and Ireland. My method of presentment therefore is to devote proportionately less space than is customary to his career before the execution of Charles I and more to his conduct as actual ruler of the country. I try to show that except in two respects — (1) expedients due to the monetary demands of the army, and (2) his attitude to religious toleration — Cromwell's policy as Protector was both conservative and dictatorial. Can it be mere coincidence that many of Cromwell's previous biographers, from Lord Tweedsmuir backwards to the French statesman Guizot, have been Conservatives?

On the whole I have resisted the temptation to indulge in modern comparisons or analogies. Herr Hitler (or is it Signor

Mussolini?) may keep a picture of Cromwell in his study, but I cannot agree with Professor Oncken, for example, that Cromwell's plan of a Protestant Union against Roman Catholics was an anticipation of Herr Hitler's 'ideological war' against Bolshevism, nor with the late M. Jacques Bainville that the Ironsides were 'Puritan Storm Troopers'. I must also apologize for my inability to paint Cromwell as black, say, as Mr. Belloc or as white as Thomas Carlyle. If my portrait is too grey I must blame it on the influence of history teachers who (unlike Croce) regard history if not as an exact science at least as demanding as impartial an approach to its raw materials as is humanly possible.

In this book I give more attention than is usual to social and economic policy. I have correspondingly reduced Cromwell's military record to a minimum, not because I regard it as unimportant but because I am sceptical of my amateur ability to say anything new about it. My impression is, however, that a good deal yet remains to be done to elucidate the battles of Edgehill and Dunbar, and if I have ventured slightly to differ from recent descriptions of the parts played by Cromwell in those battles I do so only in the hope that the professional military historians will one day discover documents that will finally establish these points. The maps, which have been drawn for me by Mr. B. Cracowski of Manchester, do not claim any great exactitude; their object is simply to illustrate the text.

On the other hand, some of the illustrations are, I believe, entirely new to a biography of Cromwell. I would draw especial attention to a Walker portrait which is one of the earliest known portraits of Oliver Cromwell and was probably painted before the execution of Charles I; to the new version of Walker's portrait of Cromwell wearing armour and a sash, in the possession of Lt.-Colonel P. R. Papillon; to the family group based on miniatures in the possession of the Duke of Buccleuch; and to the Walker portrait at Stockholm which is supposed to have been presented by Cromwell to Queen

Christina of Sweden. To the Duke of Buccleuch, Lt.-Colonel
Papillon, the Grypsholm at Stockholm, the Office of Works,
the British Museum and the Victoria and Albert Museum I
am most grateful for the permission to reproduce photographs.

I cannot pretend to have based my story on any very novel
materials, although it would be rash to assert that in the course
of time new materials bearing directly on Cromwell's career
may not be discovered. Indeed since this book was in the
press, Professor W. C. Abbott has published the first volume
of his monumental new edition of Cromwell's *Writings and
Speeches* (Harvard University Press). His four volumes will
contain altogether a hundred and fifty hitherto unpublished
Cromwellian documents of varying degrees of importance,
but, judging by the first volumes, I doubt whether had I read
them I should have altered my account; I should perhaps have
phrased some details slightly differently but then I note that
on details even Professor Abbott nods occasionally. Historians
cannot rival the accuracy of arithmeticians.

My views of Cromwell's economic policy are based on
original research, the detailed results of which were embodied
in my *Financial and Commercial Policy under the Cromwellian
Protectorate* (Oxford University Press, 1934). I have also
drawn upon the Bordeaux dispatches in the Record Office
as well as the recently published Calendar of the Venetian
ambassadors' and agents' dispatches there for some new
illustrations of Cromwell's activities. The Venetian dispatches
are so admirably edited that perhaps one may hope that
one day a French calendar will further simplify the work
of the historian of this period. A few new letters I have discovered in the British Museum are given in Appendix A and I
have indicated briefly some of my sources in Appendix B at
the end of the book.

MAURICE P. ASHLEY

Manchester
July, 1937

9

OLIVER CROMWELL
The Conservative Dictator

CHAPTER I

THE PURITAN FARMER

§ 1

'CROMWELL rules everything.' So the Imperial ambassador in England reported home in 1533. He was speaking of Sir Thomas Cromwell, later Earl of Essex, sometime merchant, moneylender, and lawyer, and general factotum to the famous Cardinal Wolsey. Three years earlier Wolsey, finally disgraced by an unsuccessful intrigue, had been buried in the 'tyrant's grave' at Leicester, and Cromwell, an ambitious self-made little man, son of a drunken Putney brewer and blacksmith, passed over to the service of King Henry VIII.

Upon Cromwell as the King's Vicar General was imposed the duty of carrying his former patron's work of uniting Church and State to its logical end. Wolsey, that magnificent 'scarlet sin' (as a Tudor playwright called him), by concentrating all the principal lay and ecclesiastical offices in his own hands, had been a living symbol of the union of priestcraft and statecraft. Rid of his greatest Minister and finally married to Anne Boleyn Henry VIII had now assumed the vast powers which his minister had monopolized, but with this difference: that whereas Wolsey had been a consistent supporter of the papacy (for he desired above all things to be Pope himself), Henry could exercise this twofold supremacy only within the framework of his kingdom. I am, he was soon able to boast, Pope and Emperor rolled into one. Thus the English Reformation ran its course, the papal authority was finally repudiated and a new 'constitution' came into being by means of which the sovereign ruled over both Church and State.

This process brought with it the suppression of the English monasteries and nunneries, not only because they were regarded as papal outposts but also because they were store-houses of wealth, and both Wolsey and Henry VIII had extravagant tastes. Thomas Cromwell had been initiated into the gentle art of suppression by his first master, and rendered such good service to his second by his skill and cunning as to win the popular (or unpopular) title of the Hammer of the Monks.

Cromwell himself found an apt pupil in this art in his sister's son Richard Williams. The families of two Putney brewers had intermarried, possibly in the way of business: Thomas Cromwell's sister Katherine had married a Welsh gentleman, Morgan Williams by name, who like her father made his money by brewing and selling beer on the banks of the Thames. Their son soon showed that he had inherited his father's native Welsh wit by adopting his mother's name, dubbing himself 'Cromwell alias Williams' as a delicate compliment to his rich and successful uncle. Sir Thomas Cromwell put Richard on his staff and virtually adopted him. Richard proved himself worthy of the honour and by fighting on the right side, by marrying in the right direction and by helping to suppress the wealthiest religious houses he amassed a fortune.

Richard Cromwell received as a gift or for a nominal payment a fine group of estates in the eastern counties, consisting of Ramsey Abbey, Sawtry Abbey, St. Neot's Priory, Hinchin-brooke Nunnery and a house of the Austin Canons in Hunt-ingdon. He also earned a knighthood from Henry VIII. Unlike his uncle Thomas, however, Sir Richard Cromwell alias Williams died in his bed, leaving his family well provided with worldly goods. It was a family that was to produce a greater and less worldly soldier; for this protégé of Thomas the Hammer was the paternal great-grandfather of Oliver Cromwell, the Lord Protector.

Sir Richard wrote numerous letters to his uncle in the course of their duties as reformers. In one of them, written on October 15th, 1538, he observed: 'Your Lordship, I think, shall shortly perceive the Prior of Ely to be of the froward [obstinate] sort, by evident witness.' He feared that like many others the Prior would refuse to acknowledge the Royal Supremacy over the Church and resist the destruction of his monastery. This Prior of Ely was named Robert Steward, and although we are assured that he was a man of uncommon life who wore and macerated his body, was lavish to the poor and despised riches and honours, he did not prove unduly 'froward' in his ecclesiastical convictions; indeed, he proved most accommodating; for with the persuasion of the Cromwells he ceased to be Catholic Prior of Ely and became instead first Protestant Dean of the Cathedral Church. In the course of his lengthy existence (he died at the age of seventy-five) he amused himself by the compilation of genealogies, including his own. He traced his descent from the same Scottish Stewards who gave Robert Bruce and King James I of England to the world. Modern genealogists have shown themselves sceptical of the Prior of Ely's reliability in this respect and have maintained that he came from the family of Stywards (or Pig-Keepers) of Norfolk. Be that as it may, the paths of the Cromwells and Stewards or Stywards were destined to cross again; for the elder brother of the Prior of Ely was the other great-grand-father of Oliver Cromwell.

§ 2

Elizabeth Steward, great-niece of the pious but amenable Robert Steward, likewise came from Ely and was twice married in the last decade of the sixteenth century. She buried her first husband and their only child in the cathedral, and two years later settled down with her second husband, Robert Cromwell, in the county town of Huntingdon and did her duty by him to the extent of at least ten children. There was nothing very unusual in this union of two respectable and well-to-do but comparatively undistinguished county families. Robert Cromwell was the younger son of Sir Henry, the heir to the enterprising Sir Richard. As such he inherited only a small share of the plunder of the monasteries, consisting of the Huntingdonshire property of the Austin Canons. He and his wife and their rapidly increasing family lived in a house formerly belonging to the Austin Canons, with 'gothic windows and projecting attics' and surrounded by a large garden watered by a tiny stream: it had once been used as a brewhouse and, standing two hundred yards from the market place, was probably among the largest in the town. Robert was a worthy and typical eastern county gentleman who took a prominent part in local affairs and had been a member of one of Queen Elizabeth's Parliaments; and there is no reason to believe that he regarded himself as a poor relation of his elder brother, the heir, who lived with their father half a mile away in the palatial manor of Hinchinbrooke, the ex-nunnery which was the fairest reward of the reforming zeal of their ancestors. As was natural and customary Robert invited his brother, whose name was Oliver, to act as godfather to his second son (his father had acted as godfather to the firstborn) and to give him his own name.

Thus the second son of Robert Cromwell was christened Oliver on April 29th, 1599, four days after he was born.

Oliver seemed chosen by all the laws of heredity to be a Protestant of Protestants. He was born and bred among the spoils of the monasteries, he passed his childhood in an area which had proved itself little resistant to the forces of the Reformation, and perhaps inherited through his mother some of the family earnestness of the apostate Prior of Ely. To the compulsions of heredity were added far stronger influences of environment. Some time after 1604, when Thomas Beard, Bachelor of Divinity, was appointed mainly on account of his Puritan orthodoxy to be Master of St. John's Hospital (or Alms House) at Huntingdon and consequently of the Free School attached to it, young Oliver became a pupil of the latter establishment and there acquired a faith and an outlook from which he never wavered throughout his whole life.

Mr., soon afterwards Doctor, Beard was by no means an obscure country schoolmaster; he was an active Protestant publicist as well as an enthusiastic and highly respected teacher. In 1614 he published a *Full Declaration of the Faith professed in the Dominions of Frederick the Elector Palatine*, in 1616 he wrote 523 pages on *A Retractive for the Romish Religion*, and in 1623 he proved in two treatises that Antichrist was the Pope of Rome and the converse proposition that the Pope of Rome was Antichrist. But his most successful work, his best seller, was *The Theatre of God's Judgments* (1597), originally translated out of the French but augmented by three hundred original examples, and three times reprinted, further improved and embellished. From the frontispiece to this book it has been deduced that in the course of his scholastic duties Doctor Beard made unsparing use both of his Eton Latin Grammar and his rod. Some of Oliver's biographers have asserted that he was frequently birched by the reverend doctor, often at his father's special request. One thing at least is certain, that, if this were so, Oliver bore him no grudge and remained his friend until death.

Part of the Grammar School where Doctor Beard taught is still standing, but the house where Oliver was born and the church which he attended have disappeared completely. In that long Huntingdon High Street where home, school and church once stood and in the flat, cold, grim countryside that surrounds it a lively imagination may envisage the earthly counterpart of the straight and narrow road to the Golden Gate which, as Beard and his fellow Puritans taught, every Christian is bound to follow.

Royalist lampooners, writing after the restoration of Charles II, relate numerous improbable anecdotes about Cromwell's youth. There are, however, only two stories for which there exists anything like independent evidence. The first is that in 1604 when King James I went to meet his second son Charles, who was being brought from Edinburgh to Whitehall, they stopped a night at Hinchinbrooke on the road. Sir Oliver

Cromwell, who had now succeeded his father as Lord of Hinchinbrooke and had been knighted for his hospitality to the King in the previous year, invited his four-year-old nephew and namesake to come over to play with the sickly infant of his sovereign. On this occasion therefore, and at this very early age, Oliver Cromwell and Charles Stuart met for the first time face to face. The other story concerns a contemporary play called *Lingua, or The Conduct of the Senses*. In the 1657 edition of the play it is stated that it was written in 1607 and first performed at Trinity College, Cambridge, and at the Free School at Huntingdon. It is alleged that Cromwell while he was at school acted the part of Tactus or the Sense of Feeling, in which he had to stumble over a royal crown, 'and took it up, and put it on, and 'twas fit and asked if it did not become him'.

On the whole we may picture Oliver as a normal schoolboy. From Doctor Beard he would have learned of the inestimable value of the Bible as a compendium of all knowledge, of the iniquity of the Catholic religion, of how after the bloody reign of Queen Mary her sister Elizabeth had beaten back King Philip of Spain and crushed his 'papist' Armada in the North Sea. At home he would have listened to his father talking of the varying price of crops and of cattle, of the problems and the virtues of country gentlemen, of the extravagance of Uncle Oliver at Hinchinbrooke and of the latest gossip from London. Sir Oliver was a Member of Parliament and his father was an ex-Member, who was naturally intensely interested in the news of what was going on at Westminster now that the old Queen was dead and the House of Commons was beginning to claim a foremost place in the counsels of the nation.

From Huntingdon school the next step was obviously Cambridge. On April 23rd, 1616 (the very day on which William Shakespeare died), Oliver Cromwell was entered at Sidney-Sussex College. The Master of Sidney at this date was Dr. Samuel Ward, an eminent Puritan divine, whose still extant diary gives a remarkable idea of his character. The following observations on Doctor Ward are taken from Mullinger's *History of the University of Cambridge*:

The category of his shortcomings [given in his diary] suggests spiritual pride and a blameless record. If he had incautiously eaten too freely at supper, if he had been conscious of feeling but inadequate compassion for some culprit flogged in the college hall, if he had felt some natural elation at being appointed to lecture in Greek, if his thoughts wandered at prayers, if he had been guilty of ostentation in the presence of strangers, if he had listened with too little interest to the catechism, or had misinterpreted or suspected another's remarks — these and suchlike peccadillos were regularly noted down at the end of the day to be a theme of sad and humiliating reflexion ere he sought the night's repose.

Ward was later appointed Lady Margaret Professor of Divinity and one of the English representatives in the Anglo-Dutch theological conferences at Dort. Cromwell as a Fellow-Commoner of the college must have come into frequent contact with this extremely introspective professor, but his own tutor was Mr. Richard Howlett, described as 'an able man and very fit for government' and 'a moderate man in his tenets, far from Doctor Ward's rigidity and his way'. Possibly the influence of Mr. Howlett modified the severe puritanical teachings of Doctors Beard and Ward.

The Cambridge of Cromwell's time did not by any means represent one theological or philosophical point of view. High Churchmen, Puritans and exponents of a 'middle course' rubbed shoulders in the Common Rooms. Nor was the study of subjects other than theology entirely unknown. Moreover, the university was not exclusively devoted to academic pursuits. Town and Gown riots occurred so often as to become questions of almost national concern. Then, as now, the university had its football fields, and it has even been said that Cromwell played this game more regularly than he studied his books. There is no doubt that he rode and hawked and hunted, just as he did at his home which was only sixteen miles' ride from the university.

On the other hand, we must believe that he pursued the theological and biblical studies into which he had been initiated by Doctor Beard. Sidney-Sussex was famous as a nursery of Puritans and regarded with grave disquiet by the High Church leaders then in power in London. At Cambridge, too, Cromwell improved on his Eton Grammar; he 'perfectly acquired unto himself the Latin tongue'. The praise of his Latin by his renowned admirer John Milton at a later date and his ability to hold diplomatic conversation with a foreign ambassador in that tongue are sufficient proofs of his proficiency.

Cromwell never underrated the importance of secular education. In the days of his greatness he supported a proposal to establish a new college at Oxford, he granted a fresh charter to the University of Edinburgh and tried to found a college at Durham.

Besides Latin his own education is said to have given him some knowledge of history and mathematics, although in placing his unbalanced budget before a Parliament in his later years he denied that he had any skill in matters of arithmetic.

The history book that he recommended was Sir Walter Ralegh's *History of the World* — 'it's a body of history and will add much more to your understanding than fragments of story', he told his son. This amazing book, written by the courtier, pirate and explorer during his imprisonment by James I, and published in 1614 when Oliver was fifteen years old, covered the history of the world from the Creation to the overthrow of Hannibal by the Romans, and was based on six hundred authorities all of which Ralegh is said to have read. He who would understand the mind of Oliver Cromwell cannot do better than read at least the introduction to this encyclopaedic folio. It is all the more necessary to appreciate its doctrine because Ralegh preaches with even more detailed illustrations the identical thesis expounded by Doctor Beard in his *Theatre of God's Judgments*. The State, wrote Ralegh, arose from necessity and is maintained by reason. The judgments of God are just and unchangeable and the prince who violates them meets with certain retribution. Lord Acton, Christian and historian, told Cambridge University that he could not maintain an opinion of conduct in one age that he did not hold in another, and that circumstances might palliate but would never excuse the wickedness of princes. Ralegh said the same thing, but went further; for he added that the careful student of history will observe that the wicked always receive the fruits of their policy here on earth, and by those fruits we can judge them. According to this test few of the kings of England or France had escaped, thought Ralegh, a richly deserved punishment, for 'ill doing hath always been attended with ill success'. The State, he said, is natural and necessary to fulfil the needs of man, but man himself is born sinful, 'so that if a man seem more noble and beautiful than dust, this proceedeth not from the diversity of his nature, but from the cunning of the Creator:

> 'For true nobility standeth in the train
> Of virtuous life; not in the fleshly line:
> For blood is brute, but gentry is divine.'

King James ordered the suppression of the *History of the World* as detracting from the dignity of kings; but when Oliver read it he may well have reflected that if a man were chosen by God to fight His battles for Him, he would come to learn that the possession of the blood royal was but a meagre foundation for the power and strength of kings.

Cromwell's studies at Cambridge were cut short. At the end of the summer term of 1617 his father was suddenly taken ill. On June 6th Robert Cromwell made his will; on June 20th he saw his daughter Margaret married; and four days later he died. Oliver had five other sisters besides Margaret, but he was himself the only son, for his two brothers had died in childhood. A few weeks after the death of his father his maternal grandfather also died. Thus his mother was left fatherless as well as again widowed, with six daughters and her Cambridge undergraduate son, turned eighteen the previous April.

§ 3

Oliver found himself upon the threshold of life in duty bound to undertake a heavy burden of family responsibility. His uncle Oliver had ten children of his own to look after. Although his maternal uncle, Sir Thomas Steward of Ely, who made him his heir, may have helped the widow and her family, in view of the stress that Oliver always laid upon the responsibilities imposed upon him by God and of the lessons to that effect which had been inculcated into him by his schoolmaster and tutors, we may rest assured that he left Cambridge after his father's death (we know he never took a degree) and devoted himself to comforting his mother, managing her estate, marrying off or educating his sisters and generally taking his place as head of the household. Indeed, the fact that Cromwell at this crucial period of adolescence was left in command of an admiring household of six women goes far to explain that power of initiative and decision which stood him in good stead in later years.

Two unrecorded years passed on in this way. In time life would have resumed its normal course for Mrs. Cromwell. She was an able, brave and affectionate woman, wrapped up in her only son and anxious not to stand in the way of his advancement. Widowhood was at least no new experience for her. It was desirable that Oliver should obtain some further preparation for his responsibilities. He was to be her brother's heir and would have to be a county magistrate, possibly a Member of Parliament, as her husband had been. He must go to London.

As no early portraits of Oliver Cromwell have yet been discovered we can only picture by means of inference how the young squire looked to Londoners when he came from the country to complete his education in life and law. There exists only one fairly early portrait, which nevertheless suggests beyond reasonable doubt his main characteristics on reaching manhood.[1] There was the long brown hair parted in the middle, a high brow, a pair of piercing eyes of mysterious colour, the long bulbous nose which dominates the face in all portraits and was the subject of many jests, and a small light coloured moustache above thinnish lips. The thick, square and determined chin was probably a later development. In height he was about five foot ten inches, he bore himself robustly and he was of a noticeably reddish countenance. 'In his rough country clothes' (as John Buchan well says), 'he must have looked at first sight like any other substantial grazier from the shires', a youth perhaps already aware of his responsibilities but, away from home, not unwilling to forget them for a while.

'He betook himself', writes an early biographer, 'to the study of law in Lincoln's Inn; that nothing may be wanting to make a complete gentleman and a good commonwealth man'. His studies, such as they were, would have been superficial enough and would certainly not have extended, as another enthusiastic early biographer suggested, to the Roman or Civil law. But it was customary in those days for country gentlemen to go to London and dabble in the Common law. The profession itself was becoming increasingly respectable. In the Middle Ages the lawyer had been somewhat despised by the aristocracy and hated by the common people; in the seventeenth century he began to govern the country. In the last Parliament of Cromwell's own epoch there were said to be a hundred and fifty lawyers who were Members of Parliament. After the country gentlemen they formed the largest social group in the House of Commons.

Whether Cromwell was actually at Lincoln's Inn or not is a little uncertain. But his presence in London in 1619-20 is sufficiently attested. It is likely that he took this first opportunity of complete freedom from the supervision of his family

[1] See portrait facing p. 46.

to enjoy himself in the normal way of a well-off young man up from the country, seeing the sights of what was even then one of the largest and most varied cities of Europe. He was provided with an introduction to the family of Sir James Bourchier, a furrier by trade but with property in Essex, who lived on the Tower Hill and made the young visitor welcome at his home. Oliver rapidly became a suitor to the daughter of the house named Elizabeth, a homely, pleasant-looking girl who never gave offence to anyone and soon became devoted to her tempestuous lover. Oliver's mother evidently approved his choice, for she allowed him to settle upon his bride 'for her jointure, all that parsonage-house of Hartford with all the glebe-lands and tythes in the county of Huntingdon', which she had inherited from her husband.

On August 22nd, 1620, Oliver Cromwell ('alias Williams'), aged twenty-one and a half years old, and Elizabeth Bourchier one year older, became man and wife. They were married in St. Giles' Church, Cripplegate, and at once left London for the country to share the home of his mother.

§ 4

Cromwell's marriage was followed by a quiet but significant period in which he settled down as a squire and farmer, and devoted himself to the cultivation of his estates and the procreation of children. The parish register of the church of St. John's, Huntingdon, which stood almost opposite to his house, is filled with entries of the births and marriages in his family during the first half of the seventeenth century; the Cromwells were obviously the largest and most prolific group of parishioners in the district. During the years which followed his marriage Oliver must have had a somewhat trying time in providing for and supporting his growing family. His father's properties are stated to have yielded not more than £300 a year and Oliver had only been able to settle £50 a year upon his wife. 'I was',

24

as he justly recalled in later years, 'by birth a gentleman neither being in any considerable height nor yet in obscurity'. His £300 were worth about four times as much as that sum to-day and in good years therefore his income would have been a comfortable one; but in bad years a real effort would have been necessary to maintain his social position and to preserve his stake in the country.

The years immediately preceding his marriage had been the worst that farming had known for twenty years. Wheat prices were appallingly low and were never in his life to fall so low again. Cattle farming was at that date equally unprofitable and there was a strong movement to prohibit the import of cattle from Ireland so as to improve English prices. In 1620 not only were the prices of wheat, cattle and wool bad but trade generally was depressed. It was not for five years that a recovery set in, the harvests of 1622 and 1623 were below the average, and in 1625 a plague in London had an adverse effect upon business generally. Even during the next five years (1626-1630), when trade was gradually getting better, wheat prices averaged nearly ten shillings a quarter less than they were to be after 1630.

Huntingdonshire was essentially a wheat-growing county. Nevertheless it had been considerably influenced by the agricultural revolution which took place in the reign of Queen Elizabeth. That revolution, which consisted of an influx of sheep farming at the expense of arable farming, had been stimulated, on the one hand, by a world fall in prices that tended to make wheat growing unprofitable and on the other by an increasing demand for English wool. The medieval strip system whereby arable land, whether belonging to the lord of the manor or to his tenants, was inextricably mixed up in small units in common fields and subjected to a strict and invariable rotation of crops hampered economic progress. So also did a lack of adequate drainage in the so-called fen counties of which Huntingdonshire was one. These handicaps invited radical changes.

25

The new class of commercially-minded landlords who appeared after the dissolution of the monasteries therefore began to organize the elimination of the strip system, replacing it with big privately-owned fields with modern ditches and hedgerows, and to advocate the draining of the fenlands. Whereas the former process, known as 'enclosure', had the consequence of creating agricultural unemployment the latter increased the acreage available for wheat growing. Nevertheless, both processes were unpopular and regarded by many as a cruel interference with the customary economy. 'Never', it was said, 'were there so many gentlemen and so little gentleness in England' as at the time of this change. In 1600-7 there were riots in the Midlands led by a half-mythical Captain Pouch against the 'heartless' enclosers, and a government investigation then carried out did in fact show that at least 3·29 per cent of Huntingdonshire, comprising 7677 acres, had been enclosed during the previous thirty years. There was probably a temporary cessation of enclosing after the commission had reported. But in 1624 certain laws for maintaining tillage were repealed and the enclosing movement was resumed. We know that when in 1636-8 fines were imposed upon landlords who had enclosed their fields during the previous twenty years in such a way as to cause unemployment (or 'depopulation' as it was then called) no less than £2747 were exacted from enclosers in Huntingdonshire. Was Cromwell an encloser? No such accusation has been made against him by his enemies and on the whole it seems likely that Cromwell did not enclose his fields, which were certainly 'open' when he inherited them from his father. Equally, although his father had been a commissioner for draining the fens, Oliver seems, as his subsequent conduct will show, to have been opposed to the capitalists concerned in the drainage enterprises, at least if their work had the consequence of encroaching upon the common pasture rights. All the indications go to show that Cromwell during these years was mainly an arable farmer working on the ancient strip system whilst owning a few horses and sheep grazing a few fields of his own or upon the common fields[1] — clinging to conservative ways of life in a fairly progressive county. He would therefore have been concerned to uphold the medieval economy. But his lot would have been hard. Yet he would have been able to contrast his own successful struggle for existence with the failure of his wealthy uncle Sir Oliver at Hinchinbrooke who, in 1627, ruined by the lavish scale on which he entertained royalty and others, as well no doubt as by bad wheat prices, was forced to sell his property to Sir Sidney Montague and retire to comparative poverty and obscurity on another estate at Ramsey. When in 1636 Cromwell inherited his property from his other uncle, he may well have regarded it as a reward from Heaven for his sobriety and conservatism during these difficult years. But if he was a conservative in his attitude to customary property rights and to agricultural methods he was no reactionary. It is noticeable that little effort was made during his Protectorate to retain or re-enact the old Tudor and Stuart laws against enclosing, and Oliver himself finally abandoned arable farming for sheep farming when in May 1631 he sold most of his properties at Huntingdon for the comparatively small sum of £1800 and moved over to St. Ives to start afresh as a grazier.

§ 5

In the years after his marriage Cromwell also underwent a profound spiritual experience. He became a fully-fledged Puritan. To appreciate this phase in his life it is necessary to consider shortly the nature of the Puritan movement which was then sweeping victoriously over England.

The English Reformation consisted of something more

---

[1] Included in his property was a malt house, which clearly points to a big barley acreage. The records speak only of two acres of pasture and four of meadowland among his properties, which could scarcely have been used except as an adjunct to arable farming. Noble: *Memoirs of the Protectoral House of Cromwell* (1787), I, 103-4.

significant than the denial of the authority of the Bishop of Rome and the abolition of the monastic system. Henry VIII had felt the pressure of a party in the English Church which demanded doctrinal reform. In 1536, therefore, he had announced in five articles on religion and five on ceremonial what the English Christian must do to be saved; and the reformers were 'rejoiced to see the scriptures and ancient creeds made the standards of the faith, without mentioning tradition or the decrees of the Church'. These were the fundamentals deemed essential to maintain unity of opinion, and although the pace was set too fast at this stage, once the medieval tradition had been abandoned the number of fundamentals was narrowed and within the requisite unity of the State Church there was scope for latitude of belief.

The door thus opened admitted the disciples of John Calvin of Geneva, who taught the doctrine of predestination, namely that faith was a consequence rather than a condition of salvation, and envisaged a Church in which those who were chosen for salvation should rule permanently over the incurably reprobate. In the last quarter of the sixteenth century Calvinism or Puritanism (the view that the Church must be purified) spread from Switzerland to England by many routes, and numerous conversions were recorded to this creed.

The Puritan movement as it existed originally in the reign of Queen Elizabeth had for its object simply sweeping out of the Church of England all the essentially Roman Catholic practices which had survived in its services. In the fifteen-sixties the question whether or not the clergy should wear vestments had threatened to split the Church in two, and as early as 1563 Convocation had actually rejected only by a single proxy vote a proposal to limit vestments to a surplice, to make Sunday a holiday, to cause the Minister to face the people when reading divine service, to omit the sign of the cross in the ceremony of baptism, to permit sick and aged communicants not to kneel and to eliminate the organ from the parish churches. Forty years later a number of Anglican ministers who had no

desire to leave the Church were putting forward similar proposals to reform 'certain ceremonies and abuses of the Church'.
Anyone who advocated this kind of reform was dubbed a
Puritan. The saintly Richard Baxter relates, for instance, how
his father 'was reviled for reading scripture when the rest were
dancing on the Lord's Day, and for praying (by a form out of
the end of the Common Prayer Book) in his house and for
reproving drunkards and swearers, and for talking sometimes
a few words of Scripture and the life to come, he was reviled
commonly by the name of Puritan, precisian and hypocrite'.

The desire for reform both of ceremonies and manners took
a very strong hold not only upon Ministers of the Church,
especially those in the towns, but also upon the House of
Commons: indeed in 1621 a certain member who ventured to
argue that the Sabbath was Saturday was obliged to apologize
on his knees for irreverence and was expelled the House. Concurrently with pressure for these reforms grew a demand for
what was termed a 'preaching Ministry' who would advocate
them before the congregations. The Puritans were willing and
eager to listen to sermons which in Anglican services, if delivered at all, had been generally read out of text books. They
sought extempore prayer and preaching instead of customary
rites and admonitions.

Gradually, however, this movement for purification of
manners, morals and services — a form of evangelical revivalism
such as is common enough in the history of the Churches —
merged naturally into another movement which concerned
itself with doctrine and Church organization. A gradual
increase of literacy and a wider diffusion of the Bible translated
into English — the Authorized Version dates from the reign
of James I — allowed a larger number of common people to
interpret the 'book of life' for themselves and induced them to
turn back to seek a model for Church organization in the
Scriptures instead of in the history of the primitive Church.
Thus, according to his lights, with the Good Book in hand,
many an independent preacher set out to regenerate the world.

In the reign of Elizabeth 'exercises' held by the clergy and the laity for the purposes of discussion came into fashion in a number of dioceses. Mere 'cowherds, clotherers and suchlike', as an aristocratic observer noted, met 'to talk of the Scriptures'. Secret conventicles gathered together, and one Henry Jacob advocated the right of independent congregations to settle their own religious practices in 'brotherly community' with the Church. But Jacob remarked that if the Church authorities rigidly enforced conformity then the independent congregations must become separatists and pursue their nonconformity outside the Church. By 1618, since no understanding had been reached between the Church and the Puritans, Henry Jacob's followers linked up with those of Robert Browne, who advocated complete separation from the established Church.

Very different in approach from the Independents and Separatists, and much more important numerically than either, were the Presbyterians who, led by some learned and influential theologians, stood primarily for a particular form of Church organization which they wished to impose at all costs on the existing establishment. Deriving encouragement from the success of John Knox in Scotland they laboured to limit bishops to purely spiritual functions and substitute as a governing body a Church directory in accordance with the principles of Calvin himself; this body, they thought, should be founded upon diocesan assemblies based in their turn upon groups of elected pastors, elders and deacons in charge of the parishes. Other minor sects also began to flourish in the early seventeenth century, ranging from the Family of Love, who believed that the resurrection of the dead was fulfilled in them, to a body which taught 'the quaint notion that women have no souls'.

All these new Christian groups had, however, a common approach to life. They stood, it has been said, for 'goodness in itself' rather than holiness in the sense of consecration. Their piety burned with fierce heat and their temper, although it derived certain springs of happiness from the secure consciousness of salvation, was grave rather than gay. In tune with this temper every department of life was held to have a sacred or at least a serious meaning. Trade became a 'calling', idleness a sin, the industrious apprentice was regarded as footing the path to Heaven and Puritan merchants believed that fluctuations in the exchanges inculcated lessons from on high. Although predestination taught that men are either chosen or not chosen to be saved, fear of the Lord, notably during the stage immediately following conversion, was to them a terrible reality and the more deeply convinced the convert the deeper would be his certainty of past sins and his apprehension of punishment.

It was a stern creed which, by teaching that all sensual experiences are evil, left little room for laughter. John Milton, the greatest of Puritan poets, ceased to write in the care-free style of *L'Allegro* in the days of the English Commonwealth, and generally the Puritan recalled that Jesus wept and the Lord was irate with him who laughed in Heaven.

The feeling against sacramental worship was heightened in the reigns of James I and Charles I by the increasing political strength of the High Church party, a minority led by William Laud, a pious but singularly unfortunate Oxford don and prelate, who taught the antagonistic doctrine that the road to salvation was to be found in a restoration of all the ancient sacraments and ceremonials and doubted the doctrine of predestination. He strove vainly to reintroduce what he termed the beauty of holiness into the churches. But the High Churchman seemed merely a thinly disguised papist to the Puritans, whose attitude to the sacraments and fear of sensual pleasure gave beauty a very low place in their scheme of values. A woman was to be loved not for her beauty but for her virtue. A poem was best if it taught the noblest moral sentiments. A sculptural figure was most to be admired if it was an accurate reproduction of the imperfect image of God. The dread of idolatrous beauty is recorded in the destruction wrought by officers of the Puritan Commonwealth and still to be seen in many a cathedral and church. Sir Robert Harley, the Puritan grandfather of the Tory minister of Queen Anne's reign, left his accounts as an example of how this work was carried out:

1644, April 19 — Receipts for 6s by Thomas Castaway from Sir Robert Harley for three days work in planing out some pictures of the Abbey. . . .

1644, September 30 — Receipt by Adam Browne from Sir Robert Harley of 2£ 19s. for work done in the Abbey, namely, cutting down the pictures over the records; taking down part of the organ loft. taking down three pictures in Queen Elizabeth's chapel and carrying them to Sir Robert Harley's house; taking down a picture in the Duke of Richmond's chapel of God the Father with Christ in his bosom. . . .

1645, January 4 — Receipt by John Rutland and Robert Hiches of 3£ 5s from Sir Robert Harley for 131 feet of new glass for glazing windows in Saint Margaret's church, Westminster.

1645, June 14 — Receipt by Richard Culmer of 5£ 11. 2d from Sir Robert Harley being the proceeds of the burning of the embroidery called the Glory, belonging to the High Altar of Canterbury Cathedral, delivered to Sir Robert Harley by the appointment of Mr. John Lade, Mayor of Canterbury. . . .

In this way the fiery zeal of the Puritan faith destroyed what it could not assimilate; every relic of superstition was plucked out and cast into the fire. Not Art, but the Sword was seized and sanctified by the service of God. To trust in Him and keep their powder dry was for the early Puritans a genuine rule of conduct which was exemplified in an instruction to the government contractor of the Commonwealth to ship out to the soldiers abroad a cargo of Bibles and a barrel of firelocks.

Such were a few at least of the superficial characteristics of Puritanism in the country over which Oliver Cromwell was to rule. Such were the elements in the atmosphere that he fully assimilated after his conversion. The immediate effect of conversion was to make the Puritan over-emphasize and exaggerate the wickedness of his daily life before he had seen the light;

and there is no solid evidence to show that Cromwell's life before his conversion was any more reprehensible than that of another famous east country convert, John Bunyan the tinker. When Bunyan was playing one day at a game of Cat, he heard a voice suddenly say, 'Wilt thou leave thy sins and go to Heaven or have thy sins and go to Hell?' From that time onward his neighbours were amazed at his great conversion 'from prodigious profaneness to something like a moral life', for he abandoned bell-ringing, dancing and swearing for ever. No graver sins than Bunyan's can be imputed to Cromwell.

Cromwell was hot-blooded both in the actual and in the figurative sense of the phrase. An ancient inhabitant of St. Ives recalled many years afterwards how he had seen Cromwell attending church there with a 'piece of red flannel round his neck, being subject to inflammation'. All his life he suffered from boils and other excrescences that come from bad blood. We have also the independent testimony of three doctors, one definitely dated 1628, that Cromwell was subject to extreme melancholia and hypochondria. Farming cares may have combined with religious doubts to lower his spirits. It seems that he belonged to that not uncommon type of psychological subject that suffers from alternating moods of profound depression and extreme exaltation. This tendency was at once receptive to and strengthened by the Puritan code that taught of the contrast of the inborn sinfulness of the human soul with its purification and purgation when chosen for salvation by a merciful Deity.

Despite the regular birth of children, his son Robert in 1621, Oliver in 1623, Richard in 1626, Henry in 1628 and his daughter Bridget in 1624, these years succeeding his marriage were therefore a time of mental stress for Oliver Cromwell. Like Bunyan he had to ask himself again and again: 'Am I one of the elect whom God has chosen to save?' The journey was for him a long and wearisome one beyond the Slough of Despond before the Delectable Mountains were attained. Mother, sisters, wife, children all dwelt together under the same roof with him. Did they accompany him upon his pilgrimage of spiritual discovery? It is more likely that, as till the end, they tended him, obeyed him and tried to comfort him, but never understood him.

His conversion must have taken place soon after his marriage. Many years afterwards he described in a letter to a woman cousin the spiritual victory that he then won in order that he might honour his God 'by declaring what He hath done for my soul'.

'Truly then I find,' he wrote:

That He giveth springs in a dry and barren wilderness where no water is. I live . . . in Mescheck which they say signifies Prolonging, in Kedar, which signifieth Blackness, yet the Lord forsaketh me not . . . The Lord . . . it is that enlighteneth our blackness, our darkness. I dare not say He hideth His face from me. He giveth me to see light in His Light. One beam in a dark place hath exceeding much refreshment in it; blessed be His Name for shining upon so dark a heart as mine!

The struggle was long and severe; but at last the conviction that he was indeed chosen to be saved was complete. His inward unhappiness yielded before the blinding light of belief, although it was also, he considered, a necessary preliminary. 'Whoever', he asked, 'tasted that the Lord is gracious without some sense of self, vanity and badness?' But that 'vanity and badness' were inevitably exaggerated with the dawn of spiritual certainty: 'I was the chief, the chief of sinners' — so it seemed in the afterglow of the days of the struggle.

How long the years of self-examination, of 'blackness' and 'darkness' endured we cannot know. But gradually beams of light pierced the gloom. By 1629 his vehement Puritanism was well known in Huntingdon and in London. Already so far as the spirit could determine he was appointed to the Chosen People of God. The teaching of the Old Testament urged him to arise and smite the Amalekites, if only there were Amalekites to smite. His lack of a fight to wage for the Lord may well explain the melancholia and hypochondria that gripped him. For his bodily and mental vigour were too powerful to be repressed or sublimated merely into religious enthusiasm. Other work, of political character, awaited him, and in time an unforeseen opportunity released his mighty store of energy and made him a leader of men.

CHAPTER II

THE LORD OF THE FENS

§ I

THE House of Commons rose to power in the sixteenth century and in the seventeenth was able to demand a very large share in the government of the country. Parliament had, it is true, been of some importance in the Middle Ages, but then it was in the House of Lords that the King's counsellors were found. The personnel of the Lords had been changed and curtailed first by the Wars of the Roses and then by the Reformation, and thence forward the country gentlemen, lawyers, merchants and soldiers who filled the Commons began to stake out a claim to be the King's advisers in most affairs of state. Henry VIII had found the Commons a useful instrument in the Reformation settlement. Queen Elizabeth made frequent if irregular use of Parliament but denied the right of the Commons to interfere in many spheres of government. The Tudors had thus taught the Commons the consciousness of their political power, and they gradually learned of themselves their economic strength. Medieval theory had identified public finance with the private finance of the King; — the King, it was said, must 'live of his own' out of the hereditary revenues derived from the royal estates and certain other long-established sources of income; but national expenditure gradually increased while the relatively stereotyped royal revenues tended to diminish in value with the world rise in prices in the sixteenth century. Consequently the sovereign who in the past had turned to the Commons only for 'extraordinary' contributions out of taxation now found himself obliged to rely upon them for regular grants to balance his accounts. In return for their financial assistance the Commons naturally asserted their right to criticize national policy in all questions of Church and State, and this was all the more significant in the first half of the century because the bulk of the members of Parliament had a wholly different view both of foreign and of ecclesiastical policy from that of the King.

The Stuart Kings clung to their ancestral powers. Although the hereditary right of King James I to the English throne was somewhat uncertain (he had actually come to an understanding with Queen Elizabeth that he would acquiesce in the execution of his own mother if Elizabeth would support his claim to the throne) he chose to adopt and to stress the doctrine that the rights of hereditary kings were derived solely and entirely from God. 'Kings', he wrote, 'are the breathing images of God upon earth;' 'they are not only God's lieutenants upon earth and set upon God's throne, but even by God himself they are called Gods.' And again, 'a good king will frame his actions according to the law; yet is he not bound thereto but of his good will and for good example-giving to his subjects'. To this challenging theory of a divinely chosen absolute monarch above the law the Commons opposed a doctrine based upon a much quoted saying of a medieval lawyer that the King is below the law. The seventeenth-century politician, while not denying to the monarch certain limited prerogative powers, asserted that the King was bound both by custom and by his coronation oath to respect the common law of the realm. And beneath the verbiage of political theory lay a dogged and scarcely reconcilable contest between divergent interests.

James I and Charles I looked to the Church of which they were Supreme Heads to bolster up their 'divine' power. They felt that the apostolic succession in Church and State went hand in hand. 'No bishop', they said, 'no king.' But the majority of the Commons had no faith either in the divine right of hereditary monarchy or in the apostolic succession, and they refused to believe that the accidents of birth or the vagaries of royal fancy were fit means for the choice of religious leaders. They advocated a radical reform of the Church to bring its organization to resemble 'the gospel ministry' of

Geneva, and sought to substitute a system of presbyters or elected elders for the bench of bishops appointed by the Crown. The constitutional history of the seventeenth century is therefore a struggle between the Commons and the Monarchy. For eleven years, from 1629 to 1640, the country was governed without the Commons. For another eleven years, from 1649 to 1660, the country was ruled without the Monarchy. Ultimately both institutions were found necessary to the harmonious working of government. But the conflict between them was long, fierce and indecisive. In 1628 Oliver Cromwell entered the arena.

§ 2

In country districts neither Reform Bills nor Ballot Acts have changed the tendency for the local squire to enjoy a prescriptive right to be elected Member of Parliament. In modern times the Verneys have represented Buckinghamshire and the Trevelyans Newcastle-on-Tyne even as they did in the seventeenth or eighteenth century. Of course some squires have moved away from their ancestral homes or a redistribution of seats has partitioned a constituency, but otherwise, whatever the alterations in the suffrage, if the squire wishes to go to Westminster he expects to be elected. Such was the position of the Cromwells at Huntingdon. Until Sir Oliver left Hinchinbrooke in 1627 he had been one of the members for the county. In 1628 his nephew became a member for the borough. It has been supposed that his well-known Puritan beliefs also commended him to the choice of his fellow-townsmen.

When Cromwell arrived in Town on his parliamentary duties in February 1628, accompanied probably by his cousin, John Hampden, the member for a neighbouring constituency, he became a spectator of, and participator in, one of the most crucial sessions in English history. The last Parliament of 1626 which disapproved of the foreign policy of Charles I and his chief adviser, the Duke of Buckingham, had refused to vote supplies for a war against Spain. 'Who rules the King? The Duke. Who rules the Duke? The Devil. Let the Duke look to it.' Charles had been driven to the 'forced' loan and an immense increase in customs duties which had hitherto been considered a hereditary royal revenue. Over seventy prominent men who refused to pay the forced loan had been imprisoned at the King's orders and held in the Tower without trial to await the royal pleasure. Beyond this the Government had billeted without payment upon wealthy families throughout the land a large number of soldiers returned from the war. Moreover, the King had shown himself a pronounced partisan of Laud's High Church group — called Arminians by their opponents. To the parliamentary Puritans the Arminians were the puppets of the Pope, and the Pope was Anti-Christ, begetter of Bloody Mary and the Spanish Armada. Finally Buckingham involved the country in a war which not only meant an attack upon fellow Protestants (the French Huguenots) but was mismanaged and unsuccessful.

Parliament therefore met in a mood of extreme wrath. The leaders of the Commons at once repudiated the King's claims to levy taxation without their consent, to imprison without trial, to countenance a new kind of Popery and to persist in a disastrous foreign policy. To do adequate justice to this session would be to write a lengthy and difficult chapter in our history. There was much to be said on the King's side, but his ministers in the Commons were few, ineffective, and lacking a caucus to cheer them on. Sir Thomas Wentworth, a fiery Yorkshire gentleman who had been imprisoned for refusing to pay the forced loan and was now released, showed himself anxious to arrange a compromise between the claims of Parliament and of the King. But his efforts were vain. Ultimately the veteran lawyer and parliamentary leader, Sir Edward Coke, who had a touching and quite unjustifiable belief in the Common Law as a panacea for all evils, drew up a petition or private Bill (the Petition of Right) which asserted that the late behaviour of the King was contrary to Magna Charta and other famous but somewhat obsolete and misunderstood medieval documents, and asked that henceforth no tax be levied 'without common consent', that no free man should be imprisoned contrary to the law of the land and that recent commissions for martial law should be withdrawn. It was all very vague and the King said 'let right be done as is desired', after he had been voted his supplies. But the Commons then took a further step to ensure their position and prepared a Bill which denied the King's right to take customs duties or 'tonnage and poundage', as they were then called. Charles, avowing that he owed no account of his actions save to God alone, prorogued Parliament, and Oliver, who had sat silent but acquiescent throughout the proceedings of the Commons, returned home to Huntingdon to see for the first time his new-born daughter, Betty.

Parliament had expected to meet again in October, and the murder of the Duke of Buckingham by a fanatic might seem to have cleared the way for an understanding between the Commons and the King. But there were still two grievances outstanding. The first was the right of the King to levy tonnage and poundage without parliamentary consent. Merchants had been actively encouraged by the Commons to refuse to obey the law, and several of them had been imprisoned at the King's order for following this welcome and authoritative advice not to pay their taxes. The complaint of one of the merchants has a modern ring: 'Merchants are in no part of the world so screwed and wrung as in England.' In the second place religious differences persisted.

On January 20th, however, Parliament had been summoned, and on the 24th the King gave way over the question of tonnage and poundage. 'It ever was', he declared, 'and still is my meaning by the gift of my people to enjoy it.' The House was not dissatisfied with its victory, but before it would pass a new tonnage and poundage Bill it returned to the religious dispute. Just before Parliament assembled the King had made a gallant effort to effect an agreement between the two great religious parties in the State. He had issued a declaration saying that the faith of the Church of England was embodied in the Thirty-nine Articles as interpreted by the King and Convocation; 'we will', he added, 'that all future curious search be laid aside', and ordered the withdrawal from circulation of a number of books written by the High Church party which had deeply offended the Puritans. This would have been excellent had it not been for the fact that the Thirty-nine Articles were universally recognized as being a typical Elizabethan and legal compromise between the points of view of those who believed in free will and those who did not. Hitherto each side had been at liberty to employ the interpretation it preferred. The fundamental difficulty now was that the King was known to be on the side of the anti-Puritan minority. One by one the Puritan Parliamentarians, led by John Pym and John Eliot, arose in their places to denounce the well-meaning royal declaration and the doctrines of the hated High Churchmen, Laud, now Archbishop of Canterbury, Bishop Neile of Winchester, Manwaring, the King's Chaplain, and others.

Oliver sat listening with approval to the full-blooded denunciations of the bishops by his fellow members. 'An Arminian is the spawn of a Papist.' How true! Some bishops might be 'fathers to all ages' — but not Doctors Laud and Neile. How right! And, talking of Bishop Neile, Oliver had an anecdote to tell against him which he had once heard related by his old schoolmaster. The story was of course somewhat of a chestnut as it concerned an incident that took place over a dozen years before, but the House was in a receptive mood. On February 11th, therefore, the junior member for Huntingdon arose and delivered his maiden speech. Mr. Cromwell related 'from the mouth of Dr. Beard' concerning a sermon which Dr. Beard had preached by way of a summing up of a previous sermon delivered at St. Paul's Cross in Spital Square when Bishop Neile, the present Bishop of Winchester, had been Bishop of Lichfield. Dr. Beard had been asked to sum up

41

(among others) a sermon delivered by a certain Dr. Alablaster — and Dr. Alablaster had uttered what he (Beard) had conceived to be Popery — 'flat Popery'. The present Bishop of Winchester, however, sent for Dr. Beard and 'charged him not to deliver anything by way of opposition against Dr. Alablaster by virtue of his canonical obedience'. Thereupon Dr. Beard went and consulted Dr. Felton, Bishop of Ely, and Dr. Felton 'charged him as a Minister to oppose it'. This Dr. Beard did 'and was sent for by Bishop Neile and was exceedingly rated for what he had done'.

The anecdote was lengthy and not very thrilling, but the House was evidently interested in the splenetic Huntingdon squire, for at least three of the members present noted his speech in their diaries, whence it comes down to us. The speaker after Cromwell 'spoke much unto the credit of Dr. Beard as an orthodox man'. Sir Robert Philips, an old stager in the House, followed with a similar episode about a Dr. Marshall, and later on the Commons decided to send for Doctors Beard and Marshall to testify personally as to the iniquities of the High Church bishops.

The King conceived that the House's interference with ecclesiastical affairs was a further encroachment upon his prerogative, and saw that in any case the debates would be interminable. He commanded the Speaker to adjourn the House. But when he rose to move the adjournment the motion was resisted on all sides. Two strong young members, one of whom was Denzil Holles the Presbyterian, seized the Speaker and thrust him back in his seat. 'God's wounds!' cried Holles, 'you shall sit till we please to rise.' Never before had the King's right to order the adjournment been questioned. Pandemonium broke loose and efforts were made to induce the Speaker to put to the House three resolutions which had been recorded by Sir John Eliot upon a piece of paper. But the Speaker would not again be browbeaten and in despair Sir John Eliot threw his paper upon the fire. The King sent the Serjeant-at-Arms to seize the mace, the symbol of its authority, and the Serjeant was followed by the Usher of the Black Rod with a royal message commanding obedience. This was a final incitement to Parliamentary defiance. Holles was able to recall the purport of Eliot's resolutions and himself put them to the House, which carried them by acclamation. The three resolutions ran:

(1) Whosoever brought in innovations of religion or favoured Popery and Arminianism should be considered capital enemies to the kingdom. (2) Whosoever should advise the taking and levying of tonnage and poundage without Parliamentary consent should likewise be considered capital enemies. (3) Any merchant who paid tonnage and poundage thus levied should be reputed a traitor to the liberties of England.

The weeping Speaker was then released from his chair and on March 10th Parliament was dissolved. The brief and exciting session was over, and Cromwell again returned home.

§ 3

Back in Huntingdon Oliver at once plunged into local politics. He first made himself prominent in the business of the new borough charter. The Huntingdon charter of incorporation had in the past been renewed at regular intervals. On July 15th, 1630, Charles I gave his assent to an instrument which substituted a mayor and twelve aldermen, who were to be appointed for life, for two bailiffs and twelve councillors annually elected. In the charter Cromwell as late member for the borough, Beard as Master of the Hospital and Robert Barnard, the leading local solicitor, were nominated Justices of the Peace, and there is no doubt that all three of them acquiesced in the change. Cromwell, however, speedily found that he disapproved of the manner in which the mayor and aldermen made use of their powers. After enlisting the support of many of the townsmen on his side, he therefore proceeded

to deliver 'disgraceful and unseemly' speeches before the town
council, and he was packed off to the Privy Council Board at
Whitehall to explain himself; for criticism of the mayor was in
a sense criticism of the King. An important peer of the realm
was thought necessary to deal with the recalcitrant ex-member
for Huntingdon and the matter was referred to the Lord Privy
Seal, Lord Manchester, elder brother of the new owner of
Hinchinbrooke. To him Oliver outlined his objections to the
functioning of the new charter. He maintained:

(1) that the mayor and aldermen were in a position to alter
the distribution of the townsmen's cattle in the common fields;

(2) that they might dispose of the town lands without the
consent of the burgesses;

(3) that they might levy excessive fines (perhaps as much as
£20) if a poor man refused to serve as alderman.

The Earl of Manchester examined these complaints and
found that although there had been no actual violation of the
charter he was himself in complete agreement with Cromwell
that to avert discontent a pronouncement on these matters was
essential. He therefore proposed to the Council that the Charter
should be amended so that:

(1) the number of cattle allowed to pasture on the town
fields might not be changed but allowed to 'common as they
have anciently done both for number and for kind';

(2) the inheritance of corporation property should not be
disposed of but by the common consent of all the burgesses
'as hath anciently been used and accustomed';

(3) the fine for refusal to be an alderman should be limited
to the sum of one pound.

His grievances having been thus remedied Cromwell
acknowledged that the words he had used to the mayor and
Mr. Barnard were spoken in heat and passion and desired that
they should be forgotten. 'I found Mr. Cromwell very willing
to hold friendship with Mr. Barnard,' reported Manchester.
Barnard accepted the apology and the two agreed to work
henceforward together for the good of their town. This

incident throws a flood of light upon Cromwell's character and outlook. A hot-tempered man, ever ready to resent an injury but willing to see reason if his point of view were accepted, he enjoyed assuming a leading part in local political affairs. Whether he himself was interested in the cattle grazing rights in the common fields (as he may well have been) we do not know with certainty. But, disinterested or not, his concern over the working of the new town charter is an excellent early illustration of the conservative mould of Cromwell's mind. He had not resisted the charter because it was anti-democratic; on the contrary, we have good reason to believe that he approved the change from elected members to aldermen appointed for life. But what he did resent was the attack upon customary property rights. He believed that other things being equal the customs that had 'anciently been used' were the best, and he resisted 'innovations' whether in matters of political and economic organization or of religion as practised in the churches.

In harmony with this point of view Cromwell maintained that Christianity as expounded by Jesus and His Disciples was a ministry of preaching, not of ceremonials. He regarded the sacramental usages which Laud and Neile valued so highly as dangerous innovations detrimental to the purity of religion. He gave a practical proof of his attitude in assisting in the creation of lectureships, that is to say, the provision throughout the country of special preachers who would reinforce the incumbents in parishes and deliver regular Sunday sermons after the accepted Puritan model. These lectureships were set up by various corporations or by *ad hoc* committees of laymen, and since in Huntingdon, despite the occasional presence of a rector, who came backwards and forwards to baptize, marry and bury, there were four parishes without a regular preacher, Dr. Beard had owed his appointment as Master of the Hospital mainly to his ability 'painfully to preach the Word of God in the Town of Huntingdon on the Sabbath Day'. For thirty years he performed this task Sabbath after Sabbath with skill

and devotion, and as he grew an old man he was anxious that
the town and townsmen he had come to know and love so well
should not be left unprovided with spiritual food when he was
forced to leave them or should die. He therefore obtained in
1625 from the burgesses permission to appoint a successor.
The authorities, and Laud in particular, objected. But the
townsmen, headed of course by Cromwell, stood by him, and
in 1631, in the preface to his third edition of *The Theatre of
God's Judgments*, he thanked the mayor, like Cromwell an
ex-pupil of his, and the corporation for their help and support.
Two years later the old Puritan Doctor, perhaps the most successful of Cromwell's mentors, died comforted by the thought
that his work for Huntingdon would be carried on by his
appointed successor.

§ 4

By this time Oliver had left Huntingdon, but his mother
remained there and his children were still baptized in the parish
church of St. John's. He had moved to the neighbouring town
of St. Ives; he had abandoned wheat growing as his main source
of livelihood after the long struggle with poor prices and
harvests and decided to embark upon sheep farming. There
was better pasture land here than at Huntingdon. Even to-day
there takes place at St. Ives every Monday one of the largest
cattle markets in the Eastern Counties. Cromwell sold his
Huntingdon property for £1800 and quickly settled down
with his family in their new home, a pleasanter spot than
Huntingdon, nestling along the banks of the river Ouse. The
Rector of St. Ives was an old friend, Henry Downhall, who
had acted as godfather to his eldest son; but Oliver evidently
did not place much reliance upon this gentleman's abilities as a
preacher, for in 1636 we find him writing to a member of the
lectureship committee in London seeking money to retain a
lecturer at St. Ives. Bishop Williams, of Lincoln, a distant

OLIVER CROMWELL
The earliest known portrait

relative of his, a man completely devoid of prejudices and consequently generally abominated by all parties, remembered in later years how Cromwell became at this time 'a common spokesman for the sectaries'. But despite his known Puritan enthusiasm he remained full of his country interests, and hunted and hawked like any other gentleman farmer. Yet one of Cromwell's Royalist biographers has a typical and unlikely story of his behaviour at St. Ives, to the effect that he used to call his family and labourers together every morning at sunrise and made them pray till nine o'clock and that the consequence was 'that the hinds and ploughmen seeing the zeal of their master, which dispensed with the profitable and most commodious part of the day for their labour, thought they might borrow the other part for their pleasure'. They therefore ploughed a couple of furrows and then took a pack of cards out of their pockets and settled down to a morning's game. Such a story implies that the man who was to organize the Roundhead army was a half-wit.

At the beginning of 1638, Oliver's maternal uncle, Sir Thomas Steward of Ely, died and left him his properties. A popular seventeenth-century story has it that Cromwell thought of profiting by this occasion to join the great Puritan exodus from East Anglia to the New World. That a man who thought as deeply about religion as he did contemplated such a step cannot be doubted, but as he regarded New England as a 'howling wilderness' it was fortunate for him that it was a step he did not feel obliged to take. Instead Oliver moved his family to Ely, where his mother joined him in the house that he had inherited in the shadow of the cathedral. He was at once made a member of the Ely Feofees Fund or Parson's Charity. A short autograph note written in this capacity has been found, addressed on September 13th, 1638, to Mr. John Hand, one of the collectors of the revenues for this charity:

'Mr. Hand, I do not doubt but I shall be as good as my word for your money. I desire you to deliver forty shillings of the town money to this bearer, to pay for the physic for Benson's cure. If the gentleman will not allow it at the time of the account, keep this note, and I will pay it out of my own purse. So I rest, your loving friend, OLIVER CROMWELL.'

Benson was an old invalid. Cromwell was not concerned solely with the spiritual welfare of his fellow-men.

In the same year Cromwell again came forward in defence of the established rights of his neighbours. In 1634 a company headed by the Earl of Bedford had been formed to drain the fens around Ely. Despite the magnitude of the task the work was declared completed three years later, and the members of the company were awarded grants of the reclaimed land which were held to infringe the rights of fishing and pasturage previously enjoyed by the Ely burgesses. Cromwell undertook to keep the draining company at suit for five years on the ground that the work was incomplete. Once more he became the self-appointed spokesman for local property rights, the defender of the three common acres and the cow. So successful was his opposition that the King intervened, and it was not until 1653 that the work was finished and the inhabitants of Ely satisfied. On more than one occasion Cromwell interested himself actively in the draining of the fens. He fully recognized the necessity and importance of the work, but insisted that the customary rights of property holders should be respected, and that if they lost their rights of pasture, of fowling and of fishing the fenmen should receive some concrete compensation in return.

Through all these years Cromwell's family continued to grow. After Betty (Elizabeth) he had two more daughters, Mary and Frances. His sons were educated, no doubt at their mother's wish, at Felsted school in Essex. In 1638 a shattering blow befell the parents in the death of their eldest son Robert, aged eighteen. Cromwell sought solace in the Scriptures, although the loss, he related, long afterwards, was 'a dagger to his heart'. But now local and family cares had to be laid aside. Parliament was once more to meet, and the struggle between King and Commons, High Churchmen and Puritans was to begin anew.

CHAPTER III

TO YOUR TENTS, O ISRAEL!

§ 1

WHILE Cromwell had been steadily occupied with local politics and family affairs, Charles I had been ruling his three kingdoms in a manner afterwards described by his enemies as an 'eleven years' tyranny'. No parliaments met to concentrate public criticism of his government, which was able to pursue its course unchecked. Cromwell and his fellow-squires might grumble at it, but as they were devoid of newspapers or other means of broadcasting their dissatisfaction they had to wait patiently until force of circumstances brought them together again at Westminster.

A long period of unaltered political supremacy, whatever its form, always invites contemporary criticism, but much has been written in modern times in praise of the English government during these years. It has been pointed out that never before had the Poor Law been administered with so much fairness and efficiency; that the central government exercised a wide and beneficent rule over the North of England through its vigorous Council at York; that small landowners were protected from the rapacity of rich men bent on enclosing the common lands for the purpose of agricultural gain; and that foreign trade steadily expanded and could well afford to pay the customs duties demanded by the Crown. This last advantage was derived from our island position; 'the wars and troubles in the neighbours' parts', said Pym in 1640, 'had brought almost the whole stream of trade into this kingdom'. In Ireland Sir Thomas Wentworth, who was created Baron Strafford and a Privy Councillor soon after the dissolution of Parliament, showed himself to be one of the ablest Protestant administrators which that country had yet known. Under his rule the Army was reformed, piracy suppressed, industry and agriculture stimulated, justice impartially administered and churches rebuilt. Both in England and Ireland there was in this decade much material prosperity, while by means of a levy of ship money from towns and counties the foundations were laid of a navy which in due course gave England the command of the seas.

But to this pleasant picture there was a dark side which has not yet been fully revealed in the publications of historians. Corruption, greed and self-seeking held sway in all high places. Royal lands in England and confiscated properties in Ireland were disposed of to courtiers at nominal prices for negligible services. High officials were bribed by business men who expected to make a fortune out of tax farming. Monopolistic commercial and manufacturing concerns, which obtained their exclusive privileges by a payment to the Crown, were not only invariably objectionable in themselves but seemed to put a premium on inefficiency. With the 'eleven years' tyranny' the names of Strafford and Laud are always associated and the labours of these two men are often especially commended, but both of them carried out their duties in the face of virulent opposition from all the other royal ministers and despite the ill-timed interferences of their master. Strafford remained cooped up in Ireland until 1639, surrounded by greedy rivals anxious to thwart him on every side. Laud asserted as his considered opinion that he stood alone 'in those things which draw not private profit after them'. A striking condemnation of the royal ministry!

Furthermore, an efficient despotism is dependent upon a strong and cunning man at the centre, but herein lay the basic weakness of the 'tyranny'. Charles I was not without his virtues; he was 'sober, grave, and sweet', he was a knowledgeable patron of the arts and his inherited Scottish accent and hesitancy of manner did not mar a charm that was capable of inspiring enduring loyalties. But the loneliness of his adolescence prevented him from acquiring many human qualities, and he was not only lacking in the deeper passions but devoid both of humour and sympathy. He was guided by his sentiments — a feeling for the dignity of his office and for the desirability of unity in the Church, for example, rather than by settled intellectual convictions. Perhaps it is unfair to blame him for the persistency with which he adhered to his prejudices or for his inability to appreciate other points of view than his own, for these after all were common failings then and are now. But if he sought to impose a benevolent tyranny firmness was at least essential. Charles I was incapable of firm rule himself and would not give a free hand to others competent to govern. Shifty and unstable by nature, he was always ready to surrender himself to the influence nearest at hand, usually that of a second-rate mind. At the beginning of his reign he was the tool of the attractive but feeble Buckingham. Next he tended to put his faith in his Lord Treasurer Weston, an inefficient nonentity. Finally Queen Henrietta Maria, a charming but superficial Frenchwoman, exercised a spasmodic and usually evil hold over her faithful husband.

Nowhere was Charles's instability and lack of statesmanship more fully exposed during this period than in the sphere of foreign affairs. He was completely lacking in any conception of a consistent or effective foreign policy. He vaguely hoped that by appealing first to one Power and then to another he could restore his worthless relatives, the princes of the German Palatinate, to their lost possessions. Neither Dutchmen, Spaniards, Germans nor Frenchmen trusted his royal word. They believed that he was perpetually trying to play off one against the other; by modern standards it is not perhaps so much to his discredit that he did so as that he let them know he was doing it. At one time he agreed to a treaty with Spain promising to attack the Dutch, whilst he was negotiating a Dutch alliance against Spain. He was a living symbol of *perfide Albion*; he made the name of England despised throughout Europe. Wrapped up in a quite unjustifiable belief in his own importance, Charles gives posterity the impression of being either a very stupid or a very dishonest man. It is probable that both these failings were rooted in his nature.

Lastly, on the debit side of Charles's 'tyranny' stands his treatment of Sir John Eliot, who together with eight others had been arrested for his part in delaying the adjournment of Parliament in 1629. He was accused of a conspiracy against the King and proudly refusing to acknowledge his offence was thrown, a prisoner without trial, into the Tower. In October 1632 he applied for leave of absence from his prison to recover his broken health, promising afterwards 'to return back to my prison there to undergo such punishment as God hath allotted to me'. His petition was twice refused. By the end of the next month he was dead. Between King Charles I and the friends and followers of Eliot, among whom Cromwell must be numbered, there was henceforward always to intervene a ghost from the Tower.

Beyond particular considerations it was later urged that the very cessation of Parliaments was a mistaken stroke of policy. Edward Hyde, in after years Earl of Clarendon and the chief architect of the Restoration, one of the noblest and most selfless of Stuart supporters, argued in this sense. He asserted in 1645, after the Royalist defeat in the first Civil War, that no man could show him 'a source from whence these waters of bitterness we now taste have more probably flown than from this unseasonable, unskilful and precipitate dissolution of parliaments'. His view was undoubtedly that of many moderate men in the sixteen-thirties. Parliament, then as now, was a microcosm of all the powerful classes in the kingdom. Had it met earlier and been treated with statesmanlike tact it is at least possible that some way of compromise might have been found between the antagonistic interests in the realm. As it was, the contrast between the comparative national prosperity of this epoch and a partially corrupt administration meant an accumulation of grievances, especially amongst the country gentry, which would be more powerfully focused at West-minster the longer the summons there of the Commons was delayed.

§ 2

Edward Hyde wrote in a passage in his autobiography, which has hitherto been accepted as a true view by all writers on this period, that in 1639 'England enjoyed the greatest measure of felicity it had ever known'. Whereas France and Spain were at war with each other and 'both with a civil war in their own bowels', whereas Germany 'was weltering in its own blood', and all the other countries of Europe engaged to a greater or less degree in destructive wars.

'Of all the Princes of Europe the King of England alone seemed to be seated upon that pleasant promontory that might safely view the tragic sufferings of all his neighbours about him, without any other concernment than what arose from his princely heart. . . . His three kingdoms flourishing in entire peace, and universal plenty; in danger of nothing but their own surfeits; and his dominions every day enlarged, by sending out colonies upon large and fruitful plantations; his strong fleets commanding all seas; and the numerous shipping of the nation bringing the trade of the world into his ports. . . .

'In this blessed conjuncture . . . a small, scarce discernible cloud arose in the North, which was shortly after attended with such a storm, that even rooted up the greatest, and tallest cedars of the three nations; blasted all its beauty and fruitfulness; brought its strength to decay, and its glory to reproach. . . .'

To understand the nature of this cloud — the Presbyterian rising in Scotland — we must revert to the ecclesiastical policy of William Laud.

Despite the violent denunciations of the proceedings of the High Church bishops by Cromwell and other Puritans in the Parliament of 1628-9, the following eleven years marked a

53

period of growth rather than decline in those forms of episcopal activity which were productive of widespread protest. In 1629 at any rate the nominal head of the Church under the King, Abbot, the Archbishop of Canterbury, 'a man of very morose manner and a very sour aspect', had himself been a Calvinist. In August 1633 William Laud, then Bishop of London, succeeded Abbot and was thus able to give an added impulse to the policy that with the approval of the King he had practised hitherto only on his own see. He therefore attacked the lecturers more vigorously and reformed the churches with greater assiduity. It was his belief that the puritanical form of worship, which centred upon the pulpit, was lacking in essential reverence for the Deity. In illustration of this he was able to point to communion tables employed as hat racks instead of altars. He could have related how in one case a woman had left her baby upon the communion table 'with consequences which may be easily imagined'. He knew that the presence of dogs in churches during service was a common occurrence, and that in the Eastern Counties Hampden and no doubt Cromwell were accustomed to drill the militia in their local cemeteries. 'Pews', wrote Bishop Corbett, 'are become tabernacles with rings and curtains on them. There wants nothing but beds to hear the word of God in.' To the Puritan contempt for the outward decencies of worship Laud opposed a revival of the sacramental observances and ceremonies of the medieval Church. In so doing he and his supporters had, as we have seen, laid themselves open to the charge of being 'papists'. Their openly expressed belief that the Church of Rome was a true branch of Christ's Church lent colour to this accusation. Court scandal heightened it further. In 1634 Lord Treasurer Weston (though an enemy of Laud) was known to have died an avowed Roman Catholic. Sir Francis Windebank, from 1632 one of the two principal Secretaries of State, was described as 'the extraordinary patron of the papists'. The Queen was surrounded by persuasive and subtle French missionaries who made numerous converts in Court circles. Her chapel was crowded for Mass each Sunday. In sum, Cromwell's conviction that there existed at Whitehall a movement to reconvert England to Popery through the agency of the established Church was not reached without circumstantial evidence.

The anti-episcopal party even at this date had its martyrs. The Puritan pamphleteers, Prynne, Burton, Bastwick and Leighton, who had published attacks on the Queen and bishops, met with the severest possible punishments short of death. In 1637 a certain John Lilburne, a Yorkshire youth of twenty, was brought before the prerogative court of the Star Chamber and accused of printing Puritan books in Holland. He refused to commit himself and was sentenced to be whipped, pilloried and imprisoned. He was lashed down the Strand and then put in the pillory in Palace Yard. Although still smarting from his wounds he exhorted the bystanders there to resist the tyranny of the bishops until at length an order arrived from the Star Chamber for him to be gagged. Afterwards he lay half-starved in the Fleet prison until Cromwell took up his case three years later.

To a convinced Puritan like Lilburne the Catholic Church was the Beast of the Revelation, the instrument chosen by Satan to destroy Christendom. A story was told in April 1630 of an oatmeal maker who had been brought before the High Commission, the prerogative court of the Church, and was ordered to take off his hat to the bishops present there. He refused. 'Will you not take off your hat to Privy Councillors?' he was asked. 'Then as you are Privy Councillors I put off my hat,' came the reply, 'but as ye are rags of the Beast, lo, I put it on again.' Towards the end of this scene Bishop Neile entered the room. 'Let us dismiss this foolish fellow,' said Neile. 'Hold thy peace', retorted the oatmeal maker, 'thou tail of the Beast that sittest at the lower end of the table.' Bishop Neile, equally obnoxious therefore to the unnamed outmeal maker and to Oliver Cromwell, was made Archbishop of York in 1634. The two archbishops were thenceforward the men most hated by the Puritan laity.

It was with the advice and assistance of these men that Charles I decided to introduce a new Prayer Book and set of canons into the presbyterian Kirk of Scotland. The framing of the Prayer Book had been entrusted to a committee of English and Scottish bishops (episcopacy had been reintroduced into Scotland in a modified form by James I). At first the Calvinist theologians hoped for better things from this committee. 'We heard the rumour', said a Scottish preacher, 'that the Bishop of Edinburgh chiefly had obtained that we should be quit of the Surplice, Cross, Apocrypha, Saints Days, and some other trash of the English liturgy'; but when it was learned that the Prayer Book was nothing but an almost unaltered version of the English book, the Scots, like the English Puritans, became convinced that this was a plot to re-establish Roman Catholicism, the religion of Charles I's beheaded grandmother, in the Church of John Knox. Riots rapidly spread from Edinburgh and Glasgow throughout the land. In February 1638 the Lord Treasurer of Scotland assured the King that if he wished to enforce his prayer book he would need an army of forty thousand men. At the very time he wrote the Scots were circulating a National Covenant for all ministers and their congregations to sign in defence of their 'true reformed religion'. The ever-warring clans and chieftains laid aside their hatreds and joined hands in defence of their drab but beloved creed. Once united the Scots were by no means willing to return to an allegiance to the bishops who offered them such 'trash'. Hence, although Charles gave way to the popular outcry against the Prayer Book, the Covenanters demanded further that their Kirk Assembly should be recognized as supreme over the bishops. The King denied their request, then hesitated, shilly-shallied, made cloudy declarations and finally declared war. His army, enlisted and maintained with the utmost difficulty, was greatly outnumbered by the Scottish *levée-en-masse*. In June 1639 Charles yielded before their superior forces at Berwick and agreed to their demands for fear they should cross the border, but in his heart he fully intended to restore the bishops to their offices at the earliest opportunity. The Covenanters understood his secret resolve and a renewal of the war seemed imminent. But meanwhile the English Army had disbanded for lack of pay, while the Scots still hovered over the frontier. At last Charles sought the advice of the one strong man among his ministers, the ex-Parliamentarian Strafford. Strafford tendered his counsel: extraordinary dangers demanded desperate measures. Parliament must be recalled.

§ 3

It has sometimes been commented on as remarkable that Cromwell had reached the age of forty before he made himself prominent in national affairs. But in reality the explanation is simple; in those days unless a man possessed either front-stair or back-stair influence at Court the only road to political success lay through the House of Commons. While Parliament was not sitting the most that a politician could hope for was to make himself so useful in local affairs as to render certain his choice as member when Parliament met again. This Cromwell had done. When Sir Oliver had sold Hinchinbrooke to the Montagues much of the Cromwell influence at Huntingdon had been lost, and with the final removal of the younger Oliver's family thence to Ely it was clear that the patronage which in effect bestowed two seats in the Commons had passed into other hands. But the name of the ex-Member for Huntingdon was known throughout the Eastern counties as that of an active, stirring Puritan, an acknowledged enemy of the 'papist' bishops and an incorruptible protector of the rights of property owners throughout the fen counties. Although it was not until 1643 that a Royalist newspaper dubbed Cromwell 'The Lord of the Fens', it was a nickname he already deserved by 1640.

A section of the Cambridge borough council therefore

decided that the late member for Huntingdon and ex-under-graduate of their local university would be a fitting representative for them in the new Parliament. One of their previous members was a certain Thomas Meautys, who was known to be a privileged person at Court. Might it not be well, they thought, in these troublous days also to have an experienced member of the Opposition? But a difficulty arose in the way of this plan; for Cromwell to represent the burgesses of Cambridge he must be a freeman of the city. However, the difficulty was overcome. According to the local charter the mayor had the right to create burgesses, and he was soon persuaded of the desirability of obtaining Cromwell's services for the borough. On January 7th, 1640, therefore, Oliver Cromwell 'of Huntingdon' was sworn a freeman of Cambridge 'on the presentation of the mayor of the town . . . gratis, on payment of one penny to the poor'.

So it was that Oliver Cromwell after eleven years' absence went back to Westminster. Apart from the Scottish war in which the Puritans openly sympathized with the Scots, the outstanding event of the sixteen-thirties had been the test case brought by Cromwell's cousin, John Hampden, before the Court of Exchequer in 1637. Hampden had refused to pay ship money, a property tax earmarked towards the cost of the fleet, which had been levied by the Crown as part of its prerogative rights not merely on the ports but also on the inland towns. Hampden's counsel argued that in a case of real national danger the subjects' and even the King's property might be forfeit to the 'law of necessity'; but to invoke the 'law of necessity' where danger was only 'apprehended' was, he said, to subject the Common Law to prerogative rule.

It was largely under the fear of such threats to the established law of the land that Cromwell and his friends went to the House of Commons in the spring of 1640, as guardians of the ancient law of England. The majority of this Short Parliament, as it was called, were — in Gardiner's exact words — 'no reformers, no followers of new ideas by which the lives of men might be

made brighter and happier than of old ... To them Parliaments were not an instrument of improvement, but an instrument to avert unpopular alterations.'

The annals of Cromwell are silent as to his part in this conservative Parliament that enjoyed its very brief career early in
1640, but he must certainly have been among the throng of
members who cried out 'a good speech!' when John Pym sat
down after his two-hour oration on April 17th. Pym was now
the accepted leader of the opposition to the Court in the Lower
House, yet he was not a Leader of the Opposition in the
modern sense. The royal ministers commanded no majority
in the House, for the King did not consider himself responsible
to Parliament. To him Parliament was merely a money-making
machine which had to be put into motion in times of financial
crisis. The new Lord Keeper Finch had said in his opening
address 'that His Majesty did not expect advice from them,
much less that they should interpose in any office of mediation,
which would not be grateful to him, but that they should, as
soon as might be, give His Majesty a supply, and that he would
give them time enough afterwards to represent any grievances
to him'. But it was far from the intentions of Pym or his supporters to let supply precede grievances. Yet in his harangue
he had been by no means truculent; he would, he said, be very
careful to express 'that modesty and humility which might be
expected by those of whose actions he was to speak'. He then
expounded in masterly fashion first the violation of parliamentary
privileges at their last meeting and in particular the imprisonment of members for their actions in the House of Commons,
from which one 'was freed by death'; second, the grievances of
religion; third, the grievance of taxation by royal prerogative,
which had increased by reason of the long intermittence of
parliaments and had only been brought to public notice by
Hampden's case. The Commons soon determined that until
the King renounced his rights to these taxes they would take
no steps to vote supplies. The conflict between the Commons
and the King was short and sharp. At first the King promised

to give way, then decided not to yield, more especially as he secretly learned that Pym would not offer him support against the Scottish Covenanters. Eighteen days after it had met the 'Short Parliament' was dissolved. Even moderate men went back to their constituencies profoundly dissatisfied with the Court.

Strafford, now King Charles's chief adviser, persuaded him that he must defeat the Scots without parliamentary aid. Money was sought in every direction in this cause. Ireland, which had voted £180,000 before the English Parliament met, was now to supply the King with 10,000 soldiers, according to the French ambassador at London, 'as well to bring to terms his English subjects as for the Scottish war'. Ship money and other prerogative taxes continued to be exacted. Strafford appealed vainly for loans to the City authorities and the Spanish ambassador; Charles, upon the advice of his wife, actually sought subsidies from the Pope! But even had he collected enough money Strafford, now a sick man, could not have invigorated a hopeless cause. The English soldiers proved mutinous and in August the Scots occupied Newcastle after routing an English force at Newburn Brook. 'Never', wrote Strafford, 'came any man to so lost a business . . . our horse all cowardly . . . an universal affright on all.' Whilst the Scots sought subsistence for their army in Northumberland, the King summoned a Great Council of Peers at York. 'Surely', he felt, 'the House of Lords will assist me.' He was mistaken. The advice tendered to him was to summon another Parliament and make peace with the Scots. In October peace negotiations were accordingly opened at Ripon and writs issued for a new Parliament.

The King's ministers made great efforts to obtain a House of Commons more favourable to them than the last. On October 2nd, Lord Keeper Finch addressed the following letter to the Mayor and Corporation of Cambridge:

'It hath pleased his Majesty to summon a Parliament to be holden at Westminster the third of November, and I hope it

will be a happy one. The last Parliament I recommended unto
you my cousin and friend Mr. Thomas Meautys, in whom I
always found ability and affection to serve you: him I shall this
time also, desire you (the rather for my sake) to make choice of
again for one of the burgesses. If you choose with him any
stranger, I build so much upon your love that I shall recom-
mend unto you my brother Sir Nathaniel Finch, knight, his
Majesty's sergeant-at-law, for whose care of you and affection
to do you any service I will undertake. But my meaning is
not that for choice of him you should praetermit [exclude] my
cousin Meautys, or any of your corporation you should have a
desire to elect, but only in case that with my cousin Meautys
you join a stranger.'

This letter was obviously aimed above all at preventing the re-
election of Cromwell. But the Lord Keeper was singularly
unsuccessful in his canvass; for not only was Cromwell chosen
but Thomas Meautys made way for a second Puritan member.
John Cleveland the poet related in after years that he had stood
for Cambridge in this election as a Royalist candidate and that
Cromwell had beaten him by one vote — 'that single vote had
ruined Church and Kingdom!' We must respect poetic licence.

§ 4

That famous assembly, the Long Parliament, which
gathered at Westminster in the first days of November 1640
contained at first only a small group of royal supporters concentrated mainly in the House of Lords. The Commons had,
even as compared with the Short Parliament, two hundred new
members, the bulk of whom had been elected, like the two
members for Cambridge, against the wishes of the Court,
while since 1629 when the Commons, under the leadership of
the martyred Sir John Eliot, had resisted for a time the order
to disperse, many Puritan politicians had died and of those who
remained the Earl of Bedford and John Pym, the leaders in
the Lords and Commons respectively, were not to survive long.

Hence Oliver Cromwell was now comparatively an old parliamentary hand and by mere reason of seniority possessed a strong claim to a seat — to use an inexact modern analogy — upon the Front Opposition Bench. He sat in the centre of a powerful and expanding phalanx of brothers-in-law, cousins' husbands and cousins once or more times removed, mostly members for the Eastern Counties. In all probability he was among those members who joined with Pym, Hampden and Sir Arthur Haselrig to keep an 'open house' as a party headquarters whither all were invited 'of whose conversion they had any hope'.

The whole House now concentrated with singleness of purpose on achieving a form of political control which hitherto it had been unable to obtain under the Stuarts. Whereas the Short Parliament had been accustomed to arise from its labours at noon, the Long Parliament generally sat on until four in the afternoon. Although Cromwell did not speak frequently in the debates we have ample proof that when he did so his words were listened to with attention, and we know that he did his duty upon many committees of the House and as a representative of his constituency with zeal and application.

The party to which Cromwell and his relatives belonged dominated the House and conceived its political programme to be essentially a conservative one, with its ultimate aim the restoration of the purity of the Constitution in Church and State. They must, said Pym, clear away the cobwebs that hung about the House lest they should breed dust in the future. They had, he thought, an unsurpassed opportunity to make their country happy by rooting out the grievances from which it had suffered during the past eleven years. They came to regard themselves as exposing and punishing the authors of a gigantic Popish Plot which had been foisted upon the King by his evil advisers. This plot, they maintained, was treasonable in the sense that it was a violation of the fundamental laws of the kingdom, involving an attack upon the Protestant religion as by law established and upon the rights and privileges of

Parliament. It was all the more dangerous because its instruments were the very men whose duty it was to manage and defend the Constitution. The judges, it was commonly asserted, had attacked the Law, and the bishops were overthrowing the Church.

What the Commons failed to realize was that the monarchy was standing upon the defensive. The noblest of the royal ministers sought nothing more than the restoration of the Crown to the position it had held in the Tudor era. Both Strafford and Pym were sticklers for the purity of the Elizabethan Constitution, but their notions of that Constitution differed as black from white. The King, said Strafford, must be a 'nursing father' to his people. But the 'people' — that is to say the well-to-do minority whose opinions really mattered — no longer needed a nursing father. Queen Elizabeth had finished all the nursing they required. Their lives and properties had ceased to be menaced from the Continent and until war should threaten again, the justification for this paternity had gone. Indeed, their royal father had become a pensioner living on their bounty and getting himself into trouble by his extravagance on undesirable escapades like the invasion of Scotland. It is significant that it was reported from Cambridgeshire, the centre of Cromwell's party, about the time that the Long Parliament met, that whereas the royal officers were able to collect ship-money from the poorer classes, the rich men steadily refused to pay. The wealthy came to Westminster armed with the ever-potent weapon of money to enforce their own political will upon the kingdom. This weapon enabled Parliament to exercise control over the Scottish Army, which was still encamped around Durham and did not intend to retreat until all its demands had been conceded. The parliamentary leaders arrived at a secret understanding with the Scottish commanders and guaranteed to pay their army until the conclusion of treaty negotiations. So long as the treaty remained unsettled Charles was wax, although slippery wax, in his Parliament's hands.

63

Meanwhile the Scots sent Commissioners to London to watch over their interests and to enter into close relations with their fellow Calvinists; among these was Robert Baillie, a Presbyterian minister and prolific letter-writer, who arrived in London on the same day as the Earl of Strafford, summoned from the North by the King. Said Baillie grimly of Strafford, 'when we get his head, all will go well'. English Parliamentarians were in full agreement with his view, and Pym determined to impeach the Earl for high treason. To both Houses Strafford seemed the spear-head of the plot against their liberties. On November 12th he was arrested, but his trial did not open till March.

The attitude of the Commons when it first met was reflected in an order made for the recall of the men who had been imprisoned three years before for libelling the Queen and the bishops and had been exiled in the obscurest corners of the kingdom. The reception given to these men on their release was extraordinary. Huge crowds went out to cheer them; they were greeted like a popular sportsman or aviator of to-day; at each halt on their road to London every form of honour and gift was showered upon them; in the City itself their path was strewn with flowers and herbs. Among them was John Lilburne, whose petition for release had been presented to the House by Cromwell, who (according to an unfriendly observer) 'aggravated the imprisonment of this man by the council-table unto that height that one would have believed the very Government itself had been in great danger by it'. Oliver was always vehement in his orations. Clarendon relates how in this same Parliament he had been the chairman of a committee upon which Cromwell sat to consider a dispute over an enclosure made by the Montagues. Their tenants petitioned against the enclosure, and Cromwell 'appeared much concerned to countenance the petitioners', seconding and enlarging 'upon what they said with great passion'. When reprimanded 'Cromwell in great fury reproached the chairman for being partial', and the committee broke up in confusion.

We may notice in passing the curiously persistent contacts between the Montagues and Oliver Cromwell throughout his life. It was the Montagues who had bought Hinchinbrooke, the ancestral home of his family. It was Henry Montague, first Earl of Manchester, before whom Cromwell had been brought to justify his attacks upon the Mayor of Huntingdon in 1633. But a few years later Cromwell violently criticized the second Earl of Manchester as a military commander, and yet as Lord Protector he entrusted this Manchester's first cousin Edward with the supreme command of his Navy. The families who governed the country were too few for their quarrels to be permanent.

The arrest of Strafford was followed by that of Laud — 'poor Canterbury ... a pendicle at the Lord-Lieutenant's ear', Baillie called him — and of other royal ministers. At the same time it was considered essential by the party opposed to the Court that Parliament should be placed in a position to prevent a recurrence of the 'tyranny' instituted by the disgraced ministers, by asserting its right to be called into regular consultation on all matters of national policy. A Bill was therefore introduced into the House of Commons to ensure an annual meeting of Parliament 'whether the King issued his writ or not', and Cromwell acted as one of its sponsors. At the request of the House of Lords it was transformed into a Triennial Bill, and although the King gave his consent with the utmost reluctance in due course it became part of the law of the land.

In January and February 1641 two significant events occurred: the first was the enforced surrender of the King to the Commons in their political demands as exemplified by the Triennial Act, and the second was the plain beginning of a split in the Commons itself over ecclesiastical policy. Almost all the members of the House agreed that the bishops had abused their powers, but whereas some thought that all would be well if their purely secular functions were taken from them, others believed that religion could not be rightly practised until episcopacy was extirpated 'root and branch' from the Church.

E
65

Cromwell was a forceful advocate of the Root-and-Branch party, whilst the bishops found moderate supporters in men like Hyde, Lord Falkland and Lord Digby. Since the King was by law the creator and protector of the bishops a nucleus was formed around which was to crystallize the Royalist side in the civil wars.

Just before Christmas the City of London, which Hyde described as 'the sink of all the ill humour of the kingdom', had presented a petition signed, it was said, by 20,000 people in favour of the abolition of episcopacy, and on February 8th the opposing parties came into the open in a great debate over it. Lord Digby maintained that the petition was 'a comet or blazing star raised and kindled out of the stench, out of the poisonous exhalation of a corrupted hierarchy', and other members of the bishops' defence group put forward the argument that the introduction of a system of elected committees to rule the Church would mean the recognition of a democratic principle, and no one in the House of Commons at that date was in the very least a democrat. Sir John Strangways asserted 'if we made a parity [equality] in the Church we must at last come to a parity in the Commonwealth', and added that the bishops were one of the three estates of the realm. Mr. Cromwell stood up next and said:

He knew no reason of those suppositions and inferences which the gentleman had made that last spake; upon this divers [members] interrupted him and called him to the Bar. Mr. Pym and Mr. Holles thereupon spake to the Orders of the House that if the gentleman had said anything that might offend, he might explain himself in his place. . . . Mr. Cromwell went on: and said he did not understand why the gentleman that last spake should make an inference of parity from the Church to the Commonwealth; not that there was any necessity of the great revenues of the bishops. He was more convinced touching the irregularity of bishops than ever before, because like the Roman hierarchy they would not endure to have their condition come to a trial.'

Although the vehemence of Cromwell's speeches had even before this caused comment in the House, the question was one which inevitably raised deep and fierce antagonisms, but for a time it was shelved and a spirit of compromise reigned. A Bill to exclude the bishops from the House of Lords and from all secular offices was sent to the Upper House with general approval, but was there mangled to such an extent as to strengthen the Root-and-Branch party in the Commons. Early in June Cromwell and other Puritans determined to bring in a Bill to abolish the bishops entirely, and this was given a first reading by 135 to 108 votes. Before we pursue the bishops further we must turn to the trial of Strafford.

The importance of that trial is that it was a final test of strength between the King and the Commons, and that it revealed in its clearest light the opposing systems of government in which each believed. So able was Strafford's defence of his administration that it seemed almost certain that the Lords acting as judges would not accept the Commons' impeachment. The leaders of the Commons therefore decided to proceed against him by an exceptional method, a Bill of Attainder, which required the assent of the Crown to become effective. The Bill passed both Houses, the Lords permitting in their political capacity what they would have refused in their judicial capacity, and it was carried up to the King. Would Charles now consent to see his faithful minister, whose only crime had been his care for the royal service, thus condemned to die? He had already done everything in his power in a roundabout way to save Strafford: he offered to banish him from England for ever; he had even attempted to smuggle him out of the Tower. But he feared that if he openly resisted the parliamentary will his wife and even his children would be menaced. His remaining councillors urged him strongly to yield. Strafford himself had already released him from his promise of protection. Like the weakling he always had been Charles gave way to this pressure. On May 11th Strafford wrote to his son from the Tower: 'the heart of man is deceitful above all things'. Did he in his last hours feel doubts about the cause and the master for whom he was now to die? The leaders of the Commons did not hesitate as to their course. The following morning the head of the man they named the Arch-Apostate fell on the scaffold.

Thenceforward the Commons were triumphant in all purely political affairs. Upon the same day that the King assented to Strafford's attainder he agreed to a Bill whereby the Long Parliament could not be dissolved without its own consent — a revolutionary measure indeed. Then followed a long-drawn-out summer session during which the Commons enacted every measure they wanted. All the taxes levied by the sole authority of the Crown were declared illegal; all the prerogative courts were abolished; a Roman Catholic persecution began; and the Scottish Treaty was signed on the Covenanters' own terms. The King showed no grace in yielding and no courage in openly resisting his triumphant Parliament. As soon as the armies were disbanded in August he left Whitehall for Scotland, in the hope of raising there a party to re-establish his dwindling rights. Yet had he in fact gauged the situation at Westminster accurately, he would have remained; for it was in England and not in Scotland, in the Church of England and not in the Presbyterian Kirk, that a Royalist party was forming, ready to fight and die for the master who had abandoned Strafford.

§ 5

In the months that followed the King's departure for Scotland the political history of England can be seen running in two main streams. The first of these consisted, as we have just indicated, in the gradual evolution of a Royalist party. As early as June the King had sent for Hyde and sought his support against the Root-and-Branch men, but it was not until that policy upon which all the members of the Commons agreed, to wit, the destruction of the prerogative courts and the execution of Strafford, had been carried out, that the cleavage in ecclesiastical affairs began to obtrude itself in the debates. In October 1641 one of the royal advisers in London was able to write to the King:

'I may not forbear to let Your Majesty know that Lord Falkland, Sir John Strangways, Mr. Waller, Mr. Edward Hyde and Mr. Holborne have lately stood as champions in maintenance of your prerogative whereof your Majesty shall do well to take some encouragement.'

Between these two parties there was an undecided minority which would not yet commit itself to the complete abolition of the bishoprics.

The other stream consisted in the intensification of the antagonism between the King and the majority in the Commons. Pym was convinced that Charles was plotting and intriguing to rescind the concessions he had made and to resuscitate the great Popish Plot that the Commons had striven to kill during the past year. In reality Charles at this time still hoped to engineer a reaction in his favour along peaceful lines through the agency of Hyde and Falkland's party in the Commons and the pro-episcopal majority in the Lords. But the actions of the Royalist extremists lent strength to Pym's worst fears and determined him at all costs to disarm the King completely. The matter was brought to a head by the rebellion that broke out in Ireland in the autumn. The Roman Catholics there, goaded to ungovernable anger by years of persecution and ill treatment, swindled out of their lands in Connaught, perceiving the new attitude adopted towards their co-religionists in England and no longer awed by the stern rule of Strafford, rose in arms against the English settlers in the hope of obtaining a guarantee of immunity for their Church similar to that which the Covenanters had gained for theirs. Here, thought the English Puritans, is the veritable Popish Plot! Cromwell had foreseen it — as early as March he had moved in committee to arrest all the 'papists' in Dublin, but had been overruled. But the question that confronted the Commons was how to provide for the suppression of the rebellion without putting into the King's hands arms which might be used against them as Strafford had proposed to turn his army against them. The only way they could find was to diminish the royal prerogative even further. Pym resolved that the Army must be managed only by officers and ministers of whom Parliament approved. In this proposal he was anticipating the modern doctrine of ministerial responsibility.

Cromwell ranged himself upon the side of the Root-and-Branch men and of Pym. In September, when Parliament met again after a brief recess, he pressed vehemently but unsuccessfully for the abolition of the Book of Common Prayer, which he regarded as a guide to superstitious papal usages in the parish churches, a view which might be sustained by any present day Evangelical. He thought that prayers were best composed by individuals themselves according to their various needs, and that the chief duty of the clergy was not to conduct set services but to preach regularly and continually. He therefore urged upon a select committee that 'sermons should be in the afternoon [of the Sabbath] in all parishes of England at the charge of those parishes where there are no sermons in the afternoon'. When in October the King appointed five new bishops, 'Mr. Cromwell renewed again', noted Sir Simon D'Ewes, M.P., in his diary, 'the motion which had been first moved by myself yesterday and was this day renewed again by Sir Walter Earle touching a conference with the Lords for the staying of the investiture of the five new bishops that were to be made and did speak somewhat bitterly against Doctor Holdsworth'. Here Cromwell seems to have seized upon the wrong victim for, according at least to D'Ewes, Holdsworth 'was a most learned man . . . ready to further a reformation in the Church'. About the same time Cromwell invented an ingenious way in which to force through the Bill to exclude the bishops from the Lords. He moved that the thirteen bishops whom the Commons had just impeached should be suspended from their right to vote in the Lords 'until after the bill was passed!' Finally he was prominent in advocating Pym's policy of disarming the King. On November 6th he helped to carry a motion ordering the Earl of Essex, who was friendly to the Puritan party, to take command of the trained bands south of the Trent and continue in command until Parliament should give further orders — a definite filching of customary monarchical rights.

Late in that same November the Houses debated a Grand Remonstrance to the King which was in fact a manifesto to all the literate in the land of the political faith of the parliamentary majority. This enormous document of two hundred and four clauses detailed the evils which had befallen the nation since Charles I ascended the throne. It described the plot that had been exposed and countered by the vigilance of the Commons to free government 'from all restraint of laws concerning our persons and estates', to re-establish Popery and to root out Puritanism. It asserted that Parliament had 'ever been careful not to desire anything that should weaken the Crown either in just profit or useful power', and demonstrated this thesis with more ingenuity than persuasiveness. In conclusion it called upon the King to employ only 'such councillors, ambassadors and other ministers . . . as the Parliament may have cause to confide in'. The Remonstrance was carried in an excited House by 159 votes to 148. The minority wished to record a protest; so violent was the feeling in the House that hands were laid upon scabbards; and as the members trooped home at four o'clock that winter morning, Cromwell is reported to have said to Falkland, one of the leading opponents of the Remonstrance, 'if it had been rejected, I would have sold all I had the next morning, and never have seen England any more'.

A few days later the King returned to London, having failed completely to form a Royalist party in Scotland. The large minority which voted against the Grand Remonstrance encouraged him to believe that he would at last find a considerable party in England. But he soon offended the Commons by

ordering that the guard around the House should be withdrawn. The wildest rumours swept the Westminster air,
many blowing across the Irish Sea. Cromwell made a valiant
attempt to find a scapegoat for the King, but again missed the
mark by naming the Earl of Bristol, one of the sanest and most
moderate of the royal counsellors. He claimed that the Earl
had earlier in the year advised the King to put his English
army (now disbanded) 'in a posture that could have no ordinary
meaning'. The Solicitor-General answered that, on the contrary, the posture had a very ordinary meaning; it was facing
the Scottish Army 'which lay near'. Cromwell was not convinced and worked in support of the parliamentary proposals
to gain complete control of the army which was to embark for
Ireland. The House of Lords resisted this basic attack on the
King's rights. But the Commons and the City of London believed that the 'papists' were everywhere rising against the true
Protestant religion. Men marched the streets crying out 'No
popery! No bishops! No popish lords!' A mob invaded the
Upper House. The Commons impeached twelve bishops for
treason and prepared to join the popish Queen with them.
Charles had long vacillated as to his best course, taking up and
then discarding first one project, then another; but this he
thought was too much. He too would impeach. He ordered
his Attorney-General to frame an indictment against five obnoxious members of the Commons and one peer, Lord Kimbolton, of whom more later, for traitorously endeavouring to
subvert the government of the kingdom, and went down in
person with his soldiers to arrest the accused. By the time he
had gained admission to the privileged precincts 'the birds had
flown'. But what was even more unfortunate for him was that
in those days when correct constitutional procedure meant so
much, he had permitted the word 'impeach' to be used, and
only the Commons had the right to impeach. The fiasco of the
unsuccessful *coup d'état* carried the Lords over to the side of
the Commons. In the City the deepest passions were aroused.
The King could no longer safely remain in London. When h e

drove in his carriage to supervise a vain search for the five members a paper was thrown at his feet 'on which was written the famous words of the ten tribes, when they forsook the foolish and wantonly tyrannical Rehoboam — "To your tents, O Israel!" ' On January 10th, 1642, Charles I left Whitehall for Hampton Court. He was not to return except as a prisoner on trial for his life.

The next eight months represent the lull which preceded the storms of civil war. The King, now supported by the Anglican or Cavalier party, and the Parliamentarians or Roundheads each prepared to fight for their privileges. Arms and money were collected by both sides. Only four days after the King had left London the Commons went into committee on 'the state of the kingdom', and Oliver Cromwell moved that a sub-committee might be named to consider means of putting the kingdom in a position of defence. Early in June he promised £500 to buy horse, money and plate for the defence of Parliament. Oliver threw himself with all the burning fervour of his nature into organizing military preparations. We shall not linger over the detailed history of the useless negotiations of these months. It suffices to say that Parliament demanded from the King absolute control of the militia and fortresses throughout the realm and the right to 'approve', in effect to appoint, all Ministers of State as well as the guardians of his children. 'Ordinances' were issued, agreed to by both Houses, which the people were ordered to regard as the equivalent of Acts of Parliament. No monarch bred in the absolutist tradition of the Tudors could admit these claims. On August 22nd Charles set up his standard at Nottingham. Ten days earlier a middle-aged member of the House of Commons buckled on his sword and rode hell-for-leather towards his constituency.

CHAPTER IV

OLD IRON-SIDES

§ I

THE great civil war, mighty sunderer of families and friends, was at least fought over matters that lie nearest to the human heart. Fear, loyalty, property rights, class instincts, religious beliefs all mingled among the motives determining individuals to cast their fortune in one scale or the other. In many cases the course of action dictated by duty seemed crystal clear; but in other cases there was a conflict of duties as potent and as shaking as any portrayed in the dramatic tragedies of ancient Greece. Some men who believed that the Church had been corrupted by the Catholic tendencies of the bishops were yet convinced that they must lay their lives at the feet of the King, were his religion theirs or not. Other men, although they trusted implicitly in the virtues of the English constitution centreing on the monarch, felt that it would never again function rightly until the evil advisers who still led Charles I astray were forcibly removed from his service.

Yet, while it must always be rash to lay down any all-inclusive generalization as to the character of the sides in this war, it is essential to appreciate that there were very definite broad social, and geographical lines of cleavage between the opposing camps. On the whole, the powerful rising economic groups of industrialists and merchants were ranged against the King. Nearly all the industrial towns were guided by Puritan ministers and lecturers; all the big ports at an early stage in the contest declared themselves on the parliamentary side; and after the war was over, among the lists of proscribed Royalists drawn up by the Cromwellian Government few names of merchants or tradesmen are to be found. On the other hand, the bulk of the wealthy landowners rallied to the defence of the Crown. Even in the Eastern counties the most solidly Puritan district in the country, men like Sir Sidney Montague and Sir Oliver Cromwell, the new and old owners of the mansion of Hinchin-brooke, stood out for the King.

To one simple-minded Cavalier indeed 'the King's side were almost all gentlemen and of the Parliament's few', but in fact many of the younger branches of established families and many well-bred tenant farmers became Roundheads. Moreover, the quality of the Royalist 'gentlemen' was not above suspicion, for as the same Cavalier (Sir John Oglander) was later to record in his commonplace book: 'Truly all the greatest part of the King's commanders were so debased by drinking, whoring and swear-ing that no man could expect God's blessing on their actions.' As for the average farm labourer, he probably continued to do uncomprehendingly what his master told him. It is related that on the eve of the battle of Marston Moor such a labourer was found by a patrol standing in the middle of the Moor. He was challenged, 'Are you for King or Parliament?' 'Whaat!' was his reply as he scratched his head, 'Has them two fallen out then?' Altogether the safest assertion that can be made about the class division in the civil war is that the new middle classes and the devotees of the new religion joined together to demand the largest share of the political powers hitherto exercised almost exclusively by the monarch and the landed aristocracy. The King would not — perhaps he could not — yield up his rights. A trial of military strength between his supporters and theirs followed.

Geographically the country was roughly divided by a line drawn in a wavering south-easterly direction from Chester to Southampton. Wales and Cornwall were staunch for the monarchy; so was the larger part of the north of England, Manchester notably excepted. Parliament drew its strength from the east, south-east, and City of London and the big seaports. The contest was in its initial stages to be concentrated in the Midlands.

In the spring of 1642 neither side possessed an army. The only military force in the kingdom consisted of the militia or trained bands, which were drilled at infrequent intervals to meet national emergencies but were much less effective than a modern territorial army and perhaps equivalent merely to a special constabulary. The only competent trained band was that of the City, which stood at the disposal of Parliament. But the King was able to call upon a potentially useful cavalry in the outdoor staffs of the richer country gentry. In the summer both King and Parliament issued proclamations to rally the local militias to their sides and made every effort to seize the stocks of arms and ammunition that were available in the county magazines.

In preparing for war Oliver Cromwell at last found an opportunity to express his innate will to lead and to act. The man who at the age of eighteen had governed the lives of six women, who had ten years later made unseemly and outspoken speeches against the government of his native town, who had been rebuked both in full session and in committee of the House of Commons for his single-minded, passionate and uncontrollable eloquence was now at forty-three to find an outlet for his exuberant nature which was in time to give the extra drive and encouragement to the Roundhead armies that would ensure their victory.

He was first able to demonstrate his military capacities in his own constituency. The town and the county of Cambridge had been recognized for some time as a centre of Roundhead enthusiasm. Early in July Cromwell had sent down arms into the county, and had moved the House of Commons to permit the townsmen of Cambridge to raise two companies of volunteers for their defence. But if the town was behind its member, the university contained a number of gentlemen, young and old, especially the old, who favoured the Royalist cause. They secretly collected arms at the Bull Hotel and elsewhere, and made ready to send their college plate northward to be melted down at the royal treasury. Cromwell soon got wind of these activities in his old university. He obtained leave of the Commons to suppress them, and at the beginning of August rode away from London along the Great North Road upon this errand.

On August 8th St. John's College had decided to dispatch 2000 ounces of plate to the King, and when Cromwell arrived and took post on the Huntingdon Road the President of Clare managed to evade his hastily raised troops and smuggled out this contribution. But here the Royalist successes ended. Leaving some of his men to guard the western outskirts, Oliver entered the town itself, determined to stop the supply of treasure at its source. He learned on his arrival that a certain Captain Docwra had just come to convoy the King's College plate to the Royalist headquarters. Cromwell immediately blockaded Docwra's company in King's College and then seized the town castle. The end of the story appears to be that both Docwra and the booty were captured. The remainder of the university plate was intercepted and was restored to the colleges. On August 17th the grateful Commons put Cambridge into Cromwell's charge and authorized him to resist forcibly all hostile attempts against it, to disarm all 'Popish recusants' and generally to preserve the peace of the neighbourhood. He at once set about carrying out his instructions by discouraging the loyalism of the leading dons. 'Down he came again', recounted one of the learned Royalist doctors four years later, 'in terrible manner with what force he could draw together, and surrounds divers Colleges, while we are at our devotions in our several chapels; taking away prisoners several doctors of divinity, heads of colleges . . . and these he carries with him to London in triumph.' Thenceforward Cambridge was to be a Roundhead stronghold where Cromwell reigned supreme.

The war had now broken out on every side, and preparations were being made in London to defeat the King before he was able to recruit his forces. A Committee of Safety under Pym had been set up, and many people hoped that since Parliament had control of the only competent militia as well as of the wealth of London with which to pay additional soldiers, the war would be speedily over and the King brought to his senses. The parliamentary procedure for enlistment was to guarantee an initial sum of £1100 to every captain who raised a troop of horse. Directly the war began Cromwell managed to collect a troop of sixty, which he later increased to eighty. He enlisted it mainly in his native county and went to Huntingdon to exhort men to join up 'for the liberty of the gospel and the laws of the land'. This became Troop No. 67 in the parliamentary cavalry under the nominal command of the new Earl of Bedford. Curiously enough Cromwell's first troop is known to history as consisting of 'arquebusiers', that is to say, armed with an old-fashioned type of musket. Actually the arquebus had by that date gone into disuse and although the name was retained it simply meant light cavalry armed only with swords and pistols.

It is arguable that the war would soon have ended had it not been for the fact that the parliamentary forces had the misfortune to be commanded by William Devereux, second Earl of Essex. This earl was the son of Queen Elizabeth's favourite, and having lost his father on the scaffold and two successive wives through divorce and infidelity he had naturally acquired a gloomy outlook on life, which was not, however, uncongenial to his Puritan admirers. At Oxford we are told he had occupied his hours in books 'that afforded most profit, not most delight'; his experience of active military service was small, but his self-satisfaction was extensive; his seriousness and earnestness, although highly commended by his contemporaries, did not altogether recompense for his all-embracing incompetence as a general. On September 9th, 1642, the Earl reluctantly led his army out of London towards Northampton, 'carrying with him his coffin and his winding sheet, together with the scutcheon that would be needed at his funeral'. Four days later Captain Cromwell's troop was ordered to join Essex's main body where it was attached to the regiment commanded by Sir Philip Stapleton. So far as we know, Oliver did not pack his coffin.

Arrived at Northampton the Earl of Essex took a rest and

allowed Charles to march as far as Chester recruiting and
collecting arms. When Charles reached Shrewsbury Essex
occupied Worcester, where he sat down again to watch events.
But it was not until eleven days after the King's army had left
Shrewsbury that Essex suddenly learned that the Cavaliers
were swiftly marching on London. Aroused from his lethargy
by these surprising tidings the parliamentary general set out
at good speed to intercept the enemy; and so great indeed was
his hurry that he was obliged to leave scattered a not incon-
siderable section of his forces. On October 23rd, 1642, the
two armies met near Banbury. The army of Essex occupied
a position about a mile in front of their base village of Kineton
after which the Roundheads named the ensuing battle.[1] The
Royalists at first drew up their forces on Edgehill — the name
by which the battle is generally known to history — a high
defensive position but useless for the purposes of attack.

At one o'clock the King's army descended from Edgehill to
begin the advance; it was inferior in infantry and in arms to
the Parliamentarians but had a thousand more cavalry and
dragoons under the command of the gallant and licentious
Prince Rupert, the King's nephew. Rupert massed the bulk
of his cavalry on the right wing, the post of honour. Both
armies had their cavalry on the wings and their infantry in the
centre. The battle opened, after a light and harmless cannonade,
with a cavalry charge by Rupert who drove back the enemy
cavalry opposed to him (one Roundhead regiment deserted),
captured the base village of Kineton and pressed on even
farther north until stopped in the early evening by the belated
arrival of two foot regiments and ten troops of horse under the
command of John Hampden, now a colonel, bringing up the
artillery from Warwick.

Meanwhile the Royalist cavalry on the left also charged
successfully, but either deliberately or by misfortune had completely missed the cavalry regiments under Sir Philip Stapleton
and Sir William Balfour opposed to it. All the Royalist horse-

[1] See map opposite p. 81.

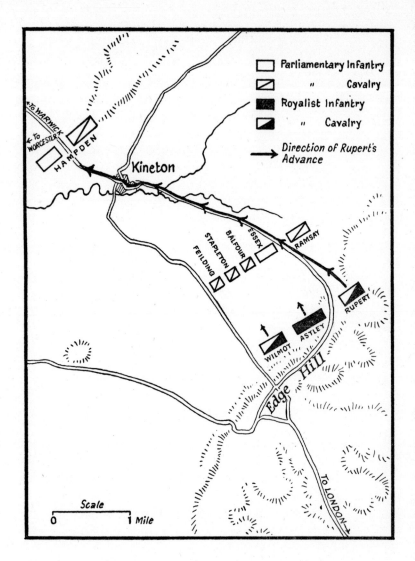

BATTLE OF EDGEHILL, OCTOBER 23, 1642

men had thus galloped energetically from the battlefield and had left two of the best Roundhead cavalry regiments to assist the numerically superior parliamentary foot soldiers against the unsupported Royalist infantry. Stapleton's horse were, however, at first repulsed by the infantry and a fierce struggle 'at push of pike' took place in the centre. At this point the pessimistic Essex, convinced that all was lost, snatched a pike from a soldier and prepared to die fighting. But Balfour's regiment overcame a regiment of the enemy foot and captured most of the cannon. Finally the bulk of the Royalist foot was assaulted by Balfour in the flank and by Stapleton in the rear while it was still struggling with the Roundhead infantry in front. One Cavalier regiment was cut to pieces, but two other regiments covered by cannon and a ditch held on till dark when the Roundhead bullet and powder were exhausted. Prince Rupert and the Royalist horse, discouraged from charging on indefinitely northwards by Hampden's whiff of shot, straggled back after dark to the field of battle in time to save the infantry from annihilation but too late to affect the issue. Hampden came up early in the morning of October 24th and pressed Essex to continue the battle. But since his men were exhausted and his reserves used Essex preferred to retreat to cover London even at the price of leaving the enemy in proud possession of the field. The King took Banbury and entered Oxford, which thenceforward became his headquarters, just as Cambridge was Cromwell's.

Some biographers have dilated imaginatively on the heroic actions performed by Captain Oliver Cromwell in the battle of Edgehill, but the truth is that we have not the means of knowing, and probably never will have, what part, if any, he played in this contest. It is of course plain that if his troop of horse had been with Sir Philip Stapleton's regiment, to which it was originally attached, from the time when the troops were first drawn up in line, he would have participated in the central movement which converted apparently certain defeat into an honourably drawn contest. But was his troop with Stapleton at that time? In support of this belief, reference is usually made to an official parliamentary account which stated that Cromwell was one of the officers 'who never stirred from their troops but they and their troops fought to the last minute'. Unfortunately, the author of this account, Nathaniel Fiennes, a lawyer who was subsequently a close collaborator with Cromwell during the Protectorate, did not leave it at that. For he mentions more casually in innocent parenthesis in the course of a letter (attached to the account) which was written about the part played by his brother John, that Cromwell's troop did not arrive on the scene of the fighting until evening approached. John Fiennes, he states, reached Kineton 'between three and four in the afternoon; there he met the parliamentary cavalry fleeing before Rupert's charge'. 'In time he gathered a pretty body together (there being ... *Captain Cromwell's troop at length come to them also*) and marched towards the town' — Kineton. Finally Fiennes joined Hampden's brigade, which had at last stopped Rupert's headlong advance. Dr. Gardiner tried to clear up this contradiction by assuming that the Captain Cromwell here mentioned was not the future Lord Protector but another man of the same name. Gardiner asserts in fact that he was Oliver's own eldest surviving son, who bore his father's Christian name. Unhappily for this theory the younger Oliver was only a cornet, not a captain, he had at that time no troop and his regiment took no part in the battle but was left behind to garrison Worcester. But even if the elder Oliver arrived only in time for the tail-end of the fighting he could still have fought 'till the last minute', and this explanation would harmonize with the assertion in Denzil Holles' *Memoirs* — Holles also fought as a Roundhead at Edgehill where he and his regiment distinguished themselves — that Cromwell lost his way to the battlefield. Oliver's may easily have been one of the scattered troops which, like Hampden's, were delayed by its duties from reaching the field in time to take part in the opening of the battle. If this is the true story about Cromwell at Edgehill there would be a touch of irony in the fact that the greatest soldier in the civil

war arrived too late for its first battle. Unlike King Frederick
the Great of Prussia, however, at the first battle of the Austro-
Prussian War, it is at least certain that once Oliver arrived
he stayed there.

A few days after Edgehill Charles marched upon London,
where Essex's army, reinforced by the new levies hastily drawn
up by the terrified city, awaited him. Although Rupert
succeeded in cutting to pieces the Roundhead outposts at
Brentford, the royal army was too inferior in numbers to
attack and after exchanging a few cannon shots at Turnham
Green withdrew slowly to Oxford. The first phase of the Civil
War was at an end.

§ 2

The easy victory anticipated by many of the Roundhead
leaders when Essex first left London with his army had not
been realized and the City had been thoroughly frightened by
the thunder of cannon close at hand. Moreover, at the beginning of 1643 the royal commanders had decided upon a
concerted plan of campaign to overwhelm the rebellious city
by advances from Cornwall eastwards and from York south-
wards, while Prince Rupert held the Earl of Essex in check
in the Midlands. The parliamentary generals had allowed the
initiative to be taken out of their hands, and even Pym and his
Committee of Safety recognized that their cause was in the
gravest danger. The change of attitude in the parliamentary
leaders was reflected in the peace propositions that were presented to the King at Oxford in March. For while the abolition of episcopacy was now for the first time included among
the terms (the Root-and-Branch party having triumphed in the
depleted Houses) other demands made in the previous year
as to the parliamentary control of the King's ministers were
much modified. But Charles, who now overestimated the
strength of the peace party and underestimated the courage of
his enemies, announced that he would not consent to any

diminution of his ancestral prerogatives. The war therefore continued and indeed spread to every corner of the kingdom.

In order the better to organize military resistance to the Royalist advance, Parliament hit on the expedient of forming the counties into associations for mutual defence. In practice this scheme only proved feasible where the counties were all predominantly Roundhead, to wit, in the Eastern Association of Cambridgeshire, Hertfordshire, Norfolk, Suffolk, Essex and Huntingdonshire. Lord Grey of Wark was put at the head of the Association, and Cromwell was made a colonel in recognition of his influence in East Anglia and of his services to Parliament during the previous year. He rapidly became the leading spirit in the new unit. A Nottinghamshire lady who was no friend of Cromwell's noted in the biography of her Roundhead husband:

'And now [1643] were all the counties in England no longer idle spectators, but several stages whereon the tragedy of the civil war was acted; except the Eastern Association, where Mr Oliver Cromwell by his diligence prevented the designs of the royal party.'

This success of Cromwell would not have been possible without the most elaborate, widespread and detailed organization for defence throughout the Eastern counties. In every town and village committees were set up to collect funds, weapons and soldiers to protect their homesteads against 'the violence, oppressions and plunderings of those wicked men, foreigners, papists, malignants and traitors, which call themselves the King's Army'. Preachers powerfully exhorted their flocks to sacrifice their all for the common good. Newspapers, fly-sheets and Association booklets were poured out as propaganda from hastily improvised printing presses. Not since the days of the Armada were so many voluntary contributions heaped together in so short a space of time. Every man gave his musket, pistol, horse or piece of silver to form a part of the sinews of war. The cry for money was persistent. Cromwell had to spend much of his time in whipping up local committees into finding pay for his men. He wrote to Suffolk: 'I am sorry I should so often trouble you about the business of money: it's no pleasant subject to be frequent upon.' To Colchester he complained on behalf of one of his captains: 'He hath been unhappy beyond others in not receiving any pay for himself, and what he had for his soldiers is out long ago.' Again, 'I beseech you hasten the supply to us: forget not money'; and again, 'If we have not money speedily, my troops will be much discouraged.' Finally in September he wrote to a close friend in London: 'Of all men I should not trouble you with money matters did not the heavy necessities my troops are in press me beyond measure. I am neglected exceedingly.' A month later when he arrived at Boston in Lincolnshire he 'wept' because he found there 'no moneys'. But although vast personal effort was essential, Cromwell's vehemence and energy achieved its purpose. The Royalist supporters throughout his association were arrested, repulsed or suppressed. A Royalist commission of array was scotched at St. Albans; Cambridge was fully fortified, the castle being strengthened with building material properly belonging to some new college buildings; and within one fortnight in March Cromwell rode from Cambridge to Norwich, from Norwich to Yarmouth and Lowestoft, from Lowestoft back to Norwich and thence to King's Lynn and back to Cambridge, besides crushing Royalist risings, and brought in Royalist gentry prisoners from various parts of the two counties.

Against such determination and enthusiasm the Royalist bands hurled themselves in vain. On April 25th 'Master Ram', the pious Puritan minister of Spalding in Lincolnshire, at last heard the good news that Crowland, the northernmost point of the Eastern Association, was about to be recaptured from the Cavaliers by three noble gentlemen including Colonel Cromwell. His Puritan soldiers did not celebrate this success with wine and carousing but contented themselves instead with making sad havoc of the painted glass windows in Peterborough Cathedral.

Cromwell was by no means satisfied merely to clear a Roundhead area of stray Royalists. He was anxious to advance against the nearest main body of the enemy, which under the Earl of Newcastle was entrenched in Yorkshire and Lincolnshire. Since the beginning of April it had been known that 'Colonel Cromwell's Cambridge men were in good readiness waiting the call and direction of my Lord General'. But my Lord General Essex was sitting placidly at Windsor, optimistically hoping that the King would see reason and treat for peace. His view and that of many other Presbyterian officers was that their function was not to fight with the other side but merely to give the King a good fright. The Royalists, however, did not appreciate these military tactics, and were concerned to beat the rebellious Roundheads in the field.

While awaiting orders Cromwell went to Huntingdonshire and paid a call upon his Royalist godfather and namesake who now dwelt half-ruined and in comparative obscurity at Ramsey. Old Sir Oliver afterwards related the story of the visit and recalled how his godson treated him with the utmost courtesy 'but at the same time not only disarmed but plundered him, for he took away all his plate'.

At length orders came from Essex and an arrangement was made for a combined attack on Lincolnshire from the Eastern Association and the Midlands. But of all the officers available only Cromwell was able to persuade his troops to move out of their home counties. On May 13th with twelve troops of horse, of whom Cromwell said 'some of them are so broken that you shall seldom see worse', he defeated a Royalist body of cavalry twice the size of his own near Grantham. 'With this handful', he reported, 'it pleased God to cast the scale of victory in our favour.' But he could not press forward alone and again sought a rendezvous with the other commanders at Nottingham. In this town he began openly to show his dissatisfaction at the mismanagement of the war. Why were not efforts to advance properly concerted by the Commander-in-Chief? he demanded. Why was the only ready money available for the payment of his troops the little that he was able to provide out of his own pocket? Why did the main Roundhead army lie idle while its officers quarrelled and disobeyed? He sent off a written complaint to London to this effect. There at least he had friends who were determined on a national victory and not merely on safeguarding their own homes.

Meanwhile the Royalists were everywhere pushing forward. In Gloucestershire a parliamentary army under the leadership of Sir William Waller, who had yet to earn his title of 'William the Conqueror', was slowly retiring before the able Cavalier general, Sir Ralph Hopton, who was about to win a crushing victory at Roundway Down. In Yorkshire a parliamentary force under two local landowners, Lord Fairfax and his son Sir Thomas, was overwhelmed by superior numbers, and the Earl of Newcastle was able to press across the Lincolnshire border. Part of Newcastle's army laid siege to the town of Gainsborough, but here Cromwell came to the rescue and achieved his first independent triumph by checking the tide of Royalist advance.

After leaving Nottingham, Oliver drove some Royalists out of Burleigh House near Stamford and then hurried north to find Colonel Cavendish, the handsome young son of the Earl of Devonshire, with a body of horse posted on a sandy plateau outside Gainsborough. The parliamentary forces consisted of cavalry, dragoons and musketeers, 1700 altogether. Cromwell's horse clambered up the hill, surmounted innumerable rabbit-holes and were at once charged by the enemy who hoped to take them at a disadvantage. 'We came up', wrote Oliver, 'horse to horse, where we disputed it with our swords and pistols a pretty time; all keeping close order so that one could not break the other.' The Royalists were routed and chased for six miles. But Cromwell, recalling the lessons of Edgehill, kept back three troops in reserve to deal with the reserve of Cavendish who was forced into a quagmire 'where', as Cromwell reported, he was slain 'with a thrust under his short ribs'. It thus pleased the Lord to give his servant 'a notable victory'.

His 'discreet and valiant carriage' was commended by the
Speaker. But more was to be done. Newcastle's entire army
lay on the other side of Gainsborough and for the time being
there was no alternative but retreat. More men were wanted.
If 200 foot could be raised 'to encounter the army of Newcastle's, to raise the siege, and to enable us to fight him', wrote
Oliver to the county committees, 'we doubt not, by the grace
of God, but that we shall be able to relieve the town [Gains-
borough] and beat the enemy [to] the other side Trent; whereas
if somewhat be not done in this, you will see Newcastle's army
march up into your bowels. . . .'

The danger was yet imminent; in August affairs still 'stood
sadly'. Despite Cromwell's successes Lincolnshire had to be
temporarily abandoned to the enemy. Cromwell was obliged to
leave campaigning and become a recruiting sergeant. In
August he went to Huntingdon, Ely, Peterborough and Cambridge to gather together horse and foot as part of 2000 men
to be provided by the six Eastern counties. By September 11th
he reported that he was ready to march against the enemy with
ten well-armed troops of horse under his command. The
position then was that the Royalist Earl of Newcastle was
besieging Sir Thomas Fairfax in Hull, whilst the Parliamentarian Earl of Manchester with an infantry force was besieging
King's Lynn in Norfolk. Cromwell visited Fairfax in Hull and
arranged that his twenty-one troops of horse should be spirited
away under Newcastle's nose, shipped down the Humber and
carried into the Lincolnshire Wolds. Both then joined Manchester, who had taken King's Lynn, and the whole force set
about reconquering Lincolnshire from the Cavaliers. Two
considerable forces met at Winceby on October 21st and the
battle resolved itself entirely into a cavalry affair. Oliver was
reluctant for the fight to take place at all that day — for his
horses were weary — but the first charge was decisive. In the
charge Cromwell's own horse was killed under him and he was
at close quarters with death, but he seized another horse,
remounted, rallied his troops and drove home the victory.

First at Grantham, then at Gainsborough and now at Winceby Colonel Cromwell's troops had proved their mettle. Gradually, although beset by every kind of difficulty, he had moulded a cavalry force capable of inflicting defeat on the most dashing of the country gentlemen. Its commander was soon nicknamed Old Ironsides, and his men took their name from his.

§ 3

No better introduction can be given to the history of the Ironsides than Cromwell's own words spoken fifteen years later in a speech in which he was hesitating whether or not he should become the King of England. When the civil war began he recalled:

I saw our men were beaten at every hand. I did indeed; and I desired him [John Hampden, his cousin] that he would make some additions to my Lord Essex's Army, of some new regiments; and I told him I would be serviceable to him in bringing such men in as I thought had a spirit that would do something in the work ... 'our troopers,' said I, 'are most of them old decayed serving-men, and tapsters, and such kind of fellows; and,' said I, 'their troopers are gentlemen's sons, younger sons and persons of quality: do you think that the spirits of such mean and base fellows will ever be able to encounter gentlemen, that have honour and courage and resolution in them?' ... 'You must get men of a spirit ... that is likely to go on as far as gentlemen will go: — or else I am sure you will be beaten still.' ... Truly I told him I could do somewhat in it. I did so, — and truly I must say this to you, — impute it to what you please — I raised such men as had the fear of God before them, and made some conscience of what they did; and from that day forward, I must say to you, they were never beaten, and whatever they engaged against the enemy, they beat continually.

This conversation with Hampden must have taken place some time during the first campaign that ended so inauspiciously for the Parliamentarians at Turnham Green. Throughout 1643 Cromwell was putting his scheme into effect. His object was to organize and drill a Roundhead cavalry large enough to withstand all the seasoned Royalist troops. At the time of the victory of Gainsborough he was already well on the road to success. Around the nucleus formed by the troop he had raised as a captain he had built a regiment fit not merely to withstand attacks but also to counter-attack the horse of the enemy. In the Ironsides of the Eastern Association there was realized a type of soldiery more efficient than the reluctant and amateur trained bands and more zealous and enthusiastic than the mercenary adventurers who tramped for hire between the capitals of Europe. Although there may be a world of difference between the 'Tommies' of modern times and these God-fearing Puritans, yet the idea of a small efficient professional army which at least until recently prevailed in Britain saw light first amid the throes of civil war. The best of the English soldiers who fought under Marlborough, Wolfe and Wellington were the direct descendants of the Cromwellian Ironsides.

After Gainsborough Colonel Cromwell pressed on with his recruiting with such vigour ('weak counsels and weak actings undo all', he murmured) that by the beginning of the next campaign he had a double regiment of picked officers and soldiers under his orders, 'a lovely company', expecting 'to be used as men'. He was fully confident of his ability to discover and enlist the best recruits available. For officers he did not rely exclusively, as Parliament itself had relied, on the most aristocratic gentlemen ready to accept a commission. His 'honoured friends' at Cambridge thought his contrary methods badly at fault; better 'plain men', he retorted, than none at all. 'I had rather have a plain russet-coated captain that knows what he fights for . . . than that which you call a gentleman and is nothing else.' One of the original captains of his fourteen new troops was his eldest surviving son Oliver, destined to be stricken down with smallpox early in 1644. The others were for the most part the celebrated Major-Generals of later years.

His privates he described as 'honest men, such as fear God . . . the freest from unjust practices of any in England, seek you soldiers where you can'. They were paid a high wage of half a crown a day and all found. (Foot soldiers were only paid ten-pence.) Throughout 1643 Cromwell evinced the deepest personal interest in their needs as to pay, food and clothing, and right up to the time of his death he was to show the same regard for the material well-being of the English soldier, a regard which can bear comparison with that of any other general who has ever commanded a British army. In return for his care Cromwell expected the strictest discipline after the Puritan manner. No swearing, gambling or plundering was allowed. A chaplain looked after the moral principles of his men and a provost-marshal saw to their practices. Lastly Cromwell gave strict orders that the regimental horses were to receive every due attention and on more than one occasion he intervened on their behalf when rash Commanders-in-Chief would have killed them through lack of proper rest. Thus when in the autumn of 1643 the second Earl of Manchester superseded Lord Grey of Wark in the generalship of the army of the Eastern Association, Cromwell as one of his four colonels was able to put at his disposal a well-paid, obedient and disciplined force of 1000 cavalrymen ready to march out and fight the enemy whenever they received orders. The cavalry was at that date overwhelmingly the decisive arm. The dragoons, infantry mounted on inferior horses for transport purposes but not for fighting, merely cleared the way by musket fire for an advance. Foot soldiers were in practice powerless against an effective cavalry charge on open ground even by much smaller numbers. The infantry consisted of musketeers and of pikemen in the ratio of about two to one. But the match-lock muskets were crude and clumsy weapons and the musket-eers had no protective armour against horsemen. Only in one battle in the civil wars did the foot play a really significant part.

Hence Cromwell's 'godly honest' cavalrymen, 'patient of wants, faithful and conscientious in employment', were to turn the military scale in the final campaigns of the war.

One reason why the cavalry became so invaluable an arm was that a change in tactics was taking place. The horsemen were no longer formed in eight ranks and no longer fired their muskets in turn at the halt before charging. They were now as a rule drawn up in three ranks or even in two and used as shock troops to bear down their opponents by weight of numbers and with their swords. These novel tactics owed much to the practice of King Gustavus Adolphus of Sweden in the Thirty Years War on the Continent and were probably acquired by Prince Rupert in Germany. But Cromwell rapidly assimilated them and his position as organizer of the cavalry of the Eastern counties put him in a favourable position to reach the first rank as a military commander. Undoubtedly he obtained his start as a soldier from his standing as a politician. As a politician, at least as a House of Commons man, he had not been especially successful. As a soldier, on the contrary, his judgment was sounder, his decisions quicker, his ability to discern the weaknesses in an opponent's case more acute. In the practice of war he was able to compensate by his unhesitating decisions for his vacillations and doubts about religion; in riding about the battlefield he could forget the hypochondria and blood weaknesses which had worried the doctors of Huntingdon. The Great War has taught us the power of politicians to observe more speedily than professional soldiers the more ingenious strategical combinations. In the comparatively amateur circumstances of the civil war, when sieges, the delight of the professional military man, took a secondary place, there was a unique chance for an adaptable man who could make up his mind rapidly as to a course of action and follow it. The Lord had spoken to Oliver, as he records, after this fashion: 'Up and be doing and I will help you and stand by you. There is nothing to be feared but sin and sloth.' It was that spirit, those powers and those opportunities that turned

Cromwell the sheep farmer into a 'natural-born' soldier. We need put no reliance upon the doubtful assumption that he studied Swedish military histories during the winter evenings at St. Ives. He acquired knowledge as he went along, profiting both from a perception of Rupert's novel tactics and of Rupert's mistakes. War fitted him as a natural sphere for his energies as it has fitted many politicians from Cleon to Churchill. His gradual acquisition of the art of generalship, however, succeeded and flowed from his constructive achievements as the architect of the New Model Army. His resourceful work in preparing this powerful and effective weapon made him, on a long view, as much the organizer of victory in the English civil war as the French Republican war minister Carnot was to be the organizer of victory in the French revolutionary wars a hundred and fifty years later. Cromwell's accomplishments as a General were a consequence, perhaps an inevitable consequence, of his unremitting efforts as a military organizer.

In two letters written by Cromwell describing his regiment he asserted that it contained no Anabaptists. This statement was not strictly true; but so strong was the Presbyterian influence within Parliament and so necessary did the politicians consider it to obtain the co-operation of the Scottish Army against the King that political expediency required that at least for a time the other Puritan sects should remain unobtrusive. This was not the last occasion on which Cromwell dissembled for political ends.

Nevertheless, it was commonly known that the soldiers of the Eastern counties, though staunch and convinced Puritans, were in the main of a different persuasion from those of the Scottish army. The largest Puritan group in England after the Presbyterians was the coalition of Brownists (or followers of Robert Browne), Independents (or Jacobites, the followers of Henry Jacob), and Separatists, but their numbers remained small until the coming of the civil war. When the Presbyterian Baillie first arrived in London, he noted that 'as for the Brownists or Separatists of many kinds, they mislike them [here] as much as we; of these there is no considerable party'. But the breakdown of Church discipline which followed the abolition of episcopacy gave an opportunity for the Independents — as the coalition came to be known collectively — to come more into the open and feed the volunteer armies. The modern descendants of the Independents are the Congregationalists, but whereas to-day there are great differences of principle between Congregationalists and Presbyterians, in the seventeenth century the only real question at issue was one of Church organization. The Independents held that every individual church or congregation was responsible to God alone and repudiated the view of the Scottish Church that there must be a general assembly possessing supreme powers to impose a uniform discipline throughout the whole realm. The natural consequence of the Independent position was that the most rigid examination had to be made of individual Christians before they were admitted as full members of the local congregation. Likewise each candidate had closely to explore the state of his soul before he was confident of his eligibility as a true 'saint'. It is thus clear that if Independency was to co-exist with Presbyterianism in England a large measure of liberty of conscience would have to be allowed to it and consequently to all nonconforming sects outside the State Church.

The Eastern counties formed the centre of the seventeenth-century Independent movement. One of its chief founders, Robert Browne, had been educated at Cambridge and first preached his gospel in that town and its neighbourhood; many of the early Elizabethan and Jacobean congregational leaders were Fellows of Cambridge colleges, and Norfolk provided two early martyrs who were hanged by Queen Elizabeth for their faith. At the beginning of the century many English Independents fled for safety from State persecution to Holland — whence some later returned to embark on the *Mayflower* for America — but by 1630 eleven Congregational churches had also grown up in London alone.

It is not, however, until 1643 that we have any definite

OLIVER CROMWELL
A new version of a famous portrait

indication of Cromwell's connection with this particular branch of the Puritan movement. In July Parliament had appointed an ecclesiastical assembly which met at Westminster, consisting of 105 clergy and a few laymen, to determine the future religious organization of the country. Cromwell and others then came forward to press for an effective Independent representation. For only five Independent ministers and two or three laymen, including Sir Henry Vane and Oliver St. John, both intimate friends of Cromwell, sustained the Congregationalist point of view; and by September a Presbyterian 'Form of Church Government' was drawn up for the approval of Parliament. Furthermore, the necessity of conciliating the Scots in order to enlist their army against Charles determined the two Houses to subscribe to a 'Solemn League and Covenant', more or less on the lines of the Scottish Covenant of 1638, which promised 'to endeavour to bring the Churches of God in the three kingdoms to the nearest ... uniformity in religion'. This seemed to imply that the religion of the Independents and of the Anabaptists (an offshoot from them) and other small Puritan groups would not be tolerated. But Cromwell's army was full of the sects, he himself was soon to earn the title of 'the Great Independent', and it was plain that undiluted Presbyterianism must split the whole army into fragments. On December 23rd, therefore, Parliament was forced to publish a declaration promising that existing congregations should not be touched. It was only some weeks after this concession had been extorted that Cromwell with the greatest reluctance subscribed his name to the Covenant.

Oliver in fact was by no means convinced, as so many of his fellow-members of Parliament were, that the employment of the Scottish Army was either advisable or necessary. He believed that Parliament could create an army of English Puritans, so steadfast in purpose and so unshakable in morale, that it could under a real commander defeat the Royalists unaided. A Presbyterian officer, speaking of the year 1643, afterwards recollected that he had often heard Cromwell say 'that it must not be [professional] soldiers or Scots that must do this work, but it must be the godly to the purpose'.

Parliament's religious concession of December 23rd was one in which John Pym would readily have acquiesced. But that superb politician was dead. Six months earlier John Hampden, who had proved himself equally proficient in statesmanship and captaincy, had been killed in an unimportant skirmish in the Midlands. What might have happened had it been Cromwell and not his cousin who was killed that year is a curious subject for speculation. Probably so far as the war was concerned much the same as in fact happened. As it was, from the beginning of 1644 Oliver Cromwell became by right of succession as well as of proved achievement a recognized Puritan leader.

CHAPTER V

THE BIG BATTALIONS

§ I

ONE of the first rewards conferred upon Cromwell by Parliament for his services in 1643 was the governorship of his home town, Ely. In the brief interval before the next campaign opened he was thus able to join his wife, mother and family under his own roof and at the same time begin his career as Governor of the town and surrounding 'island'. He was proud of the island which contained, he said, three of the finest ports in the kingdom, and bent his energies to its military, material and spiritual improvement. 'I will make the Isle of Ely', he promised his fellow-citizens, 'the strongest place in the world,' and 'I will make it a place for God to dwell in.' Laying aside his old doubts about draining the fens as an interference with property rights, he sought out the famous Dutch engineer Vermuyden for that purpose; and he begged for cannon and ammunition to be dispatched from London to protect the country from Royalist skirmishers and plunderers. The independent Fenmen rejoiced in these energetic activities of their Governor and willingly flocked to enlist under his standards. Thus the army of the Eastern Association was further weighted with the Congregational element among the Puritans.

In January 1644 Cromwell went over to Cambridge to meet the new head of the Association, Edward Montague, Earl of Manchester. This Earl was a great parliamentary hero, because by a freak of chance under his name of Kimbolton he had been linked with the notorious 'Five Members' of the House of Commons whom the King had vainly attempted to arrest in 1642. He was, however, described by contemporaries as 'a sweet, meek man', 'of a soft and obliging temper, of no great depth but universally loved'. In politics he was certainly no extremist. He felt confident that the King would sooner or later accept the parliamentary peace terms and resume his full functions as a constitutional monarch ruling a Presbyterian nation. One resounding victory, he believed, would settle the issue. Like Essex, he was far from being a man 'to ride the whirlwind and direct the storm'.

Under him the Committee of Safety now put Cromwell as his second-in-command with the title of Lieutenant-General — a General on the eve of his third campaign! — and a fierce courageous Scottish Presbyterian, by name Crawford, became his Major-General. The predominantly Independent character of the Association army, which had been steadily packed by Cromwell with sectarians, made it a command that boded ill for this uncompromising Scot. Already after the relief of Crowland in the previous year the Independents had begun circulating petitions for signature in the army advocating 'liberty of conscience'. One Presbyterian officer grimly declined and added 'if any nation in the world were in the ready way to Heaven it was the Scots'. Why should he open up by-paths from the strait and narrow way? So dissension grew in the army both among officers and men.

But at first all went well. Cromwell and Crawford could at least unite in an attack upon their common enemy, the Royalist-Anglican. At Ely Cromwell had marched his soldiers into the cathedral and pulled down from his pulpit an erstwhile friendly clergyman who had persisted with his 'unedifying' choir service contrary to the order of Parliament. At Lincoln his and Crawford's men rivalled each other in their zeal to desecrate the cathedral. In Cambridge, while Crawford was reviewing his troops in King's College Chapel, Cromwell was attending to the destruction of the superstitious ornaments in the University Church of St. Mary. Here we may pause a moment to gain a fleeting glimpse of a figure emerging from Cromwell's past to make its last appearance on the tragic stage

of History. It is Doctor Samuel Ward, Master of Sidney
Sussex, now at this time of crisis become Vice-Chancellor of
the University. He visited Cromwell in St. Mary's Church
and publicly but vainly rebuked him for allowing his soldiers
to tear down the carved reredos over the altar. It was indeed
a dramatic meeting. Little can the old Doctor have dreamed
twenty-five years before that his melancholy Puritanism would
yield such bitter fruit. He turned from the distasteful scene
and within a few months it is recorded that 'Doctor Samuel
Ward took the wings of a dove to fly away and be at rest . . .
whose dying words . . . were God Save the King'.

At first the Earl of Manchester put his entire trust in his
Lieutenant-General: 'I always placed him', he said, 'in chiefest
esteem and credit with me.' Cromwell reciprocated the
compliment, and appeared in his place in the House of
Commons to defend his superior officer against the complaints
of Lord Willoughby of Parham, who had been superseded
by Manchester in his command of Lincolnshire, which was
now absorbed into the Eastern Association. Speaking on
Manchester's behalf Cromwell asserted that Willoughby
allowed women camp-followers to attach themselves to his
army to serve 'the worst of purposes', and the thwarted evil-
doer, after vainly challenging Manchester to a duel, faded from
the scene to reappear in later years as a Royalist Governor
in the West Indies. The Eastern Association having been
purified, the campaign began.

In 1644 five separate armies took the field on behalf of
Parliament. In the first place the negotiation with the Scots
was at length completed and a Scottish army under the Earl of
Leven crossed the Border. Secondly there was the army of the
Earl of Essex, still nominally Commander-in-Chief but no
longer altogether trusted owing to his lethargy in the last
campaign. Then there was an army under Major-General
Waller, which was raised by the City of London to operate
chiefly in the South and West, and an army under Sir Thomas
Fairfax in the north of England. An Anglo-Scottish committee

known as the Committee of Both Kingdoms was formed in London, which contained all the generals, including Cromwell, and a number of leading civilians, whose duty it was to co-ordinate the movements of the different armies. King Charles remained at Oxford and hoped that by dashing out thence from time to time and attacking the various Roundhead armies as opportunities arose, he would be able to make up for his pronounced inferiority of man power by superior tactics and generalship.

The campaign began favourably for Parliament, Waller, Fairfax, and Leven all achieving successes before the spring had begun. But the Earl of Manchester with the fifth parliamentary army remained comfortably billeted on the University of Cambridge, purging the colleges of all exponents of the wrong brand of theology, whilst Prince Rupert quietly raised the siege of Newark in the north of the Association. Manchester's Lieutenant-General, however, was busily at work and did not confine his activity merely to the Eastern counties. He dispatched urgently needed ammunition to Gloucester, subdued a stubborn country-house in Buckinghamshire and finally drove back the Cavaliers on the western border of the Association into Banbury Castle. 'Cromwell hath uncattled them about Oxford,' it was reported in the newspapers. Elsewhere it was alleged that his trumpeters blew so hard as to deafen one of the bishops in the royal retinue.

It was April when the whole of Manchester's army, with Cromwell in command of the cavalry, set out into Lincolnshire. On May 6th Lincoln fell into its hands; whereupon, leaving Newark still with the enemy, it marched farther north to assist Fairfax and the Scots in the siege of York. While three parliamentary armies numbering some 27,000 men were engaged there Prince Rupert with a force of about 18,000 had captured Stockport, Bolton and Liverpool in turn, although he left Puritan Manchester severely alone. But the Earl of Newcastle's peril perturbed the Royal Court at Oxford, and Prince Rupert was called in an involved and unwise letter from

King Charles I to leave his successful Lancashire campaign, cross the Pennines and 'immediately march to the relief of York'. He obeyed his orders. On hearing of the Prince's approach Fairfax and Manchester, frightened of being caught between him and Newcastle's army in York, marched out seven miles west of the city to bar his road at Marston Moor. But Rupert slipped north and avoided them and joined Newcastle outside York. He then forcibly persuaded the courteous but cautious Newcastle on the strength of King Charles's letter to meet the Roundheads in battle on Marston Moor.

Since the Parliamentarians had 8000 more infantry than the combined forces of Newcastle and Rupert they could at first scarcely credit the news of the Prince's intention to fight. However, on the afternoon of July 2nd, with the sun shining between the showers, the two armies drew up facing each other on this Yorkshire moor amidst a field of rye. In both armies the infantry were in the centre with two lines of cavalry on each wing. Sir Thomas Fairfax took command of the Parliamentarian right opposing Lord Goring. In the centre the large mass of Roundhead foot, consisting both of Scots and of Manchester's men, were opposed by the Earl of Newcastle with the Royalist infantry. But the cream of the two armies, the Parliamentary left under Cromwell and the Royalist right wing under Rupert, both began and ultimately decided the battle. Rupert inquired of a prisoner before the battle whether Cromwell was opposite to him. 'And will they fight?' he asked. 'If they will they shall have fight enough.' 'If it please God,' retorted Oliver when he heard of the inquiry, 'so shall he.'

All that afternoon the two armies waited, and eventually Rupert, who had been dissuaded from attacking, decided that the other side also did not then intend to begin. As the Roundheads were singing their battle psalm, the Royalist officers went off to their supper. At seven o'clock, while squatting on the ground eating, Prince Rupert heard with alarm that, although a ditch and a hedge confronted his

cavalry, Oliver Cromwell had begun to advance. Prince
Rupert hurried to the field to meet his own regiment already
with its back to the enemy. "Swounds, do you run?" he cried.
'Follow me!' For the moment he succeeded in forcing back his

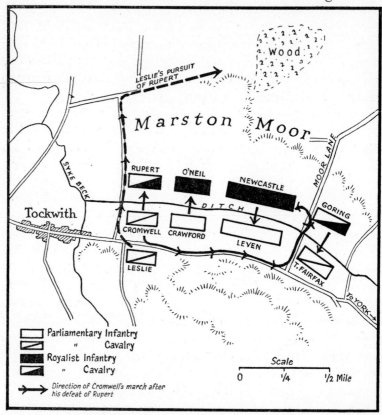

BATTLE OF MARSTON MOOR, JULY 2, 1644

enemy's line and in the mêlée Cromwell himself received a
neck wound. But his second line under the Scottish David
Leslie came on, and gave him time to rally his retreating first
line to attack Rupert in the flank. Slowly sheer weight of
numbers told. 'At last', reported his scout master, 'he brake
through them, scattering them before him like a little dust.'
Rupert was beaten; but the battle was not yet won.

Things were going badly at the other end of the line. So completely did Goring repulse the Parliamentarian right wing that old Lords Fairfax and Leven fled the battlefield. The younger Fairfax, made of sterner stuff, with a cut on his face and dust on his clothes, suddenly presented himself to Cromwell who, keeping his troops well in hand, had halted to see what was going on elsewhere amidst the smoke. Fairfax begged for help and was reassured. On hearing the bad news Cromwell did not hesitate; recalling David Leslie from his pursuit of Rupert he made his way behind the infantry, which was with difficulty holding its own, and wheeled the whole of Manchester's army, both horse and foot, until it faced south exactly where Goring had been at the opening of the battle. He thus caught the Royalist left between two fires and defeated it with expedition. Finally, with the enemy cavalry defeated on both wings, Cromwell turned again and charged Newcastle's foot to the left of the Royalist centre to complete the victory. The experienced Leslie who thus saw the victory 'plucked out of the enemy's hands professed that Europe had no better soldiers' than Cromwell's Ironsides. An eminent German military critic, who did much to elucidate Cromwell's part in the battle, has stated that 'no cavalry leader ever accomplished with so small a force such great and varied tasks as Cromwell did at Marston Moor'.

But how far was Cromwell himself really responsible for his cavalry's success? It is clear enough that when Rupert counter-charged at the outset and Oliver was wounded, much necessarily depended upon Leslie's ability to bring the second line promptly into action. On the basis of this necessity and of Leslie's wider military experience three contemporary Scots with characteristic patriotic and Presbyterian zeal asserted that Leslie was beyond all doubt the real hero of Marston Moor. Not unnaturally, Mr. John Buchan in his recent biography of Cromwell has been willing to bestow every possible credit on the Scots. It is certainly curious that Cromwell in an entirely private letter written after the battle said: 'The left wing which

I commanded, being our own horse, saving a few Scots in the rear, beat all the Prince's horse.' For since the Scots numbered 1920 out of 4200 on the left wing they were more than a few nor were they all in the rear. But the psychological explanation of Cromwell's erroneous statement is surely much less likely to have been desire to fake the facts in search of vainglory than a subconscious desire to fulfil his own previously expressed wish to beat the King without the aid of the Scots. As to his and Leslie's parts in the battle their relative skill as generals was to be demonstrated once and for all when they faced each other six years later on the field of Dunbar.

§ 2

But success as well as failure brings its problems. No sooner had this important victory been obtained than the latent causes of dissension within the Roundhead armies rose to the surface. Diametrically opposed points of view obtruded themselves both in Parliament and in the Army. On the one side Cromwell, Sir Henry Vane, the famous opponent of Strafford, Oliver St. John, a Puritan lawyer, Sir Arthur Haselrig, a Yorkshire squire, and the Independent colonels of the Eastern Association were all anxious that the King should be thoroughly beaten before he was restored to his throne, because they were convinced that, unless he were, he would at once conspire to upset any peace treaty that might be made. Whispers of deposition were even heard in this group. Meanwhile they impressed upon Parliament and the Westminster ecclesiastical assembly the necessity of devising a form of Church government which would give 'liberty of conscience' and 'liberty of worship' to those sects that did not wish to belong to a Presbyterian Church. On the other hand, the Scots, supported by the Earl of Essex, Sir William Waller, Denzil Holles and the majority of both Houses, claimed that they had a right to expect the immediate establishment of a

Presbyterian Church of England ruled by a general synod tolerating no individual sects or congregations, and that the King should at once be offered acceptable terms if he would only consent to be a Presbyterian King — 'God's Silly Vassal', — like his father when he had been only King of Scotland. The commanders of the three armies that had been victorious at Marston Moor — Leven, Fairfax and Manchester — pronounced themselves unanimously in favour of the Presbyterian policy. Manchester in particular decided to take advantage of the exhausted and depleted condition of his army to excuse himself from pressing the King's forces any further than was necessary in order that reasonable terms might be obtained from him. Therefore, when the Committee of Both Kingdoms sent him orders to pursue Rupert into Cheshire he delayed. When Cromwell urged upon him the importance of retaking Newark, he procrastinated. And when he was ordered to march westward to relieve the pressure of the Royal army on Essex (who was allowing himself to be cooped up in Cornwall) he gave the inexact character of his instructions as an excuse for remaining within the borders of his Association.

Major-General Crawford declared later in defence of Manchester's inactivity after Marston Moor that he feared mutiny in his army. This fear (overlooked by most of Cromwell's biographers) must certainly have been a very weighty one in Manchester's mind. Cromwell and Crawford were now at daggers drawn. As early as March Cromwell had accused the Major-General of wrongly arresting two of his subordinate officers merely because they were Anabaptists. In August some of the Independent colonels threatened to resign unless Crawford were dismissed. The 'sweet, mild' Manchester, concerned only for peace and 'Christ's universal discipline', recoiled before the violence of his seconds-in-command. He decided to take them both up to London and lay his troubles before the central Committee.

Cromwell took advantage of his visit to persuade his parliamentary supporters to give a definite instruction to the

Westminster Assembly that they must take into account the Independent movement in framing a new ecclesiastical government. All responsible men realized that this was no time for quarrelling. Three days before Marston Moor Waller's army had been severely repulsed in Oxfordshire. Furthermore, Waller and Essex hated each other and the latter allowed his forces to be cut off and overwhelmed on September 2nd. It was therefore essential that Waller and Manchester should advance southward and defeat the King's main army if the fruits of Marston Moor were not to be entirely dissipated. In these circumstances the 'accommodation order' desired by Cromwell was sent to the Westminster Assembly; and after he had been publicly thanked for his great services, Oliver allowed himself to be reconciled with Crawford.

Oliver was indeed fully aware of the necessity for unity and speed to save the common cause from disaster. 'Had we wings we would fly westward,' he wrote. But Manchester still refused to bestir himself. He doubted the wisdom of leaving his Association and delayed long at Reading. Eventually he joined Waller and Essex (who had deserted his army before its defeat) at Basingstoke. According to Cromwell the slowness of the subsequent march against the enemy at Newbury gave the King time to prepare. The battle of Newbury, although a nominal victory for the Roundheads, enabled Charles to retreat quietly to Oxford, and the year which had begun so auspiciously for Parliament closed in gloom and mutual recriminations.

The principal controversy that arose when the army took up its winter quarters was no longer merely between Cromwell and Crawford but between Cromwell and Manchester. Cromwell's biographers have not always done justice to the strength of his opponent's case. Yet if one is prepared to admit that war is the instrument of policy the arguments on Manchester's side are powerful.

The war had been begun to protect the rights of Parliament, the security of private property and the free expression of the growing Puritan faith. By 1644 it was clear that the tide of victory was turning against the King and that no settlement would be reached in which Charles failed to recognize his obligations in all these directions. Moreover, the war had been waged against the King's 'evil counsellors'. It was inconceivable that the restored monarch could now draw his ministers elsewhere than from the victorious party. It has been said that the King could not be trusted. But Cromwell was ready to trust him two years later. Was it not natural that Manchester with an ill-paid army divided against itself, antagonistic in the main to the army of Essex which it should have succoured, should have allowed himself to exercise what his opponents termed 'some principle of unwillingness . . . to have this war prosecuted unto a full victory'? He did not feel convinced that the more completely the King was crushed the more ready he would be to rule righteously. Manchester might well have pleaded the humanistic doctrine that the more you flog a child the more certain he is to become deceitful. But there was yet a further and perhaps deeper reason for his restraint. Cromwell had attacked the nobility and had openly avowed that 'he wished there was never a lord in England'. These radical opinions need not have been taken at their face value, for it is certain that Cromwell used them merely as a means to relieve his feelings against the military incompetence of the Earls of Manchester and Essex. But naturally they then sounded like an attack on the very institutions that many leading Parliamentarians had taken arms to defend.

Oliver's own point of view was that once begun the decision must be submitted to the test of battle, which alone would reveal the will of God. No matter that the goal changed as the war went on. No 'shuffling pretences', no personal dislikes, no religious peccadillos could excuse military failure or disobedience. But beyond all particular accusations Cromwell fully understood the fundamental difficulty that when politicians command armies their policy will determine their strategy. After a fierce quarrel between the two Houses in

December, during which each House supported its own member, Cromwell suggested a compromise: all members of Parliament who held commissions must lay them down, and the Army must be put under the care of men who were soldiers first and foremost. It must appear almost incredible to any student of human nature that a man of Cromwell's forceful personality could let himself believe that the ordinance would be allowed to apply to the hero of Marston Moor, the builder of the invincible Ironsides. But if he did so he deceived himself gravely. In any case it was not to be.

§ 3

The so-called First Self-Denying Ordinance was thrown out by the attenuated House of Lords on January 13th, 1645, for they regarded it, not unjustly, as a deliberate insult to the Earls of Essex and Manchester, whom it would deprive of their commands. The extreme Presbyterians in the Lower House looked upon it further as a calculated attack on all officers of their faith. They were to be reduced, wrote one of them, 'cast by as old Almanacs, in truth not fitted to the [Independent] Meridian'. But the majority of the Commons recognized the necessity of army reform and were ready for a bargain with the obstructive Lords. They offered to drop Cromwell's charges against Manchester if the House of Lords would accept an ordinance constituting a New Model Army. This was to consist of 20,000 men formed out of the remnants of the forces of Essex, Waller and Manchester, together with a large number of new recruits, paid for out of the national revenues instead of local funds and commanded by a general who was committed to neither religious party and whose subordinates were to be appointed by him with the approval of both Houses. The offer was reluctantly accepted and an appropriate Commander-in-Chief was found in Sir Thomas Fairfax.

Born in 1612, Fairfax was a young Yorkshire squire of considerable military experience and ability. At an early age he had served under Lord Vere of Tilbury in Flanders and had distinguished himself there by marrying the daughter of his commanding officer. Later he had taken part in King Charles's campaigns against the Scots and during the civil war had obtained several successes in his home county. Although after the siege of York he had joined his fellow generals in their pronouncement in favour of peace and Presbyterianism, he was not regarded as an enemy of the separatists. His popularity with the soldiers was witnessed by such nicknames as 'The Rider of the White Horse' and 'Black Tom'. But his constant ill health made it certain that he must be greatly dependent upon his second-in-command. Indeed an unfavourable contemporary view was that he was a man of 'natural and brutish valour, fitter to follow another man's counsel than his own'.

In the scheme for the New Model (called by its opponents the New Nodel) Army, which was necessarily the Ironside Army writ large, the name of Lieutenant-General was omitted. No one doubted that the post was intended for Cromwell. But some months were to pass before the fact was openly recognized and the Presbyterians did not abandon the idea of a Self-Denying Ordinance that would shut out the famous Independent from any further part in the war.

On January 21st Cromwell acted as one of the tellers in the vote on the New Model ordinance, which was carried by 101 votes to 69, and at the same time he took a leading part in urging upon both Houses the advisability of inviting the Scots to continue their assistance to the Roundhead cause whilst the New Model was being made ready for the field.

The exhaustion of both sides caused the campaign to open slowly. The King, who now held sway over Oxford, Wales and the South-West corner of England, was occupied in treaty negotiations with the Scots which came to nothing in face of his invincible determination not to abandon the bishops.

There were many in London who hoped that Charles would have now accepted a Presbyterian scheme of government, but Cromwell correctly anticipated his refusal. The war had to go on.

The Commons promptly showed that they did not intend to dispense with the services of their successful cavalry leader. In March they dispatched him to join Waller in an invasion of the Royalist West. Sir William was surprised and gratified to find in Cromwell an obedient officer who 'did never dispute my orders or argue upon them'. As Waller was a strict Presbyterian this is clear proof that what Cromwell disliked in Manchester was not his aristocracy but his inactivity. While Oliver was thus employed Parliament at last agreed to a Self-Denying Ordinance which ordered all its members to lay down their commissions within forty days but said nothing against re-appointments. Essex and Manchester, aghast at such ingratitude, surrendered their commissions before the Ordinance was passed and retired sulkily into civilian life. On April 19th Oliver returned from Somerset after a short but successful campaign, as if to do likewise.

Before Cromwell could reach Westminster he received from the Committee of Both Kingdoms another set of orders instructing him to march at once to prevent a juncture of Rupert and Charles at the Royalist headquarters at Oxford. He did not delay. He routed two enemy regiments, forced Bletchingdon garrison north of Oxford to surrender and finally laid siege to Faringdon, threatening its governor 'if God give you into my hands, I will not spare a man of you, if you put me to a storm'. But the governor was not intimidated, the storm was repulsed with heavy losses and Faringdon's siege is the only blot on Cromwell's military escutcheon. Three days later he was recalled to join Fairfax at Newbury, and the New Model Army prepared to justify itself by a direct attack on Oxford.

Before the siege opened Charles had escaped from Oxford and headed northward. The Marquess of Montrose, who largely for personal reasons had since 1643 been fighting on the Cavalier side in the Highlands and had there proved himself a brilliant general comparable with Rupert and Cromwell, was now in 1645 winning a series of victories over the Covenanters in the Highlands. To the hard-pressed Royalists this campaign seemed like a good dream come true. The King hoped by calling his army from the West to join Montrose in the Midlands and win back the whole of the North to his cause. A rendezvous was appointed in Leicestershire, and meanwhile the King's main army indulged in a number of raids which embarrassed the Eastern Association.

The City of London was terrified at the royal refusal to stay in Oxford and be blockaded. On May 26th Cromwell was ordered home to Ely for the purpose of protecting Cambridgeshire and Huntingdonshire from enemy attacks. As soon as he obeyed Charles's army turned away to the sack of Leicester. The Commons breathed a sigh of relief that the centre of their military strength was freed from danger and on June 10th, at the request of Fairfax, they re-appointed Cromwell to his Lieutenant-Generalship. According to the biographer of Sir Thomas Fairfax, the latter considered it 'of the utmost importance to retain Cromwell's services'! A contemporary Presbyterian seems on the other hand to have expressed the general opinion of his age when he observed that Fairfax had only the name of General. He was 'the Cypher', Cromwell 'the Figure' of the New Model Army.

It was on June 13th that Cromwell with 600 horsemen rode into Fairfax's camp eight miles from Daventry on the Northampton road. He was welcomed by the soldiers 'with a mighty shout'; 'Ironsides', they cried, 'has come to head us.' That same day General Henry Ireton, who had been dispatched by Fairfax with an advance guard, surprised twenty of Rupert's troopers playing quoits in the Northamptonshire village of Naseby. Farther north amid a group of clayey hills lay the main body of the Cavaliers with King Charles himself and the ever-impatient Rupert. Charles was

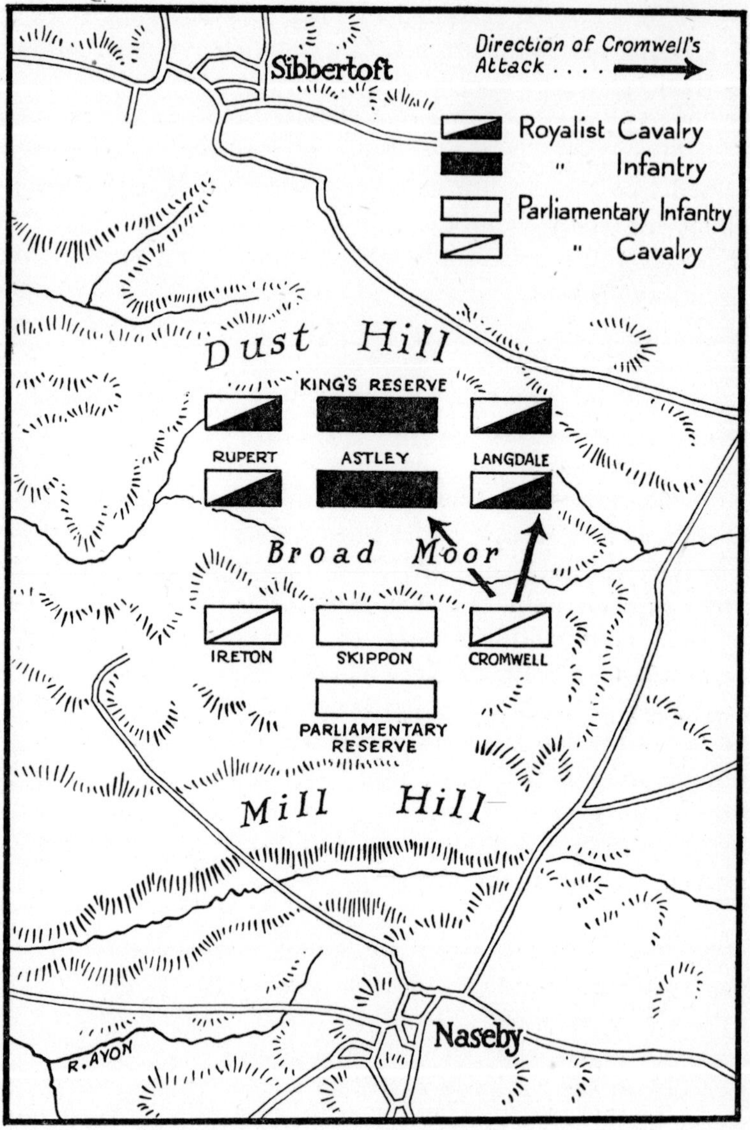
Direction of Cromwell's Attack . . . .
Royalist Cavalry
" Infantry
Parliamentary Infantry
" Cavalry
Sibbertoft
Dust Hill
KING'S RESERVE
RUPERT
ASTLEY
LANGDALE
Broad Moor
IRETON
SKIPPON
CROMWELL
PARLIAMENTARY RESERVE
Mill Hill
Naseby
R. AVON

BATTLE OF NASEBY, JUNE 14, 1645

hesitating as to his next step when Ireton's men were suddenly seen and it was known that Fairfax was following closely behind. Although the Royalists held the New Model Army in contempt they knew that they were greatly inferior in numbers to the army of Fairfax; the King had only 4000 horse against 6500 Roundheads, while he had only one-quarter the number of foot. Hence there was a natural reluctance to fight.

About nine o'clock in the morning of June 14th, however, Rupert rode out to reconnoitre. At the very moment, it seems, Cromwell had persuaded Fairfax to change the Round-head position. 'I must never forget the behaviour of Lieutenant-General Cromwell,' noted a contemporary pamphleteer, 'who as though he had received direction from God himself where to pitch the battle did advise that the battalion might stand upon such a ground though it was begun to be drawn upon another place.' Rupert made the astonishing mistake of thinking that this movement was a retreat and at once ordered the Royalists to move to a position to the right of the enemy in the hope of outflanking them; Fairfax countered by moving farther to the left and eventually the proper dispositions had been taken for battle. As usual the infantry were in the centre and the cavalry on the wings. But unlike at Marston Moor there was no direct encounter between Rupert and Oliver who each commanded their respective right wings, the posts of honour. Sir Jacob Astley was in charge of the Royalist infantry and Major-General Skippon commanded that of the Roundheads, Ireton faced Rupert and Sir Marma-duke Langdale, a Yorkshire squire, confronted Cromwell.

The Royalist foot began the advance, whilst Rupert successfully resisted a charge by Ireton's men. Ireton was wounded and for a time a prisoner, and Rupert was able to push back the Roundhead left wing in his usual headlong fashion as far as the very outskirts of Naseby. Skippon too was wounded and in the centre the fight was 'extremely hot for nearly an hour', the pikemen pushing against each other with their sixteen-foot weapons and the musketeers employing their swords and butt ends. Everything therefore depended upon Cromwell on the right; but he was beyond measure confident. 'I could not,' he said afterwards, 'riding alone about my business but smile out to God in praise in assurance of victory.' He swept back Langdale and leaving four regiments to hold him, turned against the flank of the opposing infantry. In due course Prince Rupert, who had learned nothing and forgotten nothing about the art of war, returned from his customary overrunning of the battlefield to find that all was lost. He joined King Charles, who with characteristic vacillation had rightly wanted to use his reserves against Cromwell but had been dissuaded, and the two formed a new line of battle. But the Cavalier morale was broken. The very men who, at the outset of the fight, had imagined that the Parliamentarians with their superior numbers were running away, now dared not face Cromwell again. Fairfax had drawn up his entire victorious forces in battle array. Charles and Rupert contemplated the sight for a moment, then broke and fled. Five thousand prisoners and all the royal guns and ammunition fell to the victors. 'Sir,' wrote Cromwell to the Speaker, 'this is none other but the hand of God.' As the Roundhead Army had outnumbered the Cavaliers by two to one, here, as at Marston Moor, God had shown himself on the side of the big battalions.

Oliver could not resist pressing home what he regarded as the obvious lesson of the victory in his official dispatch to Parliament. In contrast with Marston Moor, in which to his disgust and, however much he might wish to forget the fact, the Scots had materially contributed to the Parliamentary success, Naseby was the unique achievement of the New Model Army, an army based not upon intolerant Scottish Presbyterianism but upon the co-operation of the different English sects. He wrote to the Commons:

Honest men served you faithfully in this action; I beseech you in the name of God, not to discourage them. I wish this action may beget thankfulness and humility in all that are concerned in it. He that ventures his life for the liberty of his country, I wish he trust God for the liberty of his conscience, and you for the liberty he fights for.

But the predominantly Presbyterian House was so indifferent, not to say antagonistic, to Cromwell's ideas of religious toleration that this entire paragraph was suppressed in the version of the dispatch which it released for publication.

But if the Independents' cause was not yet won the King's cause was lost. His last big army was shattered. Exactly a month later the smaller army of Goring was beaten by Fairfax and Cromwell at Langport near Taunton. Goring's force was entrenched in a strong position but his cavalry was driven back by gun-fire and the way was cleared for Cromwell's victorious charge. As the reward of a vigorous pursuit Cromwell captured two guns and 1400 prisoners. In September the Scots brought to a close Montrose's remarkable career of warfare. In the autumn Cromwell took in rapid succession Bristol, the one Royalist seaport, Devizes, Winchester and Basingstoke. King Charles was obliged to beg help from abroad, and intercepted letters disclosing his efforts to buy or rather borrow a foreign army to subdue England induced Fairfax and Cromwell to accelerate the rounding up of the remaining Royalist forces. The campaign of 1646 began as early as January. In February Hopton's stubborn Cornishmen were finally subdued and in March Sir Jacob Astley surrendered with the last Royalist force, observing prophetically to his captors: 'You have done your work and may go to play; unless you will fall out amongst yourselves.'

In this falling out, implicit in the interminable quarrels between Independents and Presbyterians during the two previous years, Oliver Cromwell was also to play his part.

CHAPTER VI

THE INTRIGUER

§ I

THE records of Cromwell's life for the year 1646 are singularly sparse. His letters deal with questions of small importance and none of his speeches survive. He was for the time being mainly engaged in settling down again to civilian and parliamentary life and he was concerned with the arrangement of long-postponed family affairs. Parliament had voted him an estate worth £2500 a year for his services — a contrast with the income of £300 a year which he had earned as a farmer before the Long Parliament had met; his stake in the country had grown bigger than ever. He could afford to move his family from Ely to London. But now it had diminished in size; his two elder sons were dead, the second an indirect victim of the civil war, and his two elder daughters were married. Two daughters were still at home and his two sons, Richard and Henry, were in the Army.

Oliver was fully convinced that the war had revealed the will of God once and for all. In describing the siege of Bristol he had told the Speaker:

'He who runs may read that all this is none other than the will of God. He must be a very atheist that doth not acknowledge it.'

But among the lucky theists he demanded unity although not uniformity.

'Our desires are [he wrote in the same dispatch] that God may be glorified by the same spirit of faith. . . . Presbyterians, Independents, all had here the same spirit of faith and prayer . . . they agree, here, know no names of difference: pity it is it should be otherwise anywhere. All that believe they have the real unity. . . .'

In fact he held up the Army as an example to the Church. But so little did the Parliament agree with his view that it mutilated his dispatch just as it had done his letter after Naseby. Oliver therefore came to London, even before Oxford had fallen, in order to represent the cause of the Army and the need for unity in the Commons. If at the very beginning of the war, from the time he was known as the 'Great Independent', he had committed himself less to the teachings of any one sect than to the cause of toleration among Puritans, his experience upon the battlefield had strengthened ever more profoundly his belief in the value of Christian unity.

In the second place he now sought a constitutional settlement, a settlement that would conserve through an agreement between the Army and the Parliament that purification of the Constitution for which the war had been waged. But he had no hankering after any democratic innovations. We catch one glimpse of him in the autumn of 1646 acting as teller in the House of Commons against a proposal for the introduction of a ballot whenever offices were to be allotted. He thought that those who, like himself, were the proven vessels of the divine will should be allowed to enjoy the fruits of victory in unity and peace. The duty was incumbent upon them to take the lead. Now that the corruption in the body politic had been forcibly cut out with the sword he wanted to return to the simple and healthy life that had been lived in Elizabethan England: every man must be allowed to tend his sheep, plough his acres and say his prayers in a world made safe again both from Monarchy and from Democracy.

But confusion yet reigned.

'Sir,' Cromwell informed a correspondent in the summer of 1646, 'this is a quarrelsome age.' Two months later he repeated: 'We are full of faction and worse', and in December, although he assured Fairfax that God was in Heaven, he felt certain all was not right with the world. The complete Roundhead victory in the civil war at once brought to the surface wide differences of political and religious opinions that had until then been glossed over for the sake of unity in the face of the enemy. The three great parties that had beaten the King — the Scots, the Parliament and the New Model Army — each had special interests that they wanted to safeguard in the settlement about to be made in the two kingdoms.

The Scots wished to establish their system of Church Government throughout the island, to enforce their Covenant universally, to return to Monarchy and to receive a substantial payment for the services of their army in England. Baillie, their agent in London, doubted that this policy would find acceptance among English politicians: 'the leaders of the people', he observed, 'seem to be inclined to no shadow of a king; to have liberty for all religions, to have but a lame Erastian Presbytery; and to be so injurious to us as to chase us home by the sword'.

But Baillie's misgivings were excessive, for he described the views only of a powerful minority. The Presbyterian Party in Parliament was strengthened at the close of the war and in most respects sympathized with the Scottish claims. In the Lords the Presbyterians possessed a secure majority, while in the Commons a middle party which had supported Cromwell against Holles and other Presbyterian stalwarts on questions of military policy, turned against him on matters of religion. The English Presbyterians had consistently maintained that the war must end not in a conquest but in peace. They believed sincerely in kingship as an institution if not divine in origin at least stamped indelibly with divine approval. The Stuart monarchy they pictured as corrupted but not of its nature corrupt, and they clung to it as the surest guarantee of property rights and existing economic institutions. The King, they held therefore, should now be restored, the Presbyterian religion made national and the heretical sects suppressed. Angry feelings were roused against Cromwell and the Army, who were represented as having for their enemies the infallible combination of 'God and all good men'.

The Army itself was split into two main groups, consisting

of the Grandees or Gentlemen Independents led by Cromwell and Henry Ireton, recently become his son-in-law, and the Levellers who were inspired by John Lilburne, whom we last met as the precocious martyr of the anti-episcopal party; but they had many points in common. The first united interest of the Army was that it should be generously provided for by Parliament and its services adequately rewarded. The pay of officers and men was long in arrears and they naturally refused to disband until their accounts had been settled. In the second place they demanded that any new constitution for the Church should allow liberty of conscience to the sects, as they feared that now that the war was over Parliament might go back on the accommodation order extorted from it by Cromwell in 1644. The New Model Army, as we have seen, was predominantly sectarian because its original nucleus was the Ironsides of the Eastern Association. We are told further by a trustworthy authority that with the coming of peace Cromwell pushed forward with his scheme — begun three years before — of packing the Army with men disposed to his own religious point of view. The authority is the Reverend Richard Baxter, who though at that time obviously inclined to the Presbyterians is not counted by his biographers as a Presbyterian leader. Baxter visited the Army after the battle of Naseby and thus recorded his impressions:

When I came to the army among Cromwell's soldiers I found a new face on things which I never dreamt of: I heard the plotting heads very hot upon that which intimated their Intention to subvert both Church and State. Independency and Anabaptistry were most prevalent: Antinomianism and Arminianism [advocates of Free Will] were equally distributed; and Thomas Moor's followers (a weaver of Wisbitch and Lyn, of excellent parts) had made some shifts to join these two Extremes together. . . . There were some honest, sober, Orthodox Men, and others ready to hear the Truth, but the hot-headed Sectaries were Cromwell's chief favourites and the Soul of the Army.

The third feature in the Army's outlook was an unshakable distrust of the King. Nevertheless, Cromwell and the Grandees believed they could best protect their religion by coming to terms with him and enlisting the Royalist party on the side of the liberty of conscience as against the Parliamentary Presbyterians. But their belief in monarchy was merely opportunist and they were perfectly ready to depose Charles and substitute one of his sons for him upon the throne. The Levellers on the contrary were the earliest modern democrats — hence their name — and had also strong leanings towards republicanism. In 1645 Baillie asserted that the Anabaptists detested monarchy and when Baxter was in the Army he noted the mischief caused by the distribution of pamphlets against the King and the Ministry. 'I perceived,' he added, 'that they [the Army extremists] took the King for a Tyrant and an Enemy and intended to master him or ruin him.'

The growing republican opinions of the Levellers not only handicapped the Army leaders in their negotiations with Parliament and the King, but the democratic principles of the Levellers divided the Army into class antagonisms. Lilburne, once Cromwell's protégé and for a time Lieutenant-Colonel in the Roundhead Army, had arrived at his democratic opinions by a circuitous route. The Commons had in 1645 thrown him into Newgate for attacking the King, and unable therefore to attribute sovereignty to Parliament he discovered it in the nation as a whole. A country squire like Cromwell could neither appreciate nor value a political view which he believed to endanger the interests of property.

For a time special circumstances held together the divergent Roundhead parties. Before the fall of Oxford, the visible sign of the Cavalier defeat, the King, after vainly seeking permission to come to London, decided to surrender himself to the Scots in the hope that they would restore him to his throne at the expense of some kind of religious agreement. This step naturally united the English Parliament with the Army. Commissioners were sent to offer the King terms at

Newcastle and preparations were made to pay off the Scots. To the Newcastle Propositions Charles gave, in Cromwell's words, 'a very general answer', refusing to commit himself. He vainly tried to get something for nothing from his Scottish hosts, who thereupon took their money and handed him over to Parliament. By January 1647 the Scots had left England and Charles was installed at Holmby House in Northamptonshire under the care of Parliament, in effect a prisoner but in name still a King. But Charles, always an apt intriguer, did not despair. He believed that astute diplomacy might compensate for failure in war, and sensing the approaching clash between Parliament and the Army he prepared to profit from their dissensions by selling the divinity that doth hedge a king, while it was still marketable, to the highest bidder.

Meanwhile the Army grew more and more discontented with Parliament, and with good cause. Its first complaint was that money had been found easily enough to pay off the Scots but that English soldiers were eighteen months in arrears and there was yet no provision for them. Its feelings were further exacerbated by two petitions submitted to the Commons by the Presbyterian City of London, grumbling at the heavy expense of the Army and containing other grievances against it but failing to advance security for its arrears. Cromwell, who was now settled with his family in lodgings in Drury Lane, wrote to Fairfax commenting on these petitions. 'There want not, in all places,' he said in March 1647, 'men who have so much malice against the army as besots them.' He had reason to be angered, for not only had the Presbyterians attacked the Army but the parliamentary majority had attacked him personally. In their scheme for a peace establishment they had resolved that there should be no officer in the Army apart from Fairfax with a rank above that of colonel. This was deliberately to exclude from further service the ablest soldier in the country simply on account of his religious opinions. The Commons followed these resolutions with another to the effect that all Army officers must conform to the Church which Parliament was about to establish. The Army organized itself for resistance to these attacks on its just monetary claims, religious liberties and leader. The bitterness of Cromwell's feelings at the ingratitude of Parliament revealed itself in a remark to a fellow officer:

It is a miserable thing to serve a Parliament, to which let a man be never so faithful, if one pragmatical [meddlesome] fellow amongst them rise and asperse him, he shall never wipe it off, whereas, when one serves a general, he may do as much service, and yet be free from all blame and envy.

It is from this point — we have reached the early spring of 1647 — that Cromwell's intentions become veiled in obscurity and his conduct open to condemnation for its swift inconsistencies. It is first necessary to appreciate the alternative courses he might take. He could remain faithful to Parliament, use his influence at Westminster in favour of a reasonable disbandment and then persuade the Army to agree to the parliamentary terms. Twelve thousand men were immediately needed in Ireland where the Royalist Lord-Lieutenant, unable to suppress the Catholic rising which had begun in 1641, had laid down his commission and invited Parliament to take over the Government. Besides these there was to be a standing army of 7,000 men and there was always employment to be found in the Thirty Years War which still ravaged the Continent. If the Army agreed to disband on these terms, it might well be that Parliament would reward his efforts and a restored King prove himself not ungrateful. His position would have been in fact similar to that of Monk in 1660. His second alternative was to find a fresh outlet for his military genius, if not in Ireland, then abroad. In April he had some conversation with the Elector Palatine with a view to fighting for the cause of Calvinism in Germany. The third alternative was to exploit the discontent of the Army in order to coerce Parliament into maintaining unaltered the existing military establishment. We know that at this date he did not contemplate the view of the extreme Levellers that the monarchy must be destroyed.

What springs of action determined Cromwell's decision? The factor of personal ambition, if undoubtedly exaggerated by his contemporaries, has been strangely glossed over by many biographers. Still every one of these courses opened up genuine prospects of personal success. He had to decide which of them was the most practical. The second he speedily abandoned. Although, had he crossed the seas, he might have ended the Thirty Years War more advantageously for the Protestant cause, he was no monarch like Gustavus Adolphus, who could transport his entire army into distant lands. On the contrary, he had created a place for himself in English politics and it would have been madness for him to abandon it: nor did he do so. But if he could use his unique position with the Army and Parliament to reconcile them with each other and with the King, he might aspire to the highest rewards, and it was in this direction that he first turned.

But he had committed himself to a hopeless task. He was attempting to smooth over every contrary interest of class and religion which had been sharpened by the civil war. It was as if to reconcile Frenchman and German, Mohammedan and Hindoo, Tsarist and Bolshevist. In 1647 he was to learn by bitter experience that God had not ordained such a reign of peace on earth — and he was ever ready to interpret his experiences as the truest guides to the will of God. They formed for him 'dispensations', a phrase he constantly used to describe what historians, fortified by their later knowledge, regard as the natural sequence of events. Yet these dispensations did not bring with them any certainty of happiness but led only to conflict and struggle. And in that conflict Oliver Cromwell had to abide by the Army. He had built it out of men with whose outlook and opinions he agreed, and he had led it to victory. But if he had made it, it too had made him. Their interests could not be separated. It would again make him — or break him.

§ 2

In the middle of March 1647 the House of Commons sent a deputation to the Army headquarters at Saffron Walden near Cambridge to inform the officers of the resolutions it had passed with regard to the enlistment of soldiers for Ireland. To the immense surprise of the parliamentary commissioners the officers announced that they would not promise to carry out their orders until they knew of the detailed arrangements and whether their grievances over arrears and indemnities had been fully met. The commissioners retired in disorder while the soldiers, with the assistance and under the moderating influence of their officers, drew up a statement of their complaints which they presented to their general, Fairfax. Although Cromwell was in London at the time and can have had no direct hand in this agitation, Ireton and various personal friends of his were certainly active in the matter and a City rumour to the effect that he was about to be arrested for treason showed that the Presbyterians believed that he was behind the soldiers' demands. The Commons were infuriated at the spirit of insubordination manifested by the troops, and Denzil Holles carried a declaration that all Army petitioners were enemies of the State. A fortnight later fresh commissioners were sent down to enlist men to go to Ireland under the command of Major-General Skippon. But the officers demanded that their old leaders, Fairfax and Cromwell, should also be sent, and many cried out that all should disband or none. The privates now took a further hand in the conflict and eight regiments nominated representatives from the ranks known as Agents or Agitators, 'a novelty under the sun', to propagate and express their point of view. At the same time many of the officers drew up separate petitions to Parliament.

This was a challenge that the Commons did not dare accept and, fearful of mutiny, they changed their tone by asking

Cromwell, who had now ceased to attend their sessions, to go down with Skippon, Fleetwood and Ireton to Saffron Walden for the purpose of investigating the discontent and persuading the soldiers into accepting six weeks' pay and embarking for Ireland. Two meetings were held in Saffron Walden church, where Cromwell asserted the necessity of maintaining the authority of Parliament which the Army had fought to defend and whose interest it was yet to preserve. On May 17th he and the other commissioners reported to the Speaker that they had done their utmost to keep the soldiers in order and to satisfy them of the good intentions of the House, and would later send a full report to London. On May 20th Cromwell made his report to the effect that although the Army was still discontented it would disband but would not go to Ireland; and on the following day he received the thanks of the House for his services. But it was soon plain that he had only succeeded in patching up a temporary agreement. Three days earlier the King had at last sent a message that he was ready to accept the establishment of Presbyterianism as the national religion for a period of three years. The English Presbyterian leaders knew that the Army would resist this scheme tooth and nail. But instead of merely pressing on with the disbandment, they took the astounding step of opening negotiations with the Scots to protect themselves against their own Army. At the same time they delayed giving the 'real and visible security' they had promised to the soldiers for their arrears and ordered the disbandment at once to begin. The Army learned the proceedings of the Commons with despair and suspected their intrigues with the Scots. A rumour swept through Saffron Walden that an attempt would be made to divide officers and soldiers from each other. On May 29th Fairfax moved his headquarters to Bury St. Edmunds and here the officers voiced their dissatisfaction with the votes of the Commons, while the Agitators actively conspired against disbandment and set up a printing press to pour out statements of their case. Meanwhile a regiment at Abingdon broke into open mutiny which was quelled only with difficulty. A general rendezvous of the Army was demanded by the common soldiers to discuss the critical situation. Parliament and Army watched each other's every move with the deepest suspicion and distrust.

In these circumstances both parties attempted to enlist the influence of the prisoner of Holmby on their side. As early as April 21st Ireton had entered into secret communication with the King, who was only too eager to foment division among his opponents. But the Agitators urged on the Army leaders that it would be better to seize Charles and use him as an important piece in the game against the Presbyterians. Such was the position when on May 31st Fairfax received definite orders from Parliament to disband his artillery; he refused on the ground that the Commons had failed to satisfy the just claims of the Army as their commissioners had promised, and on the next day he summoned Cromwell from London.

But Cromwell had not remained unmoved whilst these events had been in progress. He had better means than the Agitators of knowing the exact intentions of their opponents. He therefore ordered a certain Cornet Joyce to take 500 troopers and go first to Oxford to make sure of the guns, arms and ammunition there and then to Holmby to secure the King. 'This egg', wrote Sir William Waller, who living next door to Cromwell in Drury Lane was in a position to know the facts, 'was laid in Lieutenant-General Cromwell's own chamber, and brooded between him and Commissary-General Ireton; but they were too wise to cackle; . . . Cornet Joyce was employed as the man to hatch it.' Joyce seems to have improved on his orders to the extent that he moved the King from Holmby to Newmarket where the Army could guard him more closely; but that is a minor detail. The main fact was that Cromwell had now made his first *volte-face* of 1647 and thrown in his lot completely with the Army.

§ 3

When the House of Commons learned the news of the King's seizure by the Army, it at once took alarm and adopted a mixed programme of threatening and cajoling which was obviously unlikely to prove effective. On the one hand, it took into immediate consideration the subject of the soldiers' pay; on the other hand, it prepared to resist forcibly the menaces of the Army by calling upon the aid of the City militia and even inviting the young Prince Charles (the future Charles II) to lead a Scottish army southward. It also meditated Cromwell's impeachment. But Oliver, as soon as he knew that Cornet Joyce had successfully accomplished his errand, had not stood upon the order of his going from Westminster — but had gone. When he reached the Army, however, he advocated a policy of moderation; Army, Parliament and King must be reconciled, he believed, in order to prevent the country from falling into anarchy; in pursuit of this end he gratified the Agitators by inviting them to a General Council of the Army (which he carefully deprived of all real executive power), he tried to persuade the King to return to Holmby under the care of the Army, and he drew up a letter to the authorities in the City of London defending the Army's breach with Parliament. In this letter, written from Royston near Cambridge, on June 10th, he asserted that the Army had no wish to alter the civil government of the country and merely sought the 'desire of satisfaction to our demands as soldiers'. 'We desire not', he asserted, 'to intermeddle with the settling of Presbyterian Government. Nor did we seek to open a way to licentious liberty, under pretence of obtaining ease for tender consciences.' Such statements, though soothing, were, to say the very least, ingenuous. The letter was, however, ominous enough for Londoners, since it contained the words: 'for obtaining these things, we are drawing near your City'. Was it now possible for a new and sub-dividing civil war to be averted? The victors had indeed 'fallen out among themselves'.

The declaration of June 10th that the Army had no desire to alter the civil government was promptly refuted by 'The Declaration of the Army' of June 15th, which attempted to prove that the Parliament was corrupt by appealing to a sort of doctrine of the sovereignty of the people that the Army truly represented. It required Parliament to name a date for its own dissolution (it had now sat for seven years) and to acknowledge the right of petition. At the same time the officers in the Army asked that Parliament should expel eleven of its Presbyterian members who were most obnoxious to them. After a vain attempt to raise forces for their own defence, the Commons capitulated and offered to negotiate with the Army, and the eleven proscribed members fled the City.

It was at last clear to Cromwell that the Long Parliament in particular and perhaps any Parliament that might be elected in its place would not prove a sufficient guarantor of the religious liberties and monetary claims of the Independent soldiery. The country must therefore, he decided, return to the system of constitutional monarchy from which according to the imaginative Roundhead theory the Stuarts had wickedly departed. On the very day that Parliament gave way to the Army, Cromwell wrote an urgent letter to one of his colonels to make sure that the King did not escape and ten days later Charles was brought under guard to Caversham, near Reading, the new army headquarters, where he had an interview with Cromwell. Oliver had now satisfied himself that the time was ripe for a final constitutional solution. Parliament had capitulated to the Army. If he could induce the King to accept reasonable restraints on his power, if he could hold in check the extremists in the Army and prevent the Presbyterians from flying at the Independents, the civil war might be liquidated and the causes for which it had been fought vindicated. He used every resource. Whether or not the phrase that was attributed to him by an unfriendly contemporary that 'it is lawful to play the knave with a knave' is exact, it is at least undoubted that he displayed remarkable tact in his endeavours.

How far this show of tact deserves the description of 'dissembling' attached to it by some, depends perhaps on how we define the word tact.

The ingenious and hardened general was singularly affected by the human qualities of the King, whose reunion at Caversham with three of his children Cromwell described to one of the royal intimates with tears in his eyes; but despite the satisfaction which he appeared to derive from these conversations he still distrusted Charles as a statesman. On July 16th he also had to exert all his influence and reasoning power to dissuade the army officers from immediately advancing on London. A march on London, would, he pointed out, be only a means to an end, that end being 'a general settlement of the peace of the kingdom and of the rights of the subject'. An agreement obtained by negotiation, he urged, would be of far more permanent value than one exacted by force and they must at all costs avoid a second civil war. He confessed that he himself was too much inclined to see imaginary dangers and begged them not to imitate that fault of his. He did his best to defend Parliament and pleaded this time for political unity — 'Though you be in the right and I in the wrong, if we be divided I doubt we shall all be in the wrong.' For the moment he secured his point and the Council of the Army turned to consider a plan of settlement. Three weeks later after much discussion Cromwell signified his approval of a written constitution drawn up by his son-in-law Ireton, which while it made the King's power subservient to that of Parliament also lessened the power of Parliament by making it more amenable to the control of the constituencies and by establishing liberty of conscience as a fundamental right. In accordance with the wishes of the Agitators and the Levellers certain changes were accepted by Cromwell, giving this constitution a slightly more democratic character, and it was then forwarded to the King.

But Cromwell's great efforts for unity proved to be in vain. For while these events were in progress the Presbyterians made one last effort to break away from the stranglehold of the Army. The London apprentices (very possibly incited by the City magnates) rushed into the Commons and forced the House to restore the militia to Presbyterian control. The eleven members promptly returned to the scene of their former triumphs, whereupon the Speaker and all the Independent Members of Parliament left London and threw themselves upon the protection of the Army. Cromwell was not slow to succour them. Twenty thousand men were a compelling answer to an Independent defeat in Parliament. They marched from Hounslow to Westminster, escorting back their fugitive allies and crying out 'Lords and Commons and a Free Parliament'. Finally on August 20th Cromwell, against the will of Fairfax, retorted to the apprentices' rising by coercing the Houses into declaring null and void all their proceedings in the absence of the Independent members.

The result of the Army's presence at Putney, whither it withdrew after this feat, followed as it was by a second flight of the eleven Presbyterian leaders, was to give the Independents a precarious majority in the Commons. Cromwell thenceforward assiduously attended in his place and intrigued to circumvent, though he did not openly oppose, the parliamentary peace propositions; for he was anxious to get the King to reject them in favour of the Army's plan for a written constitution. Thus, on September 22nd he exerted his influence to prevent a vote that Charles, who had refused countless different proposals submitted to him by Parliament, should no longer be permitted to receive any addresses from them. A month later Cromwell, who was described as speaking 'much on the King's behalf', made a three hours' speech in defence of monarchy. All this time the two rival parties continued both openly and secretly to press the King to declare himself on their side. Cromwell and Ireton had a series of interviews and communications with him, and although Charles had once at an earlier point almost committed himself to the Presbyterian scheme of government he announced in the autumn that he was prepared to accept the Army's 'Heads of the Proposals' in a modified form. Frequent messages passed between Charles I and Cromwell. The latter inquired casually of Sir John Berkeley, one of the Royal circle, whether it were true that a rumour was circulating that if the negotiations between them concluded successfully he was to be created Earl of Essex and Captain of the King's Guard. What a prospect opened up for Oliver if this should be! He would be as great in the counsels of a restored King Charles as his ancestor Thomas Cromwell had been in those of Henry VIII. But he might well be warned by his ancestor's fate, who having served Henry VIII's purpose perished miserably on the scaffold. Yet in the days in which we moderns live we can easily conceive of a great dictator established in power by military force, governing his country nominally under a monarch but actually holding his master in the palm of his hand. Such a dictator Cromwell might have become in the seventeenth-century terms, without even the necessity of appealing to a democratic vote to endorse his position. But this sort of dictatorship he could not attain. In any case the insincerity of the defeated monarch was patent. He continued to await which way the cat jumped. He told a confidant that he thought the Army 'ought absolutely to be well dissembled with, whilst His Majesty was in their hands, at least, that he might the better get out of them'. Furthermore, both the King and half the members of Parliament were all the time engaged, each separately, on a secret negotiation with the Scots to save themselves from the tyranny of the New Model Army. Finally, Cromwell knew that the greater part of the Army would not go with him in his schemes. So deep was the resentment aroused by his communications with the King that Cromwell had to ask Sir John Berkeley to visit him less frequently, 'the suspicion of him being so great that he was afraid to lie down in his own quarters'. The Levellers demanded a republic, not an Independent dictator. In face of all these difficulties Cromwell had perforce to abandon at least for the time being any plan along the line of enlightened despotism, and to turn once more to seek some kind of parliamentary assistance in order to regain for the nation a stable form of government which was not the half-naked rule of the sword.

§ 4

Thomas Carlyle laboured to prove that Oliver Cromwell was a Man of Truths, not of Lies. Professors Gardiner and Firth subsequently strove by a minute examination into dates and facts to refute many of the contemporary accusations of hypocrisy against their hero. Inconsistency, they claimed, is not a vice to be condemned in a statesman. So long as it can be shown that Cromwell did not pursue, as Charles I undoubtedly did pursue, two diametrically opposed lines of policy *at the same time* no stigma of hypocrisy clings to him. But though the validity of this argument will be generally admitted from a high historical standpoint one may easily understand that Cromwell's three dramatic changes of political attitude over a period of less than one year made him the object of execration to every party. In politics the time factor is all important. Over ten years a statesman's inconsistencies are forgotten, they are even regarded as a proof of his statesmanship, but over one year or less they are a natural target for adverse criticism. Consider what Cromwell did in 1647. At first he had sided with a Presbyterian Parliament against an Independent Army on the ground that Parliament was the only respectable source of authority in the country. He had then not merely upheld the Army's refusal to disband but had coerced the Parliament until it became little more than a stalking horse for the Army. Next he had turned to Charles I as the only possible person to unite the diverse political forces of the nation. In October 1647 he had defended monarchy in a three-hour speech. Within four months in the same House of Commons he was to attack the monarchic principle to such an extent that the most impartial observers were astonished at his vehemence.

The solution to each of these sudden changes of outlook on Cromwell's part has been revealed by the researches of Gardiner and Firth. Cromwell had imagined that the Presbyterian Parliament would concede the moderate demands of the Independent Army, but it had refused to do so. He had then imagined that Charles I could be persuaded into accepting the restoration of his throne on the Independent terms; but he had soon discovered that the King did not honestly intend to do anything of the kind. Finally he thought that he could establish a system of government which would not be based on mere force but on some sort of agreement between Presbyterians and Independents. Again he failed. In each case he fell a prey to self-deception. Some statesmen frankly admit that their policy has to be altered to suit circumstances. In modern times a Peel or a Gladstone or a MacDonald has deliberately made a complete political *volte-face* because some apparently unforeseeable crisis has confronted him. But Cromwell's sudden turns-about were due rather to a curious inability to digest the facts as the normal party man around him, Presbyterian, Royalist, or Leveller, was wont to do. He allowed himself to be deceived because he was too slow in taking into account in the political sphere (as he could in the military) all the factors in a given situation. Gardiner wrote in a remarkable sentence about Cromwell that by 'a strange self-delusion' he failed to recognize at the end of 1647 that he was using force to determine political action. Therein lies the clue to the whole make-up of the man. Oliver Cromwell was not a man of lies or hypocrisies, but he was the creature of strange self-delusions.

CHAPTER VII

THE KING'S HEAD

§ 1

CROMWELL's failure to obtain any settled government in the kingdom had aggravated the extreme parties beyond endurance. The Royalists were asking insistently what was the use of their defeat to the victors if they could not produce some treaty with the King. Everywhere a reaction began to show itself in favour of the Cavaliers. On the other side, the Levellers in the Army and a small group of Republicans in the Commons began to seek the deposition of the King and the establishment of a democratic republic. One of their leaders, Colonel Sexby, summed up their point of view at this time when he said: 'We have laboured to please the King, and I think, except we go about to cut all our throats we shall not please him; and we have gone to support an house which will prove rotten studs [props], I mean the Parliament which consists of a company of rotten members.'

In the circumstances Cromwell's first concern was to restore some semblance of unity in the Army. In October 1647 he took the chair at a General Council of Officers in Putney to which representatives of the Levellers, known as the 'New Agitators', were admitted. The Levellers had drawn up their own schemes for a political constitution under the titles of the 'Case of the Army' and the 'Agreement of the People'. In contrast with the officers' 'Heads of the Proposals' they made no mention of the King or House of Lords and included manhood suffrage. They sought also for a codification of the law, the restoration of enclosed lands to the commons, freedom of trade from monopolistic restrictions and the abolition of sinecures. The object of the General Council's meeting was to try to reconcile the Levellers' proposals with the officers' plan. The debates achieved no permanent result — although owing to Cromwell's able chairmanship a temporary compromise was reached — but they are important because they reveal more clearly than any of Cromwell's set speeches his true approach to political theory.

Cromwell was more concerned about the purposes than about the origin of government. But if he were asked his views about its origin he would undoubtedly have replied that it derived from a 'contract' between the governor and the governed. All medieval writers until St. Thomas Aquinas had held that the State was founded upon a convention or contract which owed its existence to the Fall of Man. John Milton was to write in tune with this ancient view that Charles I had forfeited his throne because he broke his contract. When Cromwell said later, in 1649, that 'the King is King by contract' he also accepted this traditional opinion. His ideas of the nature of this contract emerge clearly in the course of the October debates. The Agitators argued that it was necessary to settle the future of the kingdom on clearly-thought-out logical principles which they identified with 'natural' rights and to ignore all past promises and engagements. Cromwell answered that the basis of all political action was that engagements once made must be kept whether by the people or by the King unless there were overwhelming reasons for breaking them. The world, he said, expects us to make good our engagements and before God and man we cannot disregard them. But, the Levellers protested, are those engagements honest? Do they conform to right principles? But Cromwell would only commit himself to this qualification:

Circumstances may be such as I may not now break an unrighteous engagement or else I may do that which I do scandalously, though the thing be good.

Why did he believe that even an unrighteous engagement might have to be kept, and that in any case all contracts must be closely scrutinized before they could be abandoned? The answer is to be found in the logic of his opponents' case. The Agitators argued that high above the value of any agreement between men and men came the criterion of individual conscience, judging what is right and wrong. The honestly searching mind will discover what are the natural or reasonable or just rights of mankind and in terms of those rights it will criticize any and every agreement which has been concluded either in the present or in the past. But what, thought Cromwell, can these natural rights be? One set of men will say one thing, and one set another. The appeal to the conscience means in fact complete individualism, for it implies the right of any individual to find for himself the solution to every problem — and such individualism is another name for anarchy. No! he maintained the abuse of contract means the negation of peace and unity, which is the necessary condition of a successful state.

But Cromwell at least hesitated over this assumption that all contracts, however unrighteous they might appear, must be kept. His son-in-law, Henry Ireton, the chief author of the 'Heads of the Proposals' and leader of the opposition to the Levellers, had no such doubts. And there is no question that Oliver's mentor in the realm of political thought was Ireton. 'None', wrote Lord Whitelocke who should have been in a position to know, 'could prevail so much, nor order him so far as Ireton could.' Another contemporary maintained that 'Cromwell only shot the bolts that were hammered in Ireton's forge'. And Ireton's unqualified view was:

'Covenants freely entered into must be kept. Take that away, and what right has a man to anything, to his estate of lands or to his goods? You talk of "law of nature"! By the "law of nature" you have no more right to this land or anything else than I have.'

If property is based upon contract, it may be wondered how the contract which originally brought about the distribution of property was made. It is a nice problem. The Agitators and Levellers would have said that it came about by conquest. (They conceived this conquest always to be the Norman Conquest. For them the historic English world began in 1066.) But it seems safe to say that this problem never troubled Cromwell's head. It was sufficient for him that somehow at some early period God had permitted an initial distribution of property, and if God now or at a later time disapproved of the manner in which property holders lived, He would no doubt deprive them of their possessions — indeed, so far as the Cavaliers were concerned, Cromwell himself had been an agent in this duty. But it sufficed that property was the basis of the State and landed property the salt of the earth. It was a political philosophy that ruled England for hundreds of years. Professor Tawney has called it the 'freeholder' view of society; men's political rights were regarded as proportionate to their stake in the country. The 'ship of state', wrote an Interregnum pamphleteer expressing this view, is 'no slave galley', but all the passengers are 'free merchant adventurers, though each according to their proportions'. That proportional equality, indeed, Cromwell and Ireton would have agreed, was the only true equality permissible in a state, and not the inadmissible complete egalitarianism of the Levellers.

It follows as a logical deduction from his basic conception of government that Cromwell was an opponent of universal manhood suffrage. According to his principles universal suffrage led to anarchy: for if a man who possessed no property, a man who had no interest but that of breathing, were given the vote, it was clear that he would use it to obtain the goods of those who were possessors, and a war of all against all would follow. Ireton said that it was an obvious political postulate that no person had a right to participate in the affairs of government unless he had a fixed stake in the country, that is to say unless he were a landowner or a substantial tradesman. In the course of the debate on this subject Cromwell remarked that he had not heard Ireton refuted. He suggested, however, that some compromise might be arrived at between the followers of Ireton and the Agitators, and agreed that an alteration of the suffrage might be arranged which distributed the vote more widely, while securing, say, that dependent creatures like servants and the poor who were in receipt of alms should be excluded from it.

The Levellers were democrats and not Communists, but the accusation that they stood for equality of income (to use a modern phrase) was a convenient stick with which to beat them. Moreover, it is probable that the majority of their opponents, Cromwell among them, thought that political equality, the equality of those who had a stake in the country with those who merely breathed its air, would necessarily lead to a scramble for the redistribution of property. Apart from this fundamental difference there were some similarities between Ireton's constitution, the 'Heads of the Proposals', and the 'Agreement of the People'. Both believed in a re-distribution of seats, the abolition of 'rotten' boroughs and the frequent summoning of Parliament. When Cromwell became Protector he put into effect, although in a very modified way, part of the redistribution proposals. If, then, Cromwell was vehemently opposed to universal suffrage but acknow-ledged the necessity for some kind of electoral reform, what did he believe to be the best form of government? One could be a republican without being a democrat, as the cases of Athens and Venice had proved, but Cromwell was no republican. In truth, he did not attach much importance to the form: 'I am not wedded or glued to forms of government', he said, and in support of his attitude he instanced the history of the chosen people of God who, according to the Old Testa-ment, first were ruled by the heads of their families, then by judges, then by elective, and finally by hereditary monarchs; the Jews were equally happy, he urged, under all these forms of government and what mattered therefore was not the form of government but the spirit. Nevertheless, he preferred on the whole (in theory) a form of constitution which included a balance of elements; and he was by no means averse from 'something monarchical' in them. Even an autocrat with the right spirit might be a guarantee of peace and of property.

The immediate obstacle to a settlement, however, was not the idea of monarchy but the shiftiness of the existing captive monarch.

§ 2

During this time of confusion the King had succeeded in escaping from Hampton Court Palace (whither he had been ultimately transferred from Holmby) and fled to the Isle of Wight where he began to enter into deeper negotiations with the Scots. Cromwell still refused to commit himself either to Royalists or Republicans. He broke off his hopeless negotiations with the King and tried to use his influence with a distant relative of his, Colonel Robert Hammond, Governor of Carisbrooke Castle, to whose protection the King had commended himself, to prevent Charles's further escape to France or elsewhere. At the same time he suppressed a Leveller mutiny in the Army. He then returned to a policy of moderation and made a new effort to reconcile the two opposing wings of the Independent party with Parliament and the City of London. The mutineer Levellers were pardoned and various promises made to pacify the Presbyterians. His efforts were soon aided by circumstances, for at last the King's double-dealing was to render him suspect, and justly suspect, to all the English Roundhead parties.

In November 1647 Charles had dispatched an offer from the Isle of Wight to compromise with the parliamentary terms with regard to Church government and control of the Army if he could be admitted to a personal treaty in London, and he expected that Cromwell and the other Army Grandees with whom he had recently been in secret contact would support his proposal. But Cromwell would no longer trust him, and a Parliament, now mainly Independent in complexion, would only allow him to re-enter the capital if he would consent to four preliminary bills for their 'present security'. These bills were presented to Charles on Christmas Eve by a joint committee from the two Houses. But to their dismay they encountered at Carisbrooke an unwelcome rival deputation from the Scottish nobility.

Since at the end of the first civil war the Scots had surrendered the King's person to the English Parliament, there had been much political controversy in Scotland as to the wisdom of that step, especially as it was realized that the English Army did not intend to support the Covenant, as it had promised, by setting up an all-embracing Presbyterian system and fully restoring the monarchy to its old place in the constitution of the two countries. As early as July 1647 Baillie had written that 'no human hope remained' for the Scottish policy in England if the King and Army decided to seal an agreement on an Independent religious basis. To this letter he added the significant observation: 'If the King would call, I doubt not the raising of the best army ever we had for the crushing of those serpents, enemies to God and man' would best achieve their ends. But there were two parties in Scotland, one mainly lay, headed by the Duke of Hamilton, the other clerical under the Earl of Argyll, the former of which was inclined to war with England in the King's cause, as Baillie suggested, the latter against it. Gradually Hamilton's supporters gained the upper hand and enlisted a considerable measure of influential Presbyterian clerical opinion in favour of an agreement with the King. Thus it was that a Scottish commission found itself on the Isle of Wight in December 1647 with which Charles signed on Boxing Day an 'Engagement' agreeing to introduce Presbyterianism into England, to suppress all other religious sects and to grant certain wide political and trading privileges to Scotsmen. In return the Scots promised to support Charles's requests for a personal treaty and the disbandment of the English Army, and if these were not conceded, to declare war on his behalf. Although the King proceeded to bury the text of the Engagement deep in the castle garden, his rejection of the four Bills and his interview with the Scots made what had been so secretly agreed clear enough to the disgusted English Roundheads. Vane and Cromwell might be, as one Scot wrote, 'of nimble hot fancies for to put all in confusion, but not of a deep reach', but even they could penetrate the royal plotting with the Scots to renew the war.

Some years afterwards Cromwell in an expansive moment disclosed to an ex-Royalist with whom he had become intimate how in the winter of 1647 he had discovered the double-dealing of the King. A parliamentary spy in the King's service wrote to Cromwell that the bearer of a letter from the King to the Queen would be at the Blue Boar Inn at Holborn at ten o'clock a few nights hence. It was in December 1647 when the officers were billeted at Windsor that the letter came. 'Immediately upon receipt of it', related Cromwell, 'Ireton and I resolved to take one trusty fellow with us, and with troopers' habits to go to the inn in Holborn; which accordingly we did, and set our man at the gate of the inn, where the wicket only was open, to let the people in and out. Our man was to give us notice when any person came there with a saddle, whilst we, in the disguise of common troopers, called for cans of beer and continued drinking until about ten o'clock: the sentinel at the gate then gave notice that the man with the saddle was come in. Upon this we immediately arose and as the man was leading out his horse saddled, came up to him with drawn swords and told him we were to search all that went in and out there, but as he looked an honest man we would only search his saddle and so dismiss him. Upon that we ungirt the saddle and carried it into the stall where we had been drinking, and left the horseman with our sentinel. Then ripping up one of the skirts of the saddle, we there found the letter of which we had been informed; and having got it into our hands, we delivered the saddle again to the man, telling him he was an honest man and bidding him go about his business. ... As

soon as we had the letter we opened it; in which we found the
King had acquainted the Queen that he was now courted by
both factions ... but he thought he should close with the
Scots.' 'Upon this', added Cromwell, 'we took horse and
went to Windsor; and finding we were not likely to have any
tolerable terms from the King we immediately from that time
forward, resolved his ruin.'

But with or without the evidence of such a letter there was
no concealing the fact that the King was playing off Parliament
against the Scots in a last attempt to regain his power. In these
circumstances the Commons naturally enough voted that they
would make no further addresses to the King and on this
occasion Cromwell was in his place to support the resolution;
but he and Ireton still favoured the retention of monarchic
institutions with the Prince of Wales or some member of the
royal family on the throne. In the Army, while they refrained
from denying that the King was a Man of Blood, as one of the
sectarian colonels described him, they were opposed as yet
to bringing him to trial as a murderer. But this compromise
solution between the wishes of the Republicans and the
Presbyterian-Royalists pleased no party and led some to
affirm that it was merely a veiled method of substituting King
'Nol' for King Charles. This inability of the Army and
Parliament to come to terms as to the future government of the
nation contributed perhaps as much as Charles's Engagement
with the Scottish nobility to the pronounced Royalist reaction
and revival in all parts of the country. Thus for the next few
months events drifted in the direction of a second civil war.
But Cromwell himself lay seriously ill and ceased for a while
to have any influence on their course. When he recovered in
March 1648 he told Fairfax: 'It hath pleased God to raise me
out of a dangerous sickness. ... I [had] received in myself
the sentence of death. ...' Within a year he was to be God's
instrument in imposing the like sentence on another — but
without reprieve.

§ 3

The most interesting feature of the second civil war is not its military but its political aspect. The nature of the contest was plain enough in the eyes of the Independents, here typically represented by Cromwell. In their opinion the first civil war had settled the dispute between the King and the 'nation', and the series of victories won by the Roundheads was convincing proof that God was on their side. The King had 'juggled' (Cromwell was blind to his own juggling) to revive a cause already condemned in Heaven. Cromwell believed that Charles and his followers were now guilty of a triple treason. They had acted treasonably enough when they had first raised the standard of civil war in 1642; their 'iniquity' was 'double' because 'they sinned against so much light and against so many evidences of Divine Presence going along with and prospering a righteous cause'; it was a 'prodigious' triple treason because whereas 'the former quarrel . . . was that Englishmen might rule over one another, in 1648 they had allied with the Scots and thereby strove to vassalize us [English] to a foreign nation.'

In their anger at the Royalists the two wings of the Army came together; the Republicans under Colonel Ludlow united with opportunists like Cromwell and Ireton. At a conference between them on the eve of the new war, Cromwell showed his boredom with theoretical disputes by throwing a cushion at Ludlow's head and running downstairs. 'But', recorded Ludlow in his *Memoirs*, 'I overtook him with another which made him hasten down faster than he desired.' (For these stern Puritans horseplay was the sole outlet for their repressions.)

Yet although Cromwell might grow impatient with the theorists, the triumph of the Republican point of view was implicit in his characterization of the authors of the second civil war. If the Royalists had committed a 'prodigious treason', it followed that their leader must be made answerable for their crime.

If the King's trial followed as a natural result of the war, so also did the final purge of the House of Commons by the Army. The attitude of the Presbyterian Roundheads to the Scottish invasion was curiously ambiguous. The Scots declared war in March on the ground that 'the sectarian faction' was guilty of 'atrocious breaches of every article of the Covenant'. Of this accusation the English Calvinists had no criticism to make. The Presbyterian House of Lords refused to stigmatize the Scots as enemies, and the Commons continued their vain negotiations with the King in the Isle of Wight. The Army thus became the one firm uncompromising political force in the kingdom, the sole guarantee of English national independence in face of the Scots; and so ultimately in order to defend the justice of the Army's case against that of the King, Cromwell was reluctantly driven into the position of holding that Might and Right were synonymous.

In the course of the second civil war it became even clearer that the governing body in England was the Army, ruled in fact if not in name by Cromwell, and on him devolved the task of checkmating the Royalist plans. In the Isle of Wight the King was, as we have seen, under the care of Colonel Hammond, who had married a daughter of the dead John Hampden and was consequently connected with the Cromwell family; but he was also a nephew of the Reverend Henry Hammond, a loyal chaplain of the King. His position was therefore a difficult one. The Royalists felt confident that he would connive at Charles's escape, should he decide to flee the country. Cromwell, on the other hand, exercised all his powers of persuasion and all the resources of his powerful personality to prevail upon 'dear Robin', as he addressed him, to guard the royal guest more closely. In his struggle for the soul of Robin Hammond, Oliver's thoughts and feelings in 1648 are laid bare to the world. Yet at the same time he used every device from bribery to casuistry to achieve his aim. And in the end, in a large measure, he succeeded.

The King's inability to escape from Carisbrooke was the

first mishap to the Royalist plans and was followed by the delay of the Scots to enter England. When Royalist risings broke out on all sides in the spring, Hamilton ('the malignant party having prevailed in the Parliament of Scotland', as Cromwell put it) did not cross the border until July. In London a Royalist demonstration by the apprentices was prevented by Cromwell's troopers who cut them down with their swords as the mob poured out of the Strand towards Whitehall Mews. In other towns Royalist risings were equally unsuccessful. There came only from the South-East and in Wales a definite challenge to the supremacy of the Army. Fairfax took charge of the military operations in the former area and ordered Cromwell into Wales. Major-General Lambert, a Yorkshire soldier, later to be the leader of the Opposition on Cromwell's Council of State, with an inadequate force advanced from his native county to watch the movements of the Scottish army until Fairfax was ready to join him. In May Cromwell marched into Wales, took Chepstow and then moved on Pembroke Castle, the stronghold of the revolt in those parts. Its heavy-drinking, hitherto Parliamentarian Colonel was slowly starved into surrender and duly shot as a traitor. Meanwhile Fairfax had been less successful in his siege of Colchester, the centre of the resistance in the East. It was therefore left to Cromwell to repulse the Scots.

Hamilton had hesitated as to whether after the capture of Berwick and Carlisle he should continue southward by way of Lancashire or Yorkshire. Militarily speaking the route through Yorkshire offered greater advantages, and Cromwell had entered Yorkshire after the fall of Pembroke in the anticipation that the enemy would come that way. But on August 13th the Duke of Hamilton finally decided to go through Lancashire, largely because he hoped to take Manchester and obtain fresh recruits on the way. Three days later the big Scottish Army was strung out over a distance of forty miles. Sir George Monro with 3000 first-class horse and foot

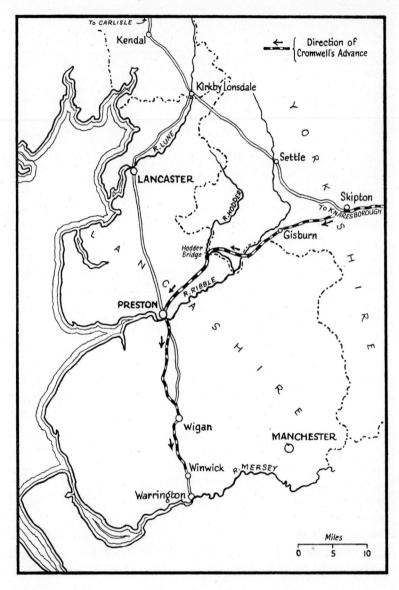

PRESTON CAMPAIGN, AUGUST, 1648

remained as a strong but useless rearguard at Kirkby Lonsdale in Westmorland. Sir Marmaduke Langdale, the gaunt opponent of Cromwell at Naseby, with 3600 English Royalists was stationed four miles east of Preston in Lancashire, guarding Hamilton's flank. Hamilton himself with the infantry was at Preston but he dispatched his two chief subordinate officers, the Earl of Callendar and General Middleton, with the bulk of the Scottish horse to Wigan, fifteen miles south of Preston. Hence although Cromwell had only some 8600 seasoned men (of whom 2500 were horse) as compared with the 24,000 under Hamilton, by practising the first principle of good generalship in keeping his army together he was at an initial advantage over the enemy.

On August 13th also, near Knaresborough in Yorkshire, Lambert had joined Cromwell who, after he had learned of Hamilton's decision to advance through Lancashire, left his artillery behind and set out secretly and swiftly across the Pennines. On August 16th he reached Hodder Bridge (the Hodder is a tributary of the Ribble) and held a council of war. The choice before the council was whether to march southward across the Ribble and block the Scots' progress through Lancashire or to march direct upon Preston and engage the main body of the enemy. 'It was decided', as Oliver explained afterwards, 'that to engage the enemy to fight was our business.' Moreover, to attack the enemy from the north-east rather than from the south was to cut them off from their communications with Scotland and to make possible not merely their defeat but their annihilation.

The Scots had not the slightest notion that Cromwell was coming upon them. Sir Marmaduke had heard a rumour that some force might be near but he imagined that it must be merely the local Lancashire levies. He was soon undeceived. On August 17th Cromwell's men encountered the Royalist foot drawn up behind the hedges on Preston Moor. 'We came to a hedge dispute', as Cromwell put it, which lasted for four hours. Despite their inferior numbers the Royalists fought heroically but after a contest at push of pike and with close firing — 'a very stiff and sturdy resistance', Cromwell admitted — the Roundhead cavalry completed the victory. By nightfall Cromwell had entered Preston itself and Hamilton, who because of the dispatch of his infantry south on the eve of the battle had been unable to bring any substantial support to Langdale, was hurrying away to join his main body of horse at Wigan. Leaving the Lancashire militia to guard 4000 prisoners in Preston, Cromwell set off next morning in pursuit; Hamilton's 'wet, hungry and weary' foot soldiers, trudging through typical Lancashire rain, were only three miles ahead of Cromwell's vanguard and many stragglers were taken or killed by the Roundheads on the road. Already the spirit of the splendid Scots army was broken. To add to the confusion General Middleton had left Wigan when Hamilton arrived; he had hastened back to Preston by another road and the two forces had missed each other. Ultimately, however, they joined north of Wigan but after contemplating putting up a fight retreated on the night of August 18th into the town while Cromwell, as he reported, 'lay that night in a field close by the enemy, being very dirty and weary, and having marched twelve miles of such ground as I never rode in my life, the day being very wet'. Nevertheless, the Scots now decided upon another night march, intending to put the Mersey between them and their implacable foe. Once more they paid the penalty of dividing their forces. On August 19th Cromwell's cavalry caught the Scottish foot at Winnick, only three miles from Wigan. After a stubborn fight 1000 Scots were killed and 2000 taken prisoners. The rest of the Scottish infantry surrendered next day, and Hamilton with his cavalry gave themselves up to Lambert in Staffordshire four days later. Meanwhile Cromwell had hurried back to Preston and was preparing to pursue Sir George Monro and the rest of the Scots from Westmorland into Scotland. The Preston campaign was perhaps the finest of all Cromwell's strategic feats. He struck his opponent in the flank (whether by accident or design) and beat him up piecemeal. The battle of Preston was Cromwell's first big independent command and his first notable victory over superior forces; although he had less than half the number of the enemy, like Napoleon afterwards he outman-œuvred them by the rapidity and secrecy of his marches. The Scottish Army was destroyed; the Lord, it appeared, had made His choice; it was the Independent Ironsides and not the Presbyterian Cavaliers who were indeed 'the apple of His eye'. A few days after the battle-and-rout of Preston, Colchester surrendered to Fairfax, and to all intents and purposes the second civil war was at an end.

Hamilton's defeat brought about an internal revolution in Scotland which Cromwell diligently fostered, threatening the Scots if they persisted with their opposition to the English with a second 'appeal to God'. Argyll and the clergy who had voted against the invasion of England at once regained the governing power and surrendered Carlisle and Berwick. Oliver did not allot to the Scots as a nation as large a share of the war guilt as he did to the King and to the Royalists. He believed his mission was to obtain an immediate, honourable and permanent peace. He seems to have been disingenuous, to say the least, in his methods of conciliating the Scottish Presbyterians. He appears to have assured a group of ministers that he was the friend of monarchy and the enemy of religious toleration! If the report of his words is accurate he was carry-ing out a principle of his — that one must speak to religious people in 'their own language' — with a vengeance. But he also addressed the clerical party in his own language. 'Give us leave to say', he addressed himself to all who had opposed Hamilton, 'as before the Lord, who knows the secrets of all hearts, that, as we think one especial end of Providence in permitting the enemies of God and goodness in both kingdoms to rise to that height, and exercise such tyranny over His people, was to show the necessity of unity amongst those of both nations, so we hope and pray that the late glorious dispensa-tion, in giving so happy success against your and our enemies in our victories, may be the foundation of union of the people of God in love and amity.'

Argyll's party was willing enough to exclude its political rivals from all part in the government and, leaving three regiments behind him in Scotland to protect its 'thriving posture', Cromwell turned back into England in October, 1648.

§ 4

As Cromwell made his way homeward the remarkable 'divided sovereignty' of the English nation daily revealed itself in a more glaring light. The Presbyterian leaders in Parliament, with the approval of General Fairfax, continued to negotiate with the King in the Isle of Wight as if he had not been directly responsible, more than any one man, for the renewal of bloodshed and of the Anglo-Scottish war. On the other hand, the English Army, independently of Cromwell — for the centre of the agitation was Fairfax's regiments in the south — petitioned against the treaty negotiations and loudly demanded the punishment of the instigators of the war. The soldiers argued that while the first war had been a righteous conflict over different principles, the second war had been a treacherous attempt to stir up strife after the sword had recorded its verdict and many of the beaten party had sworn not to take arms again. The most forward regiment in the petitioning was that of Henry Ireton, Cromwell's intelligent son-in-law and author of the 'Heads of the Proposals'. From an early stage Ireton had been convinced that no good could come of the treaty negotiations and that the Parliament should be emptied of its Presbyterians and the King punished for provoking the second civil war. He drew up a 'Remonstrance' demanding justice upon the King and royal family and the establishment of a republic based upon an electorate of property owners. General Fairfax reluctantly summoned a Council of the Army to discuss these proposals at the beginning of November. Fairfax's influence was sufficient to induce the army officers to make one last effort to persuade the King to accept an agreement whereby he would be securely bound to the Parliament and the Army; but it was generally recognized that if the King refused these terms Ireton's Remonstrance would be adopted and forced upon Parliament. The King refused and sealed his fate. Three days later the Commons postponed their consideration of Ireton's Remonstrance while they continued to negotiate with the King, and thereby as effectively sealed their own.

Oliver was in complete sympathy with Ireton's and the Army's point of view. But although no correspondence between Ireton and his father-in-law at this date survives it is improbable that Cromwell directed or influenced Ireton's course of action. He was content to follow a lead which was in tune with his own convictions. Towards the end of November he wrote both to Fairfax and to Robert Hammond in support of the Remonstrance. The King, he thought, had now thoroughly revealed his insincerity. To deal with him further was 'to meddle with an accursed thing'. Cromwell was not an enemy to monarchy — he never was — and still had some thoughts of using one of Charles's children as a puppet king, but he now maintained that Charles himself had forever forfeited his right to the throne. If that right were taken from him Cromwell hoped that peace and unity might be attained in England by a compromise between Presbyterian and Independent, a solution to the national difficulties for which he had worked consistently from the beginning of the civil wars. But first the wicked must be punished. In Scotland he had crushed the Presbyterian Royalists. In England, too, they must be treated according to their deserts. If this proposition were once granted, and it was one that was not accepted by all sections of the Army, including the Levellers, the purging of the House of Commons of all the members who had adopted an ambiguous attitude during the campaign, and the trial of the King for treason, followed naturally. When Cromwell tried to explain how it was for the people's safety that the Army had become 'a lawful power called by God to oppose and fight the King on stated grounds', that is, as apart from being the agent of Parliament, he was forced to skate on very thin ice of political theory. He was soon dissatisfied with his effort, and returned to his favourite and, to modern thought, maddening theme that was advanced by every leader and every party in those days of struggle, that God was on his side. And surely in Cromwell's case, as much as in many others, the wish was father to the thought.

On the day before Cromwell reached London, Colonel Pride with a body of musketeers, acting on the instructions of the Army Council whose 'Remonstrance' had been ignored, entered the House of Commons and drove out 143 Presbyterian members; thirty-nine of the most influential of them were confined in a tavern in Palace Yard called Hell under the charge of an officer named Devill. Only a 'rump' of the original body of 1640 was left — a sectarian rump. Five days earlier another party of soldiers seized Charles at Newport and carried him across the water to the gloomy castle of Hurst in Hampshire. As soon as he arrived in London Cromwell took command of the situation, approved Pride's Purge and arranged for the King to be transferred to Windsor, whence he was to be brought to London, not to negotiate, as so long he had pleaded, but as a prisoner on trial.

Many of the leading Army officers had, as we have noticed, long urged that Charles should be brought to trial. But in the Council of the Army there were still hesitations as to this crucial course. Oliver Cromwell was in favour of first trying the other fomenters of the second civil war before dealing with the King; and he made a special visit to the Duke of Hamilton in a vain effort to induce him to betray his English associates. In these circumstances the Council was fortunate enough to obtain the advice of Mrs. Elizabeth Poole of Abingdon, who announced that she had long been 'a Mourner for the land with great and sore lamentation' and that in this time of crisis she had been honoured with a series of visions from the Most High wherein had been manifested to her the disease and the cure of the kingdom. As she explained that the Army was undoubtedly entrusted with the Kingly Power, which had been misused both by King and Parliament, her message was warmly received by Ireton and the Council. The Royalist view that she was a witch employed by Cromwell to mould the Council to his designs has not found general acceptance among historians.

Mrs. Poole and Cromwell, however, possibly had something in common. The former advised strongly against the execution of the King and there is some flimsy evidence, mainly that of contemporary rumour, that Cromwell wished to depose and not to execute him. It is extremely likely that he hesitated, as all men hesitated, between these dire alternatives. But it is difficult to be patient with those who put forward this paltry palliative for his alleged crime. Neither he nor any of his fellow-regicides believed that they were committing a crime. Their ideas of the nature of justice may have been at fault — whose are not? — but it does not improve or detract from their decision to say that they hesitated before making it. No. The fundamental significance of Charles's condemnation is this. Every conceivable and some inconceivable crimes (including parricide) were alleged against him at his trial, but the proximate cause for which he was arraigned and found guilty was only one, the stirring up of the second civil war. That is why at the end of 1647 Cromwell had resisted the King's execution, while at the end of 1648 he acquiesced in it. In modern times newspapers and politicians urged the trial of an autocratic monarch for causing the war of 1914. There was delay and he escaped. But in the smaller and more manageable circumstances of the mid-seventeenth century the feelings of passionate anger roused against the King took an immediate form. For the crime of war guilt, and in reality for that crime only, Cromwell decided to send Charles I to the scaffold.

By the beginning of January 1649 Cromwell on those grounds had finally made up his mind. Possibly Charles's utter determination in no case to surrender his right of veto in return for his life or throne — a heroic piece of obstinacy — affected Oliver as a dispensation from Providence. At any rate he assured the House of Commons that 'the Providence of God' had cast the trial of the King upon them and 'I cannot but submit to Providence'.

The Act for constituting a High Court of Justice to try the King appointed one hundred and thirty-five commissioners, of whom Cromwell was one, to be both judges and jurors. The Act was carried in a House of Commons consisting of a mere forty-six members by a majority of twenty-six votes to twenty, and the Lords were not consulted. When the commissioners' first meeting took place only fifty-three of those nominated were present. In such unpropitious circumstances only a man of tremendous will power could have forced the issue to a conclusion. But Cromwell, his hesitations vanquished, was the man. He brushed aside the reluctant majority and the hostile minority, together with the quibbles of the lawyers. 'We will cut off the King's head with the crown on it,' he told his fellow commissioners.

When the trial opened in Westminster Hall on January 20th there were sixty-eight commissioners present but the King refused to plead; he could not recognize the legal authority of the Court or the legal accuracy of the charges of treason and tyranny preferred against him. At length, on January 26th, the sixty-two commissioners then present agreed to the death sentence, but only twenty-eight of them were willing to sign the executioner's warrant. Cromwell had been exceedingly active behind the scenes in inducing the Roundhead officers and civilians to remain steadfast in their purpose. He argued with a Scottish deputation which had come to London expressly to denounce the proceedings taken against the King. Telling them that the King, who was a King 'by contract', had broken his trust with the nation, he reminded them of the reasoning of their famous Presbyterian writer Buchanan upon this very point. He also tried to persuade his superior officer General Sir Thomas Fairfax to approve the death sentence. On

Saturday, January 27th, when the sentence was read out in court 'in the name of the people of England', the general's wife Lady Fairfax screamed from the public gallery, 'Not half or one-quarter of them! Oliver Cromwell is a traitor!' She spoke in effect the truth. For it was Cromwell — traitor or not, for all rebels are traitors to something — together with a resolute minority that determined the death of the King. That week-end was spent in collecting more signatures to the death warrant. Because Cromwell was fearful of losing the signatures already written through hesitations from men who might lose their nerve, the original date for the execution, January 27th, was rubbed out on the document and January 30th substituted. Mainly by Cromwell's personal efforts another thirty-one signatures were added. On Sunday, January 30th, with the winter sun gleaming upon him, the King stepped out from the Banqueting Hall to die the death of a traitor.

The citizens of London were silent and dispassionate as they watched, and even, says a contemporary, 'much discontented' thereby. What the people of England thought we shall never know.

In our own days we are accustomed to bow an unsuccessful monarch politely into exile so that he may find solace in some country house or library. And thus, alive and contented, he may be gradually forgotten. But to kill a king is to create a legend which does not die. Cromwell was far too much of a man of the moment, too much of a short-sighted realist, to discern the danger of a mere legend. He cut off the King's head with the crown on it — so he thought. But the crown, the child's play-thing that he affected to despise, was never to be inherited by the man who made the martyr. Only eleven years later it was to descend to the martyr's son.

CHAPTER VIII

THE LORD GENERAL

§ 1

ONCE the deed was done, Cromwell never regretted it. We cannot accept the eighteenth-century legend, that he was seen, a dark and cloaked figure, peering into the grave of Charles I and heard murmuring 'cruel necessity'. Justice, not Necessity, the tyrant's plea, was Cromwell's keyword: an exemplary justice promptly executed — for 'no other way was left'—on a ruler who had betrayed his duty to the nation. 'The King's head was not taken off', he asserted long afterwards, 'because he was King, nor the Lords laid aside because Lords ... but because they did not perform their trust.' Indeed, although Cromwell had once in a fit of temper stated that he hoped to see a time come when there were no longer noblemen in England, we know that he resisted the abolition of the Upper House after the King's death; but he was overruled, and England became a republic governed by a single chamber.

But the House of Commons that existed at the beginning of 1649 was no democratic body. It had been purged, first of all of Royalists and secondly of the strong Presbyterian party, until it had been forged into an instrument ready to do the will of the Army leaders. Its diminished size is revealed by the fact that when a Council of State of forty-one members was chosen to replace the old Committee of the Two Kingdoms as the executive organ of government it included more than half the members of the Commons. It is important to realize the very narrow character of the oligarchy which thus replaced the monarchy. What the great Republican writers of the interregnum from Vane to Milton defended in their writings was not a premature efflorescence of modern democratic government but a return to the inspired rule of the priests of Levi, in the garb of Roundhead soldiers brandishing their triumphant swords. On the other hand, to French eyes Cromwell was simply another ambitious oligarch like his contemporary Prince Condé, but without Condé's aristocratic antecedents, who had succeeded where the French prince was doomed to fail.

Nevertheless, throughout Europe the effect of the trial and execution of Charles I was electric. A King brought before a Court of Justice and condemned for violating his coronation oath! This was truly a strange and terrible doctrine. Although in the past the Dutch had broken away from Philip of Spain and set up a republic and the Swiss and Venetians had thrown off the yoke of autocracy likewise, they had at least been escaping from the hard hand of alien masters. Here was a nation that had proscribed its own anointed, hereditary king.

On February 5th, 1649, at Breda, in the private residence of the Orange Princess, Prince Charles was addressed by his chaplain as 'Your Majesty', King Charles II. This hero of modern Tory historians was not yet nineteen years old, but he had already enjoyed a vaster experience of the adventurous side of life than most men ever have. His first public appearance had been to carry his father's letter to the House of Lords in a vain last effort to save the life of Strafford. From 1642 he had been forced to flee from one part of England to another and from one country to another. Poverty (for a prince), intrigue and excitement made up the staple food of his life. He was at this early age a father, and his favourite bastard, the future Duke of Monmouth, was to be born in two months' time. The news of Charles I's death naturally overwhelmed him, but it was not unexpected and he had seen so little of his parents that the pain of his loss was less acute than it might have been. For the old Royalist counsellors who surrounded him it was like a thunderbolt dropped by Antichrist. 'My soul abhors the thought of it, of which no age ever heard the like', wrote the royal Secretary of State, Nicholas. Henceforward it was generally agreed among the Royalist exiles that any weapon might justifiably be used against the regicides. Their resolve was soon put into effect. The accredited envoys of the English Republic at the Hague and Madrid were in turn murdered by ruffian bands of Royalist fugitives. Prince Rupert, as daring at sea as he was on land, embarked on a career of piracy against all English merchant ships. In Scotland and Ireland the powerful Cavalier elements were invigorated into new life. The Dutch, French and other commercial or political rivals of England were encouraged with every promise of future reward to attack the upstart government.

The dangers facing the Council of State, of which Cromwell acted as first chairman, did not come solely from abroad, and the immediate problems with which it had to deal lay close at hand. It was first concerned with the menace from Ireland. While the second civil war was in progress in England, the Marquess of Ormond had returned to Ireland and had succeeded in uniting the English Royalists there with the larger part of the Irish Catholics, even including those who had taken part in the rebellion of 1641. Furthermore, a number of Ulster Presbyterians had thrown in their lot with Ormond, and the only military forces in Ireland that were not actively Royalist were the Ulster Catholics, led by the chieftain Owen Roe O'Neill, and three English Parliamentary garrisons at Dublin, Londonderry and Dundalk, ten miles north of Dublin. It was feared in London that Ormond's powerful military combination would not only speedily expel the three garrisons but would be able to send an expeditionary force into Wales and there revive the scarcely extinguished flames of civil war. In the light of after events we can see that the fear was unreasonable and the danger exaggerated, but it was shared by Cromwell and all the leading soldiers and politicians of the day. Consequently as early as February 19th, three weeks after the death of the King, a council of the Army voted that ten thousand men should be dispatched to Ireland and it was expected in informed circles that Oliver would be its Commander-in-Chief.

But before the arrangements could be pushed further, a

OLIVER CROMWELL
The portrait presented by him to Queen Christina of Sweden

second and graver peril confronted the Government, that of a split in the English Army itself. We have seen how the two main divisions that constituted Cromwell's victorious Army, the Grandees and the Levellers, had combined to overthrow the parliamentary Presbyterians and bring the King and other fomenters of the second civil war to trial. But the Grandees — so much is clear from the debates in the Council of the Army — never had any real intention of conceding the democratic demands of John Lilburne and his followers. Consequently as soon as the Levellers appreciated that the sole result of all their bloodshed and sacrifice had been to set up an oligarchy of well-off, although Puritan, landlords as their supreme rulers, they held that they had been grossly defrauded and had merely substituted one tyranny for another. Their attitude is summarized in the title of the pamphlet, which contained a remonstrance, submitted by eight troopers to Parliament on February 26th, 'England's New Chains'. Parliament was begged not to abdicate in favour of an arbitrarily chosen Council of State, but to remain in session until it could be replaced by a properly elected new House. The petitioners further urged the establishment of a group of executive committees, regularly answerable to Parliament, in place of the Council of State, and the revival of a Self-Denying Ordinance lest the military and political control of the country should remain permanently in the same hands. The Grandees promptly crushed the democratic movement. Five of the eight signatories were cashiered; Lilburne, for advancing other popular proposals and for asserting the obvious fact that the existing Parliament had been coerced by the Army, was arrested as a traitor; and desperate efforts were made to prevent the spread of propaganda. Although the ill success of the Leveller movement is attributed by Gardiner to the fact that its leaders 'were absolutely destitute of political tact', it is extremely doubtful whether any quantity of political tact (whatever that may be) would have reconciled the Grandees, especially in the hour of crisis, to dispensing with or even sharing their hard-won power.

Lilburne and his fellow-thinkers were particularly and not unnaturally incensed against Cromwell. His had been the voice of compromise in 1647. He it was who, while he admitted that difficult and complex questions were raised in the Levellers' ideal constitution, at the same time agreed to modify Ireton's 'Heads of the Proposals' in a sense favourable to them. Now it was Cromwell who presided over the new tyranny. 'Was there ever a generation so apostate, so false, and so perjured as these?' asked the Levellers.

'Did ever men pretend a higher degree of holiness, religion, and zeal to God and their country than these? They preach, they fast, they pray, they have nothing more frequent than sentences of sacred Scripture, the name of God and of Christ in their mouths; you shall scarce speak to Cromwell about anything but he will lay his hand on his breast, elevate his eyes, and call God to record; he will weep, howl, and repent, even while he doth smite you under the first rib. O Cromwell! whither art thou aspiring? He that runs may read and forsee the intent, a new regality.'

Cromwell respected the strength of the attack launched upon him. 'I tell you, sir', Lilburne heard him say in the Council of State, 'you have no other way to deal with these men but to break them or they will break you.' Lilburne and three of his friends were at once committed without bail to the Tower.

Cromwell and the Grandees were now assisted in their stern repressive measures by a curious event. A small group of men, about thirty in all, calling themselves 'True Levellers', suddenly emerged in Surrey as the first preaching and practising communists on the stage of English history. They were harmless enough. Seizing a small piece of public land, they proceeded to dig it and plant it that they might raise fruits from the earth 'to bring sustenance to the poor, feed the hungry and clothe the naked'. They sought by communal toil only to obtain the meagre necessities of life that they might exist without money and dwell in peace with their neighbours. They promised that they would not defend themselves with arms but would submit to authority, and it was not long before their ardent and innocent zeal was scotched by a troop of cavalry dispatched from Whitehall. But the Diggers were the proof of Cromwell and Ireton's case against all the Levellers. Their doctrines clearly involved the destruction of private property. Democracy and Socialism, reasoned the Grandees, are synony-mous. It is only in our own day that Conservative politicians have discovered that the opposite may be true.

The general discontent of the Army led speedily to mutiny. It broke out at Bishopsgate on April 26th, and Fairfax and Cromwell had to be summoned to suppress it. One trooper, Lockyer by name, was shot as an example in St. Paul's church-yard, while in the cathedral, recently converted into a cavalry stable, 'horses stamped in the Canons' stalls'. Ten days later at Banbury a certain William Thompson, a protagonist of the Lilburnian constitution, raised the standard of revolt. Crom-well, leaving his old mother who was seriously ill, chased Thompson and his comrades to Burford in Oxfordshire, where they were outnumbered and forced to surrender. Thompson was shot dead and perished, in the words of the great German historian Ranke, 'the first martyr of democracy' — executed by the servants of the first English Republic. The last trace of this revolt was found in Oxford, where a few soldiers fortified themselves in New College and thence renewed the Leveller demands. Meanwhile, over the way at All Souls College, Cromwell was lodging and dining preparatory to receiving the degree of Doctor of Civil Laws from the University, ever adulatory of the powers that be. On May 26th he returned to London, received the thanks of the House, for now the mutiny was everywhere crushed, and prepared to go to Ireland.

Cromwell had at first hesitated as to whether he should or should not accept the command, which carried with it the honourable post of Lord-Lieutenant. Before the mutiny broke out he had fathomed the aggrieved state of the Army to the extent that he had insisted that, before he definitely took up the post, Parliament should make full provision for the needs of the regiments sent on campaign. 'The work being so weighty', he related, 'I did think that it would require many things.' But of the importance and urgency of his task he had no doubts. Although there were at the same time dangers threatening from Scotland, where Argyll's party now began to draw into line with its defeated enemies against the English sectarians and Republicans, Cromwell was convinced that the fiercest enemy to the English Commonwealth was Ireland. Charles II thought likewise, and was already considering an invitation from Ormond to go over and head the Royalist forces there himself. But in the coalition lay its weakness. It would, Oliver was convinced, awaken all Englishmen to resistance, this hotch-potch of Cavaliers, Papists, Presbyterians and wild Irish, enemies alike of property and of God.

On July 14th, accompanied by his wife, Oliver arrived at Bristol. Thence he went to Milford Haven, where he inter-viewed Colonel Monk, late commander of the now surrendered Dundalk garrison, and gave his secret blessing to a neutrality agreement that Monk had concluded with O'Neill of Ulster. While he was there he also learned how Colonel Michael Jones had repulsed Ormond from Dublin with heavy losses, 'an astonishing mercy'. But Dublin and Londonderry were the only fortresses remaining in friendly hands. The way lay open for the 12,000 soldiers that Cromwell had asked from Parlia-ment and painfully collected to advance to the relief of the beleaguered garrisons.

Before he left Whitehall the Commander-in-Chief 'did ex-pound some places of scripture excellently well and pertinent to the occasion'. Then followed on August 1st a public fast ordered by Act of Parliament as a method of calling upon God to bless the Lord-Lieutenant's expedition. Encouraged by fast and sermon, and perhaps more by Jones's victory, the embark-ation of the advanced guard in thirty-two ships was completed on August 13th. The ships then raised anchor and turned their prows towards Dublin.

§ 2

A glimmer of hope had united the native Irish to the Royal-ist cause. Ormond had promised them in the Treaty of Kilkenny (1649) a substantial measure of independence if they would throw their military strength, hitherto uselessly ex-pended in rebellion, upon the Roundhead armies. A coalition was thus forged by the King's partisans in return for promises of indemnity for past crimes, security for real property and religious toleration. It was completed on the eve of Cromwell's arrival by the accession of O'Neill, whose convention with Monk had expired. The Irish hopes proved delusive; but it is easy to understand why they were eager to grasp the opportunity. The material prosperity that had dawned on Ireland in the epoch of Strafford's Lieutenancy had made the clans all the more conscious of their degradation through years of sub-jection to English rule. In 1641, with an almost spontaneous mass rising that began in Ulster, they had vainly striven to throw off their yoke. Here was another chance. But Ireland's rebirth was not to be in the seventeenth century.

The contemporary English Protestant picture of Ireland was far from being one of an oppressed people. To Puritan eyes they were a nation of robbers, murderers and thieves whose natural wickedness was aggravated and exemplified by their willingness to pounce down on England in the name of the tyrant Charles I or his son. It was usually represented in civil war tracts that thousands of innocent Protestant settlers of both sexes had been deliberately massacred in 1641 at a time of perfect peace. The association of the Royalists with the Irish clearly revealed to the triumphant Parliamentarians the stuff of which their enemies were made. Indeed a pamphlet of 1647 painted the Irish as man-eaters:

'These Irish called anciently Anthropophagi (man-eaters) have a tradition among them that when the devil showed our Saviour all the kingdoms of the earth and their glory he would not show Him Ireland, but reserved it for himself. It is most probably true; for he hath kept it ever since for his own peculiar aim. . . .'

Such was the portrait of the Irish that Cromwell had in his mind when he landed at Dublin on August 15th, 1649.

Cromwell's campaign[1] was organized as if it were taking place in a distant foreign land. Before he left London he had insisted on a most solemn promise from the Council of State of a large regular supply of stores, munitions and pay for his forces, a promise which at heavy expense was kept. Rupert and his piratical Royalists having shifted from the Irish Channel to the more hospitable waters around the Iberian peninsula, the parliamentary fleet under the future Admiral Blake commanded the seas. Throughout the earlier part of Cromwell's campaign there was a close and effective co-operation between the land and sea forces of the Republic. Ormond had put the finest troops of his new coalition, partly Irish and partly English, into Drogheda, an important seaport which blocked the road north from Dublin to Ulster. Thither Cromwell now marched with 10,000 men, taking the victorious Michael Jones as his second-in-command and Henry Ireton as his third-in-command. Before he left the capital he was careful to expel all debauched and dissolute men from the Army and to issue severe warnings against pillage. On September 3rd, a momentous date in Cromwell's life, he began the siege.

The Governor of Drogheda was Sir Arthur Aston, an English Catholic who had distinguished himself in fighting against the Turks. In the course of the civil wars he had lost a leg which was replaced by an artificial one widely reputed to be wrought of gold. Confident of the impregnability of the fortifications and the courage of the garrison, Aston at first wrote to Ormond to take no risks in coming to his relief. But his ammunition speedily ran short. On the 9th the enemy batteries began to play and on the 10th he received a letter from Cromwell summoning the town to surrender, 'to the end

[1] See map opposite page 167.

effusion of blood may be prevented'. 'If this be refused', he was warned, 'you will have no cause to blame me.' The summons was disregarded and Cromwell ordered a storm. At the first two attempts the Roundheads were repulsed, but Cromwell, sword in hand, then headed the attack himself and supported by the infantry thrust back the defenders from their entrenchments. Victory being assured, some of Cromwell's soldiers began to offer quarter to the vanquished. But Cromwell 'in the heat of the action' took upon himself to countermand the proposal. The entire garrison of some 3000 men were immediately put to the sword. Aston was among the first to fall. 'A great dispute there was', relates Ludlow, who was present, 'among the soldiers for his artificial leg, which was reputed to be of gold; but it proved to be but of wood, his girdle being found to be better booty, wherein 200 pieces of gold were found quilted.'

There is no doubt that according to the laws of war Cromwell was perfectly justified in ordering this massacre of the besieged for forcing him to storm a position incapable of defence, but both by contemporaries and by modern writers his action has been condemned as unnaturally cruel. He himself felt obliged to defend it on two grounds to Parliament:

'I am persuaded, [he wrote] that this is a righteous judgment of God upon these barbarous wretches, who have imbrued their hands in so much innocent blood; and that it will prevent the effusion of blood for the future, which are the satisfactory grounds to such actions, which otherwise cannot but work remorse and regret.'

It is difficult to find any moral standard which will accept Cromwell's first plea. 'Not a few of the most barbarous enormities in human annals have been excused on the same grounds,' commented Lord Morley. But even on the basis of an eye for an eye and a tooth for a tooth, it is certain that hardly a man in the Drogheda garrison can have been concerned in the Ulster rising of 1641. Cromwell never realized this important fact. For his second plea as a practical military argument

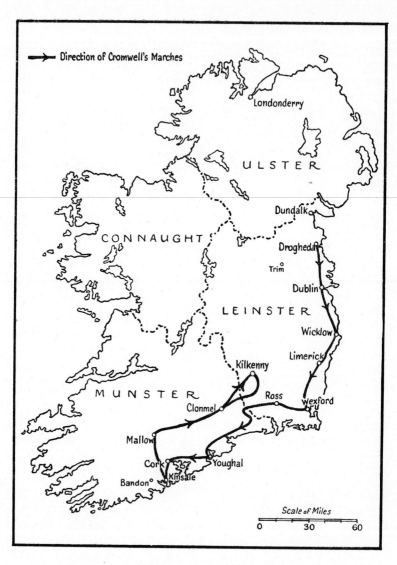

CROMWELL'S IRISH CAMPAIGNS, 1649-50

there is more to be said. Speaking of the fall of Kilkenny six months later Ludlow wrote that the garrison 'was admonished by the examples made of the friends at Tredah [Drogheda] and Wexford'. A modern clerical historian, by no means desirous of exonerating Cromwell, gave as his considered opinion that 'the speedy capture of Drogheda and the merciless massacre of its inhabitants had the effect which they desired. It spread abroad the terror of his name; it cut off the best body of Irish troops, and disheartened the rest even more fatally than the earlier defeat at Dublin.' Whether terrorism and deliberate cruelty are ever morally justifiable is another and far more doubtful question.

Cromwell now turned south to besiege Wexford in order to subject Munster, the centre of the native Irish confederacy, to the English Commonwealth. Already the appalling news from Drogheda had reached there. 'I find no resolution in the townsmen to defend the town,' wrote Sinnot, its young governor, to Ormond. Cromwell was further assisted by the treachery of one of the townsmen who, after Sinnot had refused the terms offered, admitted the besiegers into the castle. The garrison, attacked from within and without, preferred a stubborn resistance to surrender. This sealed their doom, and the massacre of Drogheda was repeated.

The character and extent of the slaughter both at Drogheda and at Wexford were grossly exaggerated after the Restoration. There is no evidence that women and children were killed at either place except accidentally. But without that the truth is sufficiently horrible. In both cases all the priests and friars were knocked on the head. Those who believe that warfare brings out the highest qualities in nations and individuals must not forget the sadism it provokes. Let them read the exultant sadism in Cromwell's description of the man who was burned alive in the church at Drogheda crying: 'God damn me, God confound me; I burn, I burn.' Yet, as we shall see in the next chapter, Cromwell was regarded by his contemporaries as a humane man. After this selfsame siege he wrote off to London seeking succour for the widow of one of his captains who was 'in great want'.

From Wexford Cromwell marched farther into Munster. He assured the governor of Ross of the reality of his intentions to save blood and preserve the town from ruin. The governor wisely surrendered. 'You may see', observed Oliver, 'how God pulls down proud stomachs.' The approach of winter prevented a similar success at Duncannon or Waterford, but Trim, Dundalk, Cork, Youghal, Kinsale and Bandon all surrendered of their own accord, so that by Christmas almost the entire Irish coast was in Cromwell's power. This achievement was not won without suffering. Cromwell described December 2nd as 'so terrible a day I never marched in all my life'. In a letter written in the same month from Cork to London he remarks upon the widespread sickness among his soldiers (who were reluctantly forced to rely on 'papist' doctors), the universal lack of food and fuel, the death of his Lieutenant-General, the gallant Jones, from a pestilential and contagious spotted fever, and the ruined condition of the country-side. These passages in the letter were carefully erased before the Government gave it to the Press.

After a very brief retirement into winter quarters the next campaign was begun with a penetration inland, first in Munster and then northward. Kilkenny was the most valuable conquest, and was due, as at Wexford, in a large measure to a frightened traitor. Gradually the English Royalist soldiers began everywhere to desert the losing cause and many of them transferred their services without regret to the other side. In England the Council of State, well satisfied with the progress that their General had made, also turned its attention to the North. The Irish question, momentarily ceasing to be a pawn in English party politics, lost its interest for both sides. It could be settled or shelved along the old lines.

Thomas Carlyle described Cromwell as the first friend that Ireland had, but would not recognize. He came, so Carlyle maintained, not armed with rose-water but proficient in skilful surgery, to revivify the body politic of the Irish people. His policy, we are told, is to be found laid down in his Declaration of 1650, 'the remarkablest State Paper' ever published by a Lord-Lieutenant; this paper has often been analysed and quoted, but no one else has been found to agree with Carlyle's extraordinary praise, which is a striking example of how hero-worship blinds the most brilliant men. If we may judge from it, Cromwell believed that the principal solution of the Irish problem was the abolition of the Roman Catholic Church. The Pope, we fancy, was at the same time of the opinion that the surest solution of the 'English problem' lay in the abolition of the Protestant Church. A powerful argument can be made out for both these points of view. But few people, whatever their religion, would acquiesce in Cromwell's theory that the massacre of soldiers and priests and the wholesale confiscation of private property must be gladly assented to by a nation because a small section of it at one time rebelled in exasperation at its undoubted wrongs. Still, as Cromwell had invested £500 in the system, he naturally upheld it and indeed extended it. No spark of imagination or originality can be detected in his dealings with the Irish, for he was simply a vigorous exponent of the ultra-Protestant thought of his own time. When he returned to England in April 1650, he left behind him a name that has been deemed a curse by all generations of Irishmen.

§ 3

Charles II, wintering in Jersey, had daily received fresh news of Cromwell's victorious career in Ireland. He was therefore forced to give up all hope of overthrowing the Roundhead cause with his Irish coalition and turned very reluctantly to investigate the possibilities in Scotland. The Scots were divided into three unequal parties. There were pure Cavaliers under the romantic and brilliant Montrose, but they formed the smallest group; there were the Engagers whom Cromwell had decisively routed at Preston; and thirdly, there were the Covenanters under Argyll, whom Cromwell had established in supreme power in the hope that they would live in peaceful friendliness with the English Commonwealth and abandon their long cherished desire of binding an intolerant Presbyterianism upon both nations. Montrose had obtained Charles's permission to raise recruits in his name in the Scandinavian countries, but the young King was too shrewd not to realize that a resounding victory could not now be won against the English Republic without the help of Argyll. But since the terms which the Covenanters determined to exact from him in return for waging war in his interests involved the repudiation of the Irish Treaty, the avowal that his martyred father had been a grievous sinner and the acceptance by himself of the full implications of the Solemn League and Covenant, he hesitated to consent until all other roads to his restoration were barred. Hence he steadily refused to commit himself to Argyll's agents and waited to see whether Montrose would achieve success on his own. At the same time he pressed plans for revolt upon the English Royalists and Presbyterians and sought subsidies from foreign courts to arm his followers.

The hopes and fears of the exiled Court were well known at Westminster. On January 8th, 1650, Parliament had ordered Cromwell's recall, but confirmation of the order was delayed and it was not until April that the Speaker received notice that the victorious General was preparing to return. At first sight it appears strange that the English Parliament insisted on Cromwell's leaving his Irish task uncompleted when Fairfax, the Commander-in-Chief of the Army, was at home and unemployed. But it is plain that, although Fairfax's military capacity was not called in question, his political faith was justly suspected. He had refused to take part in the condemnation of Charles I, and his wife, a de Vere and a Presbyterian, had created such a scene during the trial that she had been forcibly ejected from the Court. Later Fairfax had firmly refused to take the oath to be faithful to the new Republic. In these circumstances only the most optimistic could count on him to defend the Commonwealth against a Scottish attack. However, nothing was decided until the developments in the Scottish situation were known and Cromwell returned.

Parliament made ready joyfully for Cromwell's home-coming. It voted that he should be given the house near White-hall known as the Cockpit, where in later years Queen Mary II and Princess Anne were to indulge in their famous quarrels. He was also put in command of St. James's Park and con-firmed in lands sufficient to bring him an annual income of £2500. On June 1st he was greeted in royal style upon Hounslow Heath. Thither Fairfax 'with a great train of mem-bers of Parliament and Council of State' rode out to welcome him and accompanied him through cheering crowds to West-minster, where he was thanked alike by Parliament and by the City whose members 'crowned him . . . one of the wisest and most accomplished leaders among the present and past genera-tions'. After all this, Oliver was swallowed up in an 'exceeding crowd of business' (notably the dispatch of reinforcements to Ireland) and it was only when he was again on the march that he found time to reflect that 'great business in the world is not worth looking after; I should have no comfort in mine but that my hope is in the Lord's presence'.

Meanwhile events had been moving swiftly in Scotland. At the beginning of April a national fast had been ordered 'for the sin of witchcraft abundant in the land, against the increase of malignants [under Montrose] and sectaries, and that the King may grant the just desires of Kirk and Kingdom'. The fast proved efficacious. On April 27th Montrose was crushed by superior numbers at Carbisdale and promptly hanged. On May 1st Charles capitulated to the Scottish commissioners' demands in the so-called Treaty of Breda (later confirmed by the Treaty of Heligoland) and at the end of June he was able to land in Scotland. This very same day Cromwell was nominated Captain-General and Commander-in-Chief of the English forces and the Council of State declared war. Cromwell's

appointment had followed the voluntary resignation of
Fairfax, the nominal cause for which was his objection to
invading Scotland. He would, he said, take part in a defensive
but not in an offensive war. Cromwell had no such scruples.
'I think', he argued, 'we have a most just cause to begin or
rather to return and requite their hostility first begun upon
us. . . .' Surely it is better, he added, to have the war 'in the
bowels of another country' than in our own. Fairfax thereupon
retired into dignified solitude, to emerge at the Restoration
with the plea that he had never waged war against the monarchic cause after the execution of Charles I and that it was
because of his noble resolve to avoid doing so that he had lost
his commission.

The crowds continued to cheer as Cromwell wended his way
northward. Lambert, who accompanied him as Lieutenant-
General, is reported to have observed that he was glad to see
they had the nation on their side; to which Cromwell replied:
'Do not trust to that, for these very persons would shout as
much if you and I were going to be hanged.' On July 22nd
the army of some 16,000 men crossed the border at Berwick.
David Leslie, who was in effective command of the Scottish
forces, was in confident mood. In number, if not in experience,
his army was vastly superior; it was operating on inner lines;
and he ordered the withdrawal of all male civilians within the
walls of Edinburgh and the destruction of supplies south of it
in the hope of starving out the enemy. But Cromwell also had
definite advantages. His men were trained veterans; he knew
the country from his campaign of 1648; and as the Scots had
no navy, so long as he hugged the coast he could draw food and
ammunition from the supply ships that accompanied him by
sea. As in Ireland, close co-operation was maintained between
Army and Navy, and in both cases it was a decisive factor in
Cromwell's success.

Cromwell's object was to bring on a battle, Leslie's to delay
it so that the English Army should wear itself out far from
home. An initial stab made by Cromwell at the Scots was

repulsed and followed up by a counter-attack, and Cromwell regretfully concluded that it was inadvisable 'to attempt upon the enemy, lying as he doth'. He determined instead to provoke a fight by pushing his way past Edinburgh so as to menace the capital and endanger its supplies from the north. But he was outmanœuvred by Leslie who intercepted him at an impregnable position between two lakes at Corstorphine, south of the road to Queensferry and, as Cromwell's supplies soon gave out and he felt himself in danger of being cut off from the ships, he was obliged to retreat and retired very dispiritedly to Dunbar by the sea, followed closely by the Scots who succeeded in cutting him off from the land route to England. On September 2nd he wrote thence a letter to Haselrig, the commander at Newcastle, in which he explained that Leslie's forces were so drawn up on the Doon Hill in front of him that they could not be assailed, while the English were ravaged by disease and had lost nearly 5000 men since they entered Scotland. His only hopes lay in reinforcements and in the Lord. So perilous appeared the position that 500 sick men and the heavy baggage had been embarked on ship-board and it was strongly urged in the English camp that the entire army should retreat to England.

The subsequent decisive defeat of Leslie was only explicable to the Scots on the assumption that their general had been either bought or befooled. But the main fault did not lie with Leslie at all. His army was the army of the Kirk and it behoved him to obey the ministry. Thus many of the finest soldiers were dismissed right up to the eve of the fight because their fidelity to Calvinist dogma was not above suspicion. Then when the army was safely ensconced on Doon Hill the ministers, relying on the text in Judges which describes Ehud as going down from the mountain and slaying the Moabites, pressed on the general an immediate descent. The extreme inclemency of the weather on the hill-top combined with the erroneous rumour that Cromwell had shipped half his forces induced Leslie to accept the priestly counsel, although he would have preferred to wait until circumstances had forced the English to try to retreat and thus enabled the Scots to fall on their rear.

But Cromwell was not meditating flight. On the contrary, when he saw the position occupied by the Scots after their descent from the hill he detected a surprising opportunity. The situation of the armies on September 2nd was this: Be-

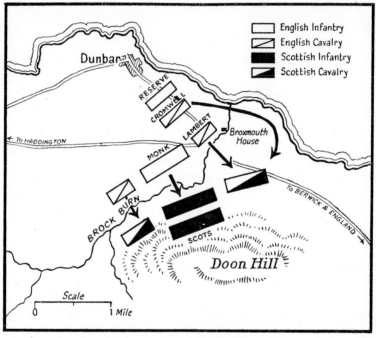

BATTLE OF DUNBAR, SEPTEMBER 3, 1650

tween the two armies was a rivulet, the Brock burn, running from Doon Hill into the sea. Leslie drew up the greater part of his cavalry on his right wing behind the burn in order that it should obtain the advantage of a good slope down which to charge and in order to cut off a possible line of escape for the English along the Berwick Road. He supported his right-wing cavalry with a body of foot, while the rest of his infantry, forming the centre, were massed half a mile farther west. Still farther west the Scottish left consisting of 1500 or 2000 horse was posted on a narrow strip of ground between the deeper clough through which went the upper reaches of the Brock burn and the steeper side of Doon Hill. Cromwell's army had marched to the edge of the north side of the burn and he had posted his artillery along the burn at regular intervals, so creating a strong defensive position.

Thus the English had taken the defensive while the Scots had adopted a formation which was primarily intended for offence. Cromwell perceived, however, that if he could force the Scots to act defensively their formation would expose weaknesses; for if the Scottish right were forced back it would have to fall back upon its cramped left wing. With the full approval therefore of Lambert and of Colonel Monk (the future hero of the Restoration), who at his insistence had been given a regiment in the Army, Oliver matured a plan to surprise the Scots in the pouring rain. All night long 'old Nol' rode, as one of his captains related, 'through the several regiments by torchlight, upon a little Scots nag, biting his lip till the blood ran down his cheek without his perceiving it, his thoughts being busily employed to be ready for the action now at hand'.

The wetness of the night — the moon did not appear until four — confused the Scots. They had stood to their arms crouching amid the long grass during the evening, fearful of a surprise attack. But when nothing happened the Scottish commanders were convinced that the enemy had no such intention. The men bivouacked as best they could and the officers retired to their tents or to beds in neighbouring farm-houses. But Cromwell ignored the deluge. Early on the morning of September 3rd while the bulk of the Scots still slept he launched his attack. He had ordered the cavalry to ford the burn at three different points. Lambert and Fleetwood had six regiments facing the Scottish right at the most fordable parts of the burn. Cromwell held his own cavalry regiment in reserve against all contingencies. Monk with most of the foot faced the Scottish centre, and a small cavalry force on the right was ordered to feint against the Scottish left.

The Scots do not appear to have been taken entirely by surprise. For when Monk's infantry began the attack at the centre it encountered a Scottish party also advancing across the burn. At first the battle went against the English, who were outnumbered both in horse and foot. Lambert's first charge was repulsed by the Scottish lancers and Monk's foot were driven back by sheer weight of numbers. But at the crucial moment Cromwell brought his reserve into action. Crossing the burn at a point near to the sea on the extreme left of his line he made a swift detour of about a mile and succeeded in attacking the flank of the Scottish right across the Berwick road. This movement at the far easterly corner of the battlefield distracted the attention of the Scottish cavalry from the frontal offensive, for the Scottish commanders imagined that the numbers involved were far larger than one regiment. At the same time as he attacked with his cavalry Cromwell threw in two reserve foot regiments against the advancing Scottish infantry, while at an opportune moment he brought a third foot regiment to support his successful flank attack.

Denuded of its cavalry support the Scottish centre broke. As the English generals had anticipated, the Scottish right was forced back upon the centre and in the confined space could get no help from its inactive and unbeaten left wing. The Scots were made, said Oliver, 'by the Lord of Hosts as stubble to our swords'. Three thousand were killed and 10,000 taken prisoners. A captain who was present recorded:

And, the sun appearing upon the sea, I heard Nol say, 'Now let God arise and his enemies be scattered'; and he following us, as we slowly marched, I heard him say, 'I profess they run!' and there was the Scots army all in disorder and running, both right wing and left and main battle.

The discomfited ministers were the first to flee from the field. After the victory a relieved Oliver wrote to his Elizabeth:

The Lord hath showed us an exceeding mercy; and who can tell how great it is. My faith hath been upheld. I have been in my inward man marvellously supported; though I assure thee, I grow an old man, and feel the infirmities of age marvellously upon me.

The siege of Edinburgh followed upon the Scots' defeat, but Cromwell was careful not to use the downright methods which had brought about his conquests in Ireland. Now he felt he was dealing with the 'godly', and he employed all his persuasive powers to convince the governor of Edinburgh Castle that the Scots had no cause to fight him. He pointed out that the power given by the Presbyterians to their ministers was of the same kind that the papists gave to the Pope. He urged that Dunbar had been a trial of strength between them to discover on which side God stood. Both had prayed to Him before the battle; but only one side had its prayers heard. When the Scots retorted that they had not so learned Christ as to hang the equity of their cause upon events, Oliver could only shake his head and say he pitied their weak understandings. However, after a long correspondence with the governor and some few fire-balls had been thrown in, the castle was surrendered. In the meantime the remainder of the Scottish Army had retreated to Stirling, the Scottish Parliament had gathered at Perth and Charles II was crowned a covenanted King at Scone.

One result of Dunbar had been to encourage the King to adopt a bolder attitude towards his Scottish subjects. Since the Presbyterian clergy had been responsible for the disaster he was able to argue that their policy of exclusiveness was wrong and that if they wished to beat the English they must take into their ranks their old opponents, the Engagers. But ancient enmities were not easily forgotten and Cromwell did not fail to profit from the dissensions among his foes.

While he was at Edinburgh in the early months of 1651 the English commander remained comparatively inactive, partly on account of the weather and partly because he hoped to detach some of the Covenanters to his own side; he was able to find time to suppress the bandits or moss troopers in the neighbourhood, to have his bust engraved, to design a commemorative medal, to accept the Chancellorship of Oxford University and to lend his support to the project of a college at Durham. About March he was taken ill, but recovered sufficiently to go to Glasgow (which had surrendered the previous October) and give the inhabitants 'a friendly Christian meeting'. Lack of forage and a recurrence of fever soon forced him to return to Edinburgh. His enforced inactivity caused him to become sensible of impending old age, though he was barely fifty. In June he was able to tell the Council of State that the Lord 'hath plucked me out of the grave' and at last he advanced northward, as he might have done four months earlier had it not been for his illness. Yet when the English Army came within reach of the Scots they found the position taken up by Leslie, protected by the Carron river and the Firth of Forth, unassailable.

'The beauty of the summer is passing away very fast,' grumbled one who was present, 'and yet we are not upon any action. The enemy lieth so that we cannot engage them.' The English soldiers were sick, wet, unfed and largely unpaid, and there was therefore pressing need to finish the war during the campaign. Another Scottish winter might prove fatal. In these circumstances Cromwell decided that the only way to dislodge Leslie, well warned by his terrible experience on Doon Hill, was to cut off his supplies and reinforcements by crossing the Firth and attacking Perth. A party sent by Leslie in an effort to ward off this blow was cut in half by Lambert (to the delight of the English main body who, through their 'prospective glasses' saw the enemy fleeing) and by August the manœuvre had been successfully carried out. Cromwell advanced with his main body and occupied Perth; but he first took the precaution of sending General Harrison to the English border with instructions to check the Scots if they chose to march into England. As soon as Perth had surrendered, Cromwell learned that the Scottish Army had indeed made the obvious move left open to them in the chess game of war and were heading south for England.

The English General had by no means been outwitted, as was plain from his letter to the Commons of August 4th in which he wrote:

Indeed this is our comfort that in simplicity of heart towards God we have done to the best of our judgments, knowing that if some issue were not put to this business it would occasion another winter's war to the ruin of your soldiery, for whom the Scots are too hard in respect of enduring winter difficulties of this country, and have been under the endless expense of the treasure of England in prosecuting this war. It may be supposed that we might have kept the enemy from this by interposing between him and England; which truly I believe we might, but how to remove him out of this place without doing what we have done, unless we had a commanding army on both sides of the river Forth is not clear to me.

Leslie in fact had fallen into a trap. But if in London little fear was felt the news of the invasion was heard in the north of England with dismay. Yet the demoralization of the Scots was patent. Indeed, one of them frankly confessed 'they had quitted their country, being scarcely able to maintain it' for which they had 'but one stout argument — despair'.

The Scots advanced through Lancashire, where Lambert and Harrison failed to stop them, and thence they made for the Welsh border. Very few Royalist sympathizers joined Charles II, the King of the Scots, as he rode south, the English with ever-swelling forces hastening behind. On August 27th Cromwell having come through Yorkshire reached Evesham with 28,000 men. Charles II and the 16,000 Scots had meanwhile taken and were trying to fortify Worcester. Here the invaders were caught. For once superiority of numbers enabled Cromwell to take the risk of dividing his army; one half on the right took post on the road to London, the other half on the left attacked the city from the south-west. Although the bridges across the Severn had been broken, bridges of boats conveyed the English soldiers across; but here the Scots put up a strong resistance. Cromwell himself went across the

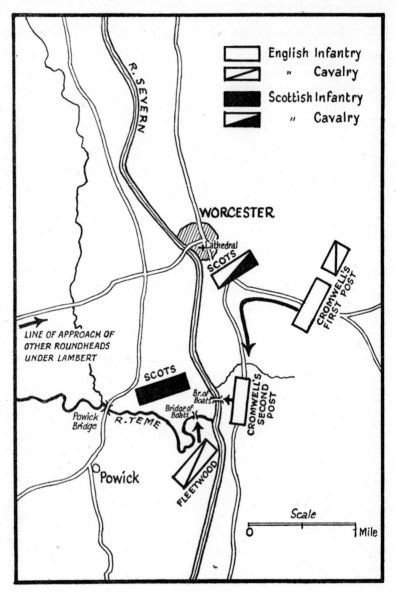

BATTLE OF WORCESTER, SEPTEMBER 3, 1651

Severn to help. Encouraged by his absence, Charles II launched
a counter-attack upon the depleted English forces on the London road. The dangers involved in dividing any army were
thus made obvious. Cromwell had to hurry back again to
direct the second struggle. Altogether the Scots put up 'as
stiff a contest for four or five hours' as Cromwell had ever
known. But Cromwell's division of his forces had the ultimate
consequence of ensuring that the Scottish Army was not merely
beaten but destroyed. The date was September 3rd, exactly a
year after Dunbar and two years after Drogheda. Six days
later, whilst Charles II crouched in hiding in the priest's hole
at Mosely Hall, the victorious commander was invited by
Parliament to return to London and honour them with his
advice. His sword was now to be replaced finally in its sheath.
Henceforward he must govern instead of fight.

§ 4

When Cromwell returned from Worcester, he was, according to Ludlow, 'a haughty gentleman. . . . In a word, so much
was he elevated with that success, that Mr Hugh Peters [one
of the Army chaplains] as he since told me, took so much notice
of it, as to say in confidence to a friend upon the road on his
return from Worcester, that Cromwell would make himself
king.' Oliver had reason to feel satisfied. Since 1648 God had
steadily guided him along the path to victory. Might it not be,
he asked himself, that he was in truth a Moses chosen to lead
his people into the Promised Land?

He was welcomed home with every sign of enthusiasm.
Four thousand pounds were added to his income; Hampton
Court was put at his disposal as a country residence; and at
the next election for the Council of State he was carried to the
top of the poll. In the House of Commons his influence was
sufficient to obtain first consideration for the measures that he
favoured. On his advice an Act of Oblivion for Royalists —

talked about since 1649 — was at last put on the statute book. The proposal to elect a new Parliament was revived. A committee sat down every Wednesday morning to discuss the reform of the law relating to real property. For all these things Cromwell had long shown himself anxious. Now that the civil wars were finally ended, he wished to secure peace and unity at home and to reconcile the defeated party to the new regime. As to the Parliament he had expressed long ago in the Council of the Army his opinion that it would be 'honourable and convenient' for the Long Parliament 'to put a period to themselves', and this was one of the few subjects on which he had not changed his mind. His wish was gratified on November 14th when he was teller for the ayes in a vote which declared that the present Parliament should fix a date for its dissolution, and it was settled that it should not sit beyond November 3rd, 1654.

Lastly, his views on law reform were well known from an exhortation in his Dunbar dispatch:

Relieve the oppressed, hear the groans of the poor prisoners in England; be pleased to reform the abuses of all professions; and if there be any one that makes many poor to make a few rich [i.e. the lawyers] that suits not a Commonwealth.

It was a sentence that had warmed and still warmed the Republican Ludlow's heart.

His domestic projects having been put into motion, Oliver turned his attention, possibly for the first time, to the study of foreign affairs. Although hitherto, we, like Cromwell, have concentrated our attention on the internal struggles of the Commonwealth, it is necessary to remember that throughout 1650 and 1651 English commerce had been subjected to every kind of outrage from Royalist privateers and foreign ships either friendly to the Royalist cause or at least willing to take advantage of the difficulties of the revolutionary government. In effect, if not in name, a state of naval warfare existed between England, on the one side, and France, Holland and Portugal on the other. To protect commerce and the trade routes the Rump Parliament had been obliged to build a big navy, and they were fortunate in finding an admiral of genius in Robert Blake. It was none the less essential for the English Government to gain as wide a recognition from foreign Powers as possible lest Charles II and the exiled Cavaliers should succeed in welding an alliance and winning a restoration by foreign arms.

Spain, the enemy alike of Portugal, France and Holland, was the first country to recognize the English Republic. Portugal was slowly but definitely subdued by Blake. France was divided by civil wars and the opposing sides each sought to buy the use of Cromwell's splendid military machine. But the Dutch Republic, whose hereditary rulers, the Princes of Orange, had intermarried with the Stuarts and whose merchant adventurers competed with their younger English rivals in three continents, remained bitterly antagonistic to the Long Parliament.

Cromwell, as he examined the situation, was guided by two main principles, the 'Protestant interest' and national ambition. He knew that in France there was an important Protestant sect, the Huguenots. He was aware that the French regency during the minority of Louis XIV, headed by the Machiavellian Cardinal Mazarin, was harassed both by aristocratic intriguers and by a drawn-out war with Spain, and might easily be persuaded to cede territory to England as well as to promise increased liberties to its Protestant subjects in return for powerful military aid; and since he felt no sympathy with Spain, the home of the Inquisition and from his youth the traditional enemy of England, and did not desire a war with the Protestant Dutch, he was naturally inclined towards a French alliance if favourable terms could be arranged.

In these circumstances, without consulting the Council of State, Cromwell took the astonishing step of opening negotiations with Mazarin for the surrender to England of the port of Dunkirk — (in the Spanish Netherlands but precariously held by a French garrison) in exchange for Ironside assistance, while to press his point he listened blandly to the proposals of Mazarin's enemies. At the same time that he was forwarding these negotiations, Cromwell was laying before a meeting of Members of Parliament and army officers a constitutional settlement 'with somewhat of monarchical power in it'. Perhaps we are not wrong in concluding from the Dunkirk negotiations that 'somewhat of monarchical' or at least dictatorial power was already in existence.

All these schemes were brought to a temporary stop by the war that broke out almost spontaneously in July 1652 between the English and the Dutch Republics. Fomented by the East India Company, desired by the strongly Republican fleet and encouraged (on the Dutch side) by the exiled Royalists, the conflict was peculiarly offensive to Cromwell and many of the sterner Puritan officers, who looked upon it as nothing less than fratricide. A prophecy that the war would be a short one proved, like most such prophecies, to be delusive. Whilst closely contested sea battles raged, the Wednesday committee on law reform, abandoning its vain but well-meaning attempt to define an 'incumbrance', ceased to sit; all thoughts of a general election were suspended; Dunkirk was reconquered by Spain; and Cromwell, still turning over in his mind the nature of divinely chosen kingship, grew discontented.

The Army had been very much reduced in numbers after the battle of Worcester, but there were still 25,000 soldiers unemployed in England. Many of the men who had been disbanded had difficulty in finding work and those who remained were frightened lest they likewise should be thrown by Parliament on to the labour market in the cause of retrenchment. In this Army the most influential officers after Cromwell were Lambert and Major-General Harrison. The former had at one time hoped to be made Lord Deputy in place of Ireton who, to Cromwell's deep sorrow, had died in 1651, but in a fit of economy Parliament abolished the post, whereupon Lambert in revenge devoted his energies to abolishing the Parliament. Harrison was a good soldier and an uncouth, ambitious and fanatical Christian. He had gradually drifted into the ranks of the Fifth Monarchy sect, which believed in the imminent return of Christ in person to rule His people and in the necessity of a government of 'saints' as an interregnum. Harrison was now the recognized leader of the Fifth Monarchy men and he and Lambert therefore both had personal reasons for urging on Cromwell the desirability of forcibly dismissing the 'Rump' Parliament. 'I am pushed on by two parties to do that', Cromwell is reported as saying, 'the consideration of the issue whereof makes my hair stand on end.' For some months he preferred to act as mediator between Parliament and the Army. In August 1652 he supported a petition submitted by the Army to Parliament asking for the payment of its arrears, the reform of the law, the abolition of tithes and the provision of employment for the demobilized. A demand for the immediate dissolution of Parliament was on his advice shelved. But so slow was the response of Parliament to these somewhat extensive requests that Oliver thought that they were having very little consideration or no consideration at all. Nor did discussions promoted by him in the autumn between the officers and the members of Parliament yield any positive results. A remarkable conversation which Cromwell had in November with a lawyer named Whitelocke, who was like himself a leading member of the Council of State and opposed to the Dutch War, reveals his thoughts of exploiting the Army's discontent with Parliament to become King. He was never, as we have seen, a Republican, or indeed a fanatical admirer of any form of government and had frequently suggested that Charles I's youngest son, the Duke of Gloucester, should be made monarch under a Roundhead regency. The course of recent events, however, had convinced him that he himself might be destined for a higher office even than that of regent. Thomas Carlyle dismissed Whitelocke's record of the conversation as not genuine, but it is too much in accordance with previous and subsequent evidence to be lightly disregarded. Lord Morley's opinion was that 'we need invoke neither craft nor ambition to explain the rise of the thought in Cromwell's mind that he was perhaps himself called to take the place and burden of chief governor'. It may be that it was neither conscious craft nor conscious ambition; but what other word than ambition can a modern give for the force that drove Cromwell on to the supreme heights of power? With regard to the Rump, which he described to Whitelocke as consisting of corrupt self-seekers, Cromwell allowed himself to be deluded. They were not for the most part wicked, selfish or greedy, and indeed a contemporary French observer gave emphatic testimony to their single-minded devotion to what they held were the national interests. Four years later Cromwell alleged that he had been made the mere 'drudge' of the Army in dissolving the Long Parliament, but that is only one facet of the truth. He let himself be convinced that Parliament did not intend to fulfil the Army petition and had no intention of dissolving itself when it had promised. Neither of these assumptions was capable of proof. Lord Morley pointed out that what Cromwell himself appeared to envisage was a 'Constituent Assembly', that is to say, a body of men who would draw up a new constitution for the State, but whereas the surviving members of the Long Parliament naturally wished to belong to the Constitutional Assembly, Cromwell favoured the nomination of an entirely new set of politicians. Cromwell in fact distrusted the Rump because he had come to look upon it as an ungodly assembly, but the Rump itself was convinced that it, too, was a chosen vessel of Puritan power and alone could be trusted.

Throughout the spring of 1653, exactly as throughout the spring of 1647, Cromwell hesitated as to his course of action. At first he tried to arrange a compromise with the Republican members of Parliament. He exerted his influence to moderate 'the preaching people' who were 'violent against this Parliament', as they had been against all Parliaments. He urged upon the officers that so long as peace negotiations were in progress with the Dutch no unconsidered action should be taken. Nevertheless he was said to be offended because his views in favour of peace with Holland had not met with general acceptance in Parliament, and in April he was involved in a bad-tempered scene in the Commons when to his demand for a new Parliament the reply was made that there was 'no more fitting moment to change the Lord General'. The story was told that on another occasion he had been accidentally locked out of the House of Commons and that he angrily observed that 'just as the door had been shut upon him that day it would be closed against the whole Parliament some other day'. He began ominously to absent himself both from the Council of State and from the Commons and to conspire openly with his Army adherents. At length on April 19th he put forward the suggestion that the present House should at once itself nominate a Constituent Assembly. Vane and his friends were not pleased but, according to Cromwell, promised to sleep on the suggestion and to try to suspend further proceedings with their own constitutional Bill until the two parties conferred again.

The following morning Harrison discovered that the rank-and-file of the Commons had no intention of being bound by any promises exacted from their leaders. He at once sent a message to Cromwell to come to the House, because, he said, the armistice concluded the night before was being violated. The Commons was indeed preparing to rush through a Bill which would perpetuate its own power. The Lord General arrived with every sign of cold wrath and of haste, dressed in plain black clothes and grey worsted stockings but accompanied by forty musketeers. For a while he sat and listened to the debate which (asserted a Royalist newsletter) 'did so enflame Oliver and his attending myrmidons that he threw himself forth into the midst of the House, his hat cocked and with the very breath of his mouth', more potent 'than Guy Faux's powder, he blew up the Parliament and Commonwealth in an instant'. 'Come, come,' he exclaimed, 'I will put an end to your prating. You are no Parliament.' He ordered his musketeers to clear the House and began to hurl abusive epithets at the members as they were seized and hurried out. After the mace — that jester's 'bauble', as he then described it — had been taken away the doors were locked. 'He called the members', says the same newsletter, 'a company of oppressive, perfidious fellows; and commanded and by Captain Hewson enforced the unwilling Speaker to leave his beloved chair and mace. This last, with the books and keys, he secured, and gave contumelious speech to Sir Henry Vane the younger, Henry Marten "the broadfaced adulterer" and to others.' It was but another example of those violent natural explosions from deep down inside him which Cromwell let loose only at times of crisis. Finally Oliver carried off the disputed Bill under his cloak. Thus the exact nature of the measure which so aroused his wrath may never be known with complete certainty to posterity.

§ 5

The news of the breaking of the Rump had a mixed reception. According to Cromwell, 'scarce a dog barked'. The Army rejoiced, for the fear of unemployment now faded from the horizon. The Fifth Monarchy men and other sectarian preachers prophesied the coming of a Golden Age. Merchants applauded the closing of the 'talking shop' and averred that the change had taken place without noise or sorrow: 'we hope better things of ten than two hundred, greater secrecy, more promptitude, less speechifying, more work. . . .' On the other hand, the officials of the City of London drew up a firm protest and urged on Cromwell the recall of the Long Parliament. They were told to mind their own business. At the same time the French ambassador, M. Bordeaux, reported home from London that the civilian population was discontented at the thought of being governed by the Army officers and disgusted both at the loss of its privileges and at the suppression of Parliament.

For a month Cromwell delayed over his next step. There

were strong rumours that he would, as he had hinted to Whitelocke, take it upon himself to be a King. But he decided at
length in favour of a Constituent Assembly. He was guided in
his decision, as he afterwards related, by 'a desire ... sinful
enough, to be quit of the Power God had most clearly by His
Providence put into my hand'. He therefore assented to a compromise between the wishes of Lambert and Harrison by
calling on his own responsibility an assembly of 'divers persons,
fearing God, and of approved fidelity and honesty' nominated
by himself on the advice of the Army Council. One hundred
and twenty-nine 'notables' were called altogether from different
parts of the country as well as five from Scotland and six from
Ireland.

The assembly gathered on July 4th and listened in a swelter-
ing heat to a two-hour speech from the Lord General. He
exonerated himself at length for turning out the Rump and
condemned especially its 'utter inability of working reform' —
a reflection perhaps of the impatience of the military man with
the talking shop. He even apologized — significantly enough
— for not now retaining all power in his own hands and he
then proceeded to offer broad advice upon how the new assembly should make use of its opportunity. They were, he
reminded them, a people chosen by God (through the instru-
mentality of himself and his Army) to do His work and show
forth His praise. First and foremost they must promote the
Gospel and be tender to the 'good' people of the nation. Unhappily God had not yet, in his opinion, fitted the ordinary
elector to choose his representatives, although He might one
day do so. Meanwhile let them conduct themselves in the true
spirit of the Testaments. They hardly needed such counsel.
After they had voted themselves a Parliament which is known
to history indifferently as the Nominated, Little or 'Barebones'
Parliament, they immediately settled down to extempore
prayer, each member taking his turn to lead his fellows. 'The
new Parliament', reported Bordeaux, 'is composed of persons
who believe themselves inspired.' Sir Henry Vane, despite the

opprobrious remarks thrust at him by Cromwell two months before, was invited to become a member of the new Council of State; but he replied that 'he believed the reign of the Saints would now begin, but, for his part, he was willing to defer his share in it until he came to Heaven'.

The saints began to rule under most favourable auspices. On July 31st Blake won the decisive victory of the Texel over the Dutch, and it was openly said in Holland that the English ruled the seas. Cromwell at once began negotiations with the Dutch Republic for a close Protestant union between the two states and followed these with a proposal that they should divide the world between them. The Dutch commissioners were surprised but not very receptive, and the war dragged on. Some of the Fifth Monarchy men even made the claim that God had given Holland into English hands.

Meanwhile the Little Parliament began its labours and gave its attention with inexhaustible energy to projects of social and economic reform. Twelve committees were appointed and the whole House was soon vigorously discussing the abolition of tithes and lay patronage, the improvement of the Commonwealth system of taxation, the civil registration of marriages and the general reform of the law. They had for their guidance Cromwell's advice to the Long Parliament after Dunbar and his avowed intention to Ludlow in 1650 to 'contribute the utmost of his endeavours' to 'a thorough reformation of the clergy and the law'.

It is often said that the revolutionary zeal of the Little Parliament carried them to excesses, and the fact that they put no lawyer on their committee for law reform is an instance charged against them. Still, they showed a praiseworthy zeal for action, which is usually supposed to be absent from parliamentary governments, and — as to the lawyers — Parliament feared that their advice would be tempered by their vested interests. Yet the parliamentary saints failed to please their masters.

Oliver soon grew dissatisfied at the vigorous manner in which his own nominees were attacking established property rights, turning all things to confusion and trying to replace the Common Law by the Law of Moses. He was particularly taken aback at the curious unwillingness of the Parliament of his own choosing, which, when all was said and done, was dependent upon him and his army for its very existence, to seek his advice. 'Fain would I have my service accepted by the Saints,' he complained to his son-in-law Charles Fleetwood in August, 'but it is not so.' He was jealous that the saints appeared to prefer the counsels of a wild Fifth Monarchy preacher of Blackfriars, a man who earlier that year had ventured to assert in public that 'the General was not the man that the Lord had chosen to sit at the helm'.

Of all the sudden changes of front in Cromwell's career none is more remarkable or less commented on than the change in his attitude to this Parliament of his own creation. Carlyle did not even trouble to face the problem, as he imagined quite wrongly that the destruction of the Little Parliament was merely the work of disgruntled lawyers. Gardiner, however, proved beyond dispute that it was Cromwell's own dissatisfaction with it that encouraged the military Grandees under Lambert to break up the saintly congress. It is true that the Army was afraid a threatened reform of taxation would endanger its pay, despite the fact that the ordinary revenue was voted without reduction in November. But if this fear gave the initiative to the Army, that was not the reason afterwards given by Oliver himself for his acquiescence in this deed of wrath. 'What did the convention of *your* naming?' he asked the Army officers in 1657. 'Fly at liberty and property, insomuch as if one man had twelve cows, they held another that wanted cows ought to take a share with his neighbour. Who could say anything was their own, if they had gone on?' (Here he was expressing the same dread that six years earlier had turned him against the democratic theories of the Levellers.) Indeed, when Colonel Sydenham (at Lambert's request) successfully proposed to the 'moderate' minority of the assembly on December 12th that they should give back their power to the General from whom it came, it was precisely on the ground that the majority were aiming at the destruction of the clergy, the law and the property of the individual. (The remaining members had to be impressed by the argument of a file of musketeers.)

It was therefore Cromwell's concern for the security of private property and well-established rights which caused him to destroy that aristocracy of saints, that high-water mark of the Calvinistic conception of a ruling class, which men like Milton and Algernon Sidney had held to be the ideal Republican form of government. Three months before Oliver had significantly observed, 'I am now more troubled with the fool than with the knave', thus summarizing his respective opinions of the typical member of the Little and the Rump Parliaments. In his view the Rump members had endangered the rights of private property by their self-seeking greed, the 'Saints' of the Little Parliament by their reforming folly, and he fully realized that the basis of authority in a state is the support of the propertied interests. As the ally of those interests and at the desire of the Army he now took upon himself to be Lord Protector — a conservative dictator.

CHAPTER IX

THE FAMILY MAN

§ I

BEFORE we turn to the career of Oliver Cromwell as Lord Protector, let us attempt to obtain a picture of what he was like as a man, not the official nor the successful statesman or soldier, but simply an ordinary individual who slept and ate and lived and died and passed his evenings in the family circle after the day's work was over. How did he strike his intimates and what were his daily habits? What, in fact, was the character of his private life?

Oliver Cromwell was tallish in stature, a couple of inches under six feet, upright and dignified in his gait. His long hair flowed down his neck, coloured brown in his youth, then grey and finally marked with that bald spot which cares of office bring. He wore a moustache and a scanty beard and his reddish face was a matter of frequent comment. His large grey-blue eyes were one of his most impressive features, for none could fathom what it was they saw in them: fanaticism, enthusiasm, ambition? — perhaps all or none of these, in the determined eyes set off by the big aquiline nose. His complexion was described as 'olive' by a Venetian envoy writing during the Protectorate. Although he led a healthy and active life he was afflicted with serious blood trouble and never enjoyed entirely good health. Apart from the famous wart above his right eyebrow he was always having pimples, boils and abscesses on his back which at times forced him to keep to his bed. He is said to have suffered when a young man from hypochondria, but this was evidently a psychological rather than a physical condition. In the summer of 1647 he was dangerously ill with an abscess on the head. When in Ireland in 1649 he wrote home to say that his health had been 'crazy' of late. He was again extremely ill in 1651. In the later years of the Protectorate he was frequently unwell; he was made miserable by gout and the stone; finally he caught and recovered from an ague, but contracted it again in a fiercer form and, worn out by an over-strenuous existence, died of it.

His appearance in the House of Commons in the Short Parliament of 1640 is the subject of a well-known description in the *Memoirs* of the Royalist Sir Philip Warwick, who recalled how one day on entering the House he perceived an unknown speaker 'in a plain cloth suit, which seemed to have been made by an ill country tailor; his linen was plain, and not very clean; and I remember a speck or two of blood [the work no doubt of some seventeenth-century razor] upon his band, which was not much larger than his collar. His stature was of a good size; his sword stuck close to his side; his countenance swollen and reddish, his voice sharp and untuneable, and his eloquence full of fervour.' But not even Cromwell's enemies denied him dignity, and in the well-bred country gentleman of genteel descent there was no strain of that curious vulgarity which lay so near the surface of the first Napoleon.

Perhaps the most extraordinary and least known of Cromwell's personal characteristics was his intensely human attitude to all individual cases of affliction and distress. The man who put the Irish garrison to the sword on political and military grounds would not spare himself in striving to alleviate any personal sufferings of which he had first-hand knowledge, nor could he bear to learn of the infliction of unnecessary pain because of a lack of the necessities of life. Few people will dispute the accuracy of the proverb that no man is a hero to his own valet, and this strengthens the value of the testimony to Cromwell's humaneness written in a private letter six months after his death by his household steward, John Maidston:

He was naturally compassionate towards objects in distress, even to an effeminate measure; though God had made him a heart, wherein was left little room for any fear, but what was due to Himself, of which there was a large proportion, yet did he exceed in tenderness towards sufferers. A larger soul, I think, hath seldom dwelt in a house of clay than his was.

Cromwell's care for the material welfare of his soldiers is celebrated. Towards the end of the Protectorate, because the Exchequer was behindhand with their pay, he gave a large sum out of his own pocket to provide them with boots and clothing. When part of the Army had to be disbanded he exerted himself to find work for the demobilized; military and naval hospitals were always a first charge on his budget; and he is said to have subscribed generously out of his Civil List to other charitable institutions. Long before he became Protector he used his influence with Parliament on behalf of women who had been widowed and children who had been orphaned in the Roundhead cause: in one letter, speaking of a faithful and gallant colonel, he wrote: 'He hath left some behind him to inherit a father's honour, and a sad widow: both now to the interest of the Commonwealth'; and of another: 'He left a wife and three small children but meanly provided for. Upon his deathbed, he commended this desire to me, that I should befriend his family to the Parliament or to your Excellency [Fairfax]. His wife will attend you for letters to the Parliament, which I beseech you to take into a tender consideration.'

Nor was Cromwell's sensibility confined to material suffering. He himself had plumbed the depths of mental agony when he lost in swift succession his two eldest sons, Robert and Oliver, both promising youths in their teens. His letter written after the battle of Marston Moor to break the news to Colonel Valentine Walton of the death of his son is, if we appreciate the Puritan point of view, one of the finest and most sensitive letters of condolence ever penned:

It's our duty to sympathise in all mercies; that we may praise the Lord together in chastisements or trials, that so we may sorrow together. . . .
Sir, God hath taken away your eldest son by a cannon shot. It

break his leg. We were necessitated to have it cut off, whereof he died.

Sir, you know my trials this way: but the Lord supported me with this, that the Lord took him [young Oliver] into the happiness we all pant after and live for. There is your precious child full of glory, to know sin nor sorrow any more. He was a gallant young man, exceeding gracious. God give you His comfort.

Furthermore it cannot be said that Cromwell was a vindictive opponent towards individuals. He agreed to the execution of the King, largely, as has been argued, because of his belief that Charles had been guilty of wantonly shedding innocent blood. But he treated the ordinary harmless Royalist or Anglican with consideration and even kindness. He interceded for the life of Lord Derby in 1651, and he actually ordered the release of the poet Cleveland when arrested by one of the Major-Generals, in spite of his acknowledged authorship of the lines:

> What's a Protector? He's a stately thing
> That apes it in the non-age of a King.

An anecdote is told of Oliver's courtesy even in wartime. After he captured Hilsden House in Buckinghamshire in 1644 one of his soldiers stole the hat belonging to the Royalist commander. 'Sir,' Cromwell is reported to have said, 'if you can point out the man or I can discover him, I promise you he shall not go unpunished. In the meantime (taking off a new beaver hat which he had on his head) be pleased to accept of this hat instead of your own.'

Like all famous men Cromwell has been credited with a mistress, but there is sounder evidence that the henpecked Duke of Marlborough was unfaithful to his marriage-bed than that Cromwell was. Indeed, he laid strong emphasis on his duty to his family, and even when writing to a bishop — and we know that bishops were anathema to him — because he was a very distant cousin, Oliver promised to study to serve him 'for kindred's sake'.

His mother, like old Madame Bonaparte, followed him fearfully to the heights of his splendour. A Venetian envoy described her as 'a woman of ripe wisdom and great prudence'. She survived her illness of 1649 and predeceased her son by but four years, reaching her eighty-ninth birthday in the palace of the kings. Cromwell's sons and his daughters' husbands were all given high positions in his government of which they were not unworthy, but not one of them, except perhaps Ireton who died before the protectorate, rivalled his powerful personality. Richard, his eldest son, a gentle young man who inherited his father's long nose but not his ability, seems to have pressed on his father a match with a country girl that involved long settlement negotiations, and the pair then spent a contented idle life in Whitehall, occasionally finding leisure to make a journey into the country 'to eat cherries'. This conduct was not at all pleasing to the father, who expected from his children a Puritan sanctification of their daily life and solemnly reproved Dick and Doll's idleness, yet was prepared to forgive his daughter-in-law so long as she was fruitful of 'little brats'. But he complained 'she is too modest to tell me whether she breeds or no'. In 1657 Richard was gradually brought into the political limelight and was forced to gaze with a troubled eye upon a world 'sick of plenty and mad with liberty', but he really had no idea what to do about it all. He once wrote to his brother Henry explaining how much he hated writing letters, which is of course a common failing, but one that shows he was hardly of the stuff of which tyrants are made. He enjoyed his brief hour of authority, forced upon him by the dying wishes of his father, but once he had resigned his Protectorate he made no effort to regain his lost power.

The younger son, Henry, an abler man who came to understand and appreciate the problems of Ireland when set to rule it, lacked the enthusiastic religious convictions and the strict morality of his parents. Henry fell in love with the attractive and charming Dorothy Osborne, daughter of a Guernsey Royalist. He presented her with an Irish greyhound. His gift was accepted but his suit was rejected, and he soon consoled himself by marrying instead the beautiful sixteen-year-old Elizabeth Russell, of a rather obscure Cambridgeshire family. He took his young wife with him to Ireland. Here the course of their married life was not unruffled. A letter written to Henry by his sister Mary in December 1651 speaks reprovingly of a mysterious lady in the Dublin household 'who rules much in your family' and is reported to be 'a discountenancer of the godly people'. Whatever this lady's capacity for mischief-making may have been her reign was plainly short; for a few months later in another letter Henry Cromwell's mother-in-law was able to thank him for 'loving her daughter so well'. Neither of Oliver's sons inherited the strong religious enthusiasm of their father, who once sadly confessed in public that 'often the children of great men have not the fear of God before their eyes'. The character of these two sons was admirably summed up by the contemporary French ambassador to England when he said of them: 'Few people believe that the Protector's sons are capable of sustaining the heavy burden of supreme power, his elder being more devoted to wine and to hunting than to business. The younger has more ambition and is in the army, but is little respected and less loved.'

Of his four daughters Bridget, the eldest, was the best behaved, but his favourite was Betty (Elizabeth Claypole). Although she married a comparatively unimportant Lincolnshire gentleman she came 'to act the part of a princess very naturally'. Cromwell told his wife on more than one occasion that Betty was far too subject to worldly vanities — the clothes she wore were over rich for a Puritan princess — but he granted her the indulgences of the most precious of children. She was a beautiful wilful creature who intervened once or twice successfully with her father on behalf of Royalist petitioners for his mercy, and was instrumental in saving from destruction a manuscript of the famous republican philosopher James Harrington for which he lived to bless her. She flattered the important statesmen, snubbed the lesser ladies of her father's court, and then

CROMWELL AND HIS FAMILY

Left to Right: Richard Cromwell, Mary Cromwell, Oliver Cromwell, Mrs.
Oliver Cromwell, Elizabeth (Betty) Cromwell and Henry Cromwell

died suddenly, worn out by successive illnesses and child-bearing, before her youthful spirit had deserted her. Oliver felt her loss bitterly, and it hastened on the failure of his own spirit. Bridget married Henry Ireton, her father's friend and fellow-thinker, to please her parents, and a year after his death married Major-General Charles Fleetwood to please her parents again. In writing to this daughter about her first husband Cromwell advised her 'that which is best worthy of love in thy husband is that of the image of Christ he bears'. She lived on to the age of seventy-six and was seen by Dean Swift at the Court of Queen Anne, who noted that she was very like her father.

Cromwell's two younger daughters, Mary (Mall) and Frances (Frankie), whom their father described as his 'two little wenches' when he was concerned about their dowries in 1648, were brought up in the enjoyment of each other's company which they continued to share after their elder sisters were married. Like Bridget, Mary married according to her father's wish. The entire machinery of government, through Secretary of State, ambassador and diplomatic correspondence, was brought into use in order to bring Lord Fauconberg, the son-in-law-elect, to the point of proposal. Writing a fortnight after her wedding Mary confessed that God 'had been pleased to dispose of my heart so as that I have been obliged to my parents'. But she was content to note that her husband was 'a sober person' that 'hath a greater kindness than ever I might have expected'. She invoked her brother Henry's prayers for their marital happiness. As things turned out, the two of them fared together for better or worse for half a century. After the Restoration Fauconberg, son of a Royalist, was allowed to take an honourable position in society and Bishop Burnet thought Lady Fauconberg 'a wise and worthy woman' who had she worn breeches instead of petticoats would have made a more capable Protector than either of her brothers.

Frances, like Mary, married into the aristocracy, but here was a case of love victorious over parental obstacles. Her chosen suitor was Robert Rich, a grandson of the Earl of Warwick. The settlement negotiations dragged on interminably and Mary revealed to her brother Henry that the difficulty was not so much over the estate 'as some private reasons that my father confided to none but my sister Frances and his own family which was a dislike of the young man which he had from some reports of his being a vicious man given to play and suchlike things'. But for once the mighty Oliver met with resistance from his womenfolk. Frances denied the charges against her young man as mere malicious tittle-tattle calculated to ruin the match, and insisted on the wedding taking place. 'To tell you the truth', oberved her sister, 'they were so much engaged in affection before this that she could not think of breaking it off.' The two younger daughters were married within a week of each other. But poor Frances, who had fought so hard and waited so long for the man she loved, was a bare three months later at the age of eighteen to become a widow.

In contrast with his daughters or even with old Mrs. Cromwell, Oliver's wife remains a somewhat shadowy figure. A plain, plump personage, we may suspect she did what she was told and did not ask questions, although she occasionally made complaints. We know that she disliked her son Henry's exile in Ireland, and he was probably her favourite. One letter written by her to her husband survives. It is a curious, possibly a significant, fragment. Oliver had evidently upbraided her for not writing oftener, to which she gently rejoins that she writes thrice as often as he, that her letters must have gone astray and that she has seldom had any satisfactory answer from him. She tells him how deeply she misses him when he is away up in Scotland badgering obstinate Presbyterians — 'my life is but half a life in your absence' — and finishes by urging him to write to his friends and colleagues, almost hinting that his not doing so implies overmuch independence of them. Three of Cromwell's letters to his wife are known. The first, written after Dunbar, tells her, 'Thou art dearer to me than any living creature; let that suffice.' All three of them are

noticeably simple in tone when contrasted with many of Cromwell's other letters with their fervent appeals to the witness of
God. Indeed, if one compares the letters written by other
Puritans of this time to their wives, with their lengthy discur-
sions on the state of their spiritual health and lists of appropriate texts, these three short missives of Cromwell, though
certainly Puritanical in tone, appear like a pleasing oasis in a
rolling desert of words. Mrs. Elizabeth Cromwell had a country
upbringing and the aristocracy laughed at her as unfit for her
great position in her husband's world, but it was said that she
was an admirable housewife and had secret passages constructed
in the palace of Whitehall in order to watch her steward at
work. After the abdication of her son Richard she quickly
vanished back into the oblivion of the country-side.

Who were Cromwell's friends and in whom did he repose
his trust? Here we find a problem which reflects the tragic side
of dictatorship. In the unique letter of his wife she refers to
'his dear friend', Chief Justice St. John. In after years Oliver
St. John denied that he had approved Cromwell's assumption
of the Protectorate, and as Chief Justice he at least once gave
a decision unfavourable to Cromwell's Government. Although
there was no quarrel it seems certain that the man whom
Cromwell trusted as much as any one up to 1651 gradually
drifted away from him. Another friend whom he lost, quite
certainly on account of his destruction of the Long Parliament
and of his later policy, was Henry Vane the younger. In a
letter written by Oliver Cromwell to St. John in 1648 he
sends a message to 'my dear brother', Henry Vane, and in
two of the three letters to his wife he alludes to him as to a
close intimate of the family. He nicknamed him 'brother
Heron' ('The Heron' was the name of an inn where they had
been wont to meet as young men) and his name was the last
on Cromwell's lips as he drove out the 'Rump' Parliament in
1653. Some two years later Vane published a pamphlet
attacking Oliver's Government, urging that the Republican
cause was as good as ever and its exponents as virtuous;

Cromwell sent for him to try to effect a reconciliation, but in vain. Just as such civilian friends tended to leave him when he overthrew Parliament, so his soldier friends were alienated by his anxiety to become King in 1657, while two of his closest friends, John Hampden and Henry Ireton, met premature deaths. So intimate was the relationship of Ireton and Cromwell that some thought, not without a show of reason, that had Ireton lived, Cromwell would have taken a different path from the one which he chose alone.

It has been said of Cromwell that in his later years he had no friends, only agents. At least one exception can be made to this statement. His most valuable agent was his most devoted friend. John Thurloe, barrister of Lincoln's Inn, received the patronage of Oliver St. John and through him became secretary to the Council of State. After the formation of the Protectorate he became Cromwell's sole Secretary of State and served him with unswerving devotion till the day of his death and after. Thurloe guarded Oliver by his wonderful system of espionage against the many enemies who conspired and plotted at home and abroad, while he kept in his own hands the detail of all diplomatic negotiations, and from 1656 defended the Government's policy in person in Parliament. 'The little secretary', as a contemporary called him, ceaselessly active in toil and yet finding a few leisure hours to spend on his recreations of French and mathematics, is a pleasing figure whose absence of religious enthusiasm offered a marked contrast to that of his chief. They must have looked an odd pair, too, as they sat in consultation or took exercise in Hyde Park, Cromwell horsed, Thurloe in the coach behind. Only on Oliver's death was the pen of the secretary moved to emotion; and it was he who received the injunction to nominate Richard as his father's successor and strove against an active and powerful opposition to effect the wishes of his dead master. After the Restoration it was said that Charles II often begged Thurloe to put his unrivalled knowledge of foreign affairs at the disposal of the Government, but he preferred to remain quietly in his rooms at Lincoln's Inn, pondering the past.

Cromwell did not deny himself relaxation and in his family circle allowed himself to put off his official worries and take his ease. He hunted and hawked with enthusiasm or played bowls, especially as he grew conscious of middle age. He loved horses — white Arabs were his favourites — and cared for them in a way befitting one who was perhaps the finest cavalry leader in English history. Of an evening he would sit smoking a pipe or drinking small ale, listening to music, instrumental as well as vocal, of which he was extremely fond, or even watching a 'mixed dancing' which scandalized his Puritan subjects.

But if he sometimes broke the conventions, on the whole he accepted the Puritan approach to life. He enjoyed attending the interminable sermons of his numerous chaplains. He spoke of a choir service as 'unedifying and offensive', and of sacramental rites as 'foolery'. The Spring Gardens of Whitehall, which under Charles I had been the meeting place of ladies and gallants, remained closed throughout the Protectorate. Although we may take with a pinch of salt a Venetian story that he used to go round visiting the London churches with a great Bible under his arm, in appreciating Cromwell's humanity let us not forget his fundamental Puritanism.

Directly he assumed the Protectorate the Master of Ceremonies made it known that in all ceremonial matters the usage should be that practised under the kings, and when Louis XIV of France refused to address Cromwell as 'brother', his Secretary of State announced that 'cousin' was the least that would satisfy him. From the Cockpit, the residence that had been allotted to him as General, he moved with his family into Whitehall Palace itself, a very different place from the modern home of bureaucracy, for of Cromwell's Whitehall only the Banqueting Hall remains. The Palace gardens extended to the Thames, and the river, to which Whitehall stairs gave access, was a busy highway. John Evelyn the diarist visited Whitehall in 1656 and found it 'very glorious and well furnished'. But at the week-end Cromwell left the Palace and enjoyed driving down to Hampton Court in coach-and-four and practising the diversions of the country. In these days, too, he wore better-tailored clothes, attempted to gather the old aristocracy round him, and created a new one. Thus his Court lacked no pomp and was not unmindful of its pride. An amusing though possibly apocryphal story is told of it. One of Cromwell's chaplains, a Mr. White, had ventured to make secret love to his attractive youngest daughter, Frances, whose marriage was to bring the 'mixed dancing' with it. The Protector discovered White one day on his knees before the young lady and sternly inquired what he did there. Certain of reprimand if he told the truth, White said that he was enamoured of the Lady Frances's chambermaid and was interceding with her mistress on behalf of his rejected suit, for the maid had been cold to him. Cromwell addressed himself thereon to the chambermaid, 'What, will you not take my good friend, Mr. White?' The girl, who wanted nothing better, affirmed that she would, and the Protector sent for a clergyman and had them married there and then. Be that story true or not, it is certain that the wearing of the cloak of royalty by Cromwell was equally offensive alike to the bulk of the Stuart supporters, the old Republicans, many of the Puritans and to his late comrades in arms. And at the very end of his life when his family were wishing 'that he were equally distant from both his childhoods', he remained a somewhat lonely and forbidding figure to the outer world.

His enemies made the most of his superficial faults. He admitted himself that he had a sudden and fierce temper, which flamed and died often enough before it had brought trouble in its train. One odd characteristic was his faculty for bursting into tears. To his enemies they were the tears of a hypocrite produced with the ease of a modern film star. But it is more likely that it was a not unusual phenomenon in so highly strung a Puritan. In a moment of stress he occasionally vented his psychological reaction in an outburst of horseplay. His cushion-throwing with Ludlow at the crucial period of 1647 has already been noticed. Another instance is the famous story, which is not intrinsically improbable, that when signing the death warrant of Charles I he drew an inky pen across the face of a fellow signatory. Although it is likely that these wild outbursts only showed themselves at times of extraordinary mental agony, there is some reason to suppose that Cromwell (in common with many other soldiers of all ages) lacked a genuine sense of humour. While the Royalist anecdotes about his wild youth, when he was alleged to have robbed orchards and so on, need not be taken seriously, there was possibly some fire behind the smoke of the elaborate stories told by many writers that before his conversion the exuberance of his spirits had been revealed in youthful escapades. Richard Baxter described him as having been 'a prodigal in his youth' but in late life as being 'of a sanguine complexion, naturally of such vivacity, hilarity, and alacrity, as another man is when he hath drunken a cup of wine too much'. Captain Hodgson, who was with him in Scotland in 1650, recounted an anecdote illustrative of his taste in jokes:

Our officers were looking out at a window, hearing a great shout amongst the soldiers, they spied a soldier with a Scots kirn [churn] on his head. Some of them had been purveying abroad, and had found a vessel filled with Scots cream; and bringing the reversions to their tents, some got dishfuls, and some hatfuls; and the cream growing low in the vessel, one would have a modest drink, and lifting up the kirn, another lifts it up, and the man was lost in it, and all the cream trickles down his apparel, and his head fast in the tub; this was a merriment to the officers, as Oliver loved an innocent jest.

He is also related to have sported with his soldiers, but 'sober cheerfulness', an expression once used of him by an intimate in 1657, probably more aptly describes his normal temper in later life. There is an odd story, not without some semblance of authority, in an old manuscript to the effect that, at his youngest daughter's wedding, 'the Protector threw sack posset [a sticky drink] among the ladies to soil their rich clothes and daubed the stools where they were to sit with sweetmeats'; but it must surely be one of the thousands of lampoons merely caricaturing the foibles of a great man.

Oliver Cromwell was not, as some of his more devoted literary adherents affirm, a good speaker. His sentences were involved and difficult and he frequently lost the thread of his discourse and wandered from political facts into matter on which sermons are based. No one who reads his conciliatory speeches in the Army Council of 1647 and contrasts them with the other speeches made there can deny that they were lacking in clarity; and even practice could not create an orator out of one who was most unskilled in the accents of command, and his 'untuneable voice' could only form the music of prose when it thundered forth the words of the psalmist. In private he seems to have been equally prone to longwindedness, and when he took the floor in the Council Chamber his councillors had been known to fall asleep. In conversing with Ludlow one occasion he began by reciting the whole of the Hundred and Tenth Psalm. He believed in using the personal interview as a means of conciliating his opponents, but this method never seems to have met with success. He was deeply interested in varieties of Protestant religious opinion, in favour of which from his earliest years of power he advocated liberty of conscience, and he was interviewing George Fox, the father of the Quakers, only a few weeks before his death.

No one to-day troubles to question the reality of Cromwell's personal religion; yet we are not perhaps wrong in thinking that there was always in it that terrible Puritan conflict between consciousness of personal self-righteousness and knowledge of personal sinfulness. On the one hand, he was convinced that all who were chosen by God to rule on earth and to attain eternal bliss in the next life were imbued by Him with the spirit of grace, and that just as the Pillar of Fire appeared over the Israelites in the wilderness to lead them into the Promised

Land, so those who in the seventeenth century knew themselves destined from the moment of their conversion to take a lead in determining the affairs of the English people were able to recognize by signs that the grace of God was on them, and that, though they might err, He would never abandon them. Cromwell felt this most confidently; according to Bishop Burnet his favourite doctrine was 'once a child of God always a child of God'. Throughout his life he asserted his firm belief that he was indeed a chosen leader of the people of God. Yet although he was certain that he had been elected to do God's work for Him, he was never entirely sure of the exact character of the task that he had been set to do. In his younger days he helped very largely to guide the political and constitutional changes that were taking place, and having guided them, he could interpret them as divine dispensations. But he had too acute a mind not to have an occasional doubt of their validity. 'Remember my love to my dear brother H[enry] V[ane],' he wrote to St. John in 1648, 'I pray he make not too little, *nor I too much, of outward dispensations.*' As he grew older his control over circumstances grew weaker, and thus when he became Protector he began to have doubts as to his wisest course of action. Even Thurloe, best trained of civil service minds, once complained of Cromwell's proneness as Protector to follow the advice of others. Indeed, Lord Morley argued that from as early as 1647 Cromwell showed himself readier to follow the trend of events than to lead the way. But in reality this was his practice throughout his whole public career, particularly in the last phase we are about to describe, and it was his practice because it was his religious and political creed that the synthesis of events is the measure of God's necessity, which knows no law but the obligation of the just man to recognize it and to obey.

CHAPTER X

THE LORD PROTECTOR

§ I

THE Nominated Parliament committed suicide in a placid and somewhat undignified manner by giving back its power to the General from whom it had come. But before doing so the Council of the Army had made provision for its successor and had given birth to the first Written Constitution in English history, known as the Instrument of Government.

Under the Instrument Oliver Cromwell was made Lord Protector of the Commonwealth of England, Scotland and Ireland and the executive power was conferred upon him and a Council of State which it named. The Council consisted of seven officers and eight civilians. A pretty personal touch was given to the civilian membership by the inclusion of Henry Lawrence, who had been Cromwell's landlord at St. Ives, and of Richard Mayor, the father-in-law of Richard Cromwell. With the advice of the Council Cromwell might issue ordinances, levy necessary taxation and control the militia. The legislative power devolved upon an elective single chamber which was to meet for at least five months every three years. The Protector had no power to veto Acts of Parliament.

Oliver had acquiesced in the new constitution with considerable misgivings, not through any reluctance to assume the heavy responsibilities that were thrust upon him by it, but, on the contrary, because he doubted whether he was justified in accepting any limitations at all upon his authority. Gradually he was coming to believe, for so the Lord's dispensations through past events had revealed it to him, that he was destined to be the supreme ruler of the State. Six years earlier when the Long Parliament was still sitting he had been within distance of persuading himself and trying to persuade others that the Army was a power called by God to govern the country. When he had dissolved the Long Parliament he had hesitated to create another legislative body in its place because he was uncertain whether it was not sinful for him to surrender to others the obligations of government. Now once again, with the failure of his carefully chosen nominees, the question confronted him whether it was not his duty to seize without any hampering restrictions upon the helm of government. Not only did there seem to him to be many signs from the Lord that he was the new Moses, but, he asked, had not the destruction both of the throne and of Parliament left him 'the only constituted Power' in the State? Had he not been appointed General by a properly elected Parliament? 'My power,' he explained later in a public speech, had through the self-destruction of the Little Parliament become 'as boundless and unlimited as before. . . .' The obvious weakness of this extraordinary argument — for who had made him the only constituted power but himself? — does not appear to have occurred to him. But the Army officers were determined to prevent their general from becoming a dictator above their reach. Hence they induced him to accept the Instrument of Government which at least on paper limited his powers. Hence, too, some of the officers were even ready to offer him the title of King, since it seemed plain that after Parliament's painful experience with James I and Charles I a King's powers would inevitably be narrowly circumscribed. Oliver refused at this time to become King; but he hesitated before he accepted a constitution which aimed at preventing him from becoming a dictator.

The officers who framed this scheme of government were in fact anxious to avoid any suspicion of establishing a military dictatorship. Their scheme clearly envisaged a 'mixed' or 'constitutional' monarchy, wherein the elements of monarchy (the Protector), aristocracy (the nominated Council) and democracy (the elective Parliament) were judiciously mixed.

Such a government had been constantly advocated as an ideal during the negotiations with Charles I in the 'forties and was to be the staple food of advanced political thinkers until the days of William III. The only important difference between it and those paper constitutions put forward earlier was that since more confidence was placed in Cromwell than in Charles I, the powers of the executive were correspondingly greater. Also it was extended to apply to Scotland and Ireland conquered by Cromwell, which were given thirty seats each for the first time in the history of the British Parliament. The Levellers criticized it because the suffrage, based on the £200 property owner, was obviously not democratic and the lawyers apparently would have preferred it to have been more avowedly monarchical. When we moderns peel off the constitutional skin with which it was covered we find the new rule nothing more or less than the old General with his Army Council and 'purged' Parliament governing in unmilitary guise. Cromwell symbolized this transformation when at the installation ceremony he exchanged his own for a civic sword. In one sense the establishment of the Protectorate was a triumph for the more worldly Lambert over the Fifth Monarchy Harrison. When asked by Ludlow why he had supported Cromwell in 1653, Harrison replied because he stood for 'a higher principle than that of civil liberty', in a word, for the rule of the godly. The Parliament of Nominated Saints had been a concession to Harrison, but now that a Parliament elected not by the Chosen People but by the well-to-do was in prospect he saw that the good days were over. He refused to acknowledge the Protectorate and retired in dudgeon to his home in the country, leaving the Fifth Monarchy preachers to expound as best they might their thesis that Jesus Christ was preferable to Oliver Cromwell. Among the tergiversations of John Lambert can be discerned the hope of one day succeeding to the protectoral throne. Meanwhile he was content with being a power behind it.

Turning from the ambitions of individuals to the general

desires of the politically conscious we find that they relied on Cromwell chiefly to give them peace. Peace was to be sought both at home and abroad. The expensive Dutch war, so antagonistic to the religious instincts of the true Puritan, must be brought to a speedy and happy end. The perpetual naval conflicts between England and other nations, terribly injurious to commerce, must also cease. Merchants declared that there was no greater enemy to trade than war 'be it in what country you will'. At home the military system created by the civil wars must be modified now that the battles were over. The Royalists should be induced to accept the new government by kindness instead of cruelty. Beyond this there was among those who trusted that the wars had not been waged vainly a demand for retrenchment and reform, the two things that the Nominated Parliament had tried to achieve, and would perhaps have achieved had they not so unwisely attacked the rights of property. It was clear — this is the essential fact about the Protectorate — that efforts in these directions would be certain to provoke a passionate dispute between the leaders of the army and the rest of the victorious middle-class leaders.

But at first the problem was shelved and Cromwell devoted himself to establishing peace. He was aided in his work by an able new class of administrators which the revolution had produced, men like Whitelocke, Dr. John Pell, an eminent mathematician, George Downing, after whom the present Downing Street is named, and, above all, the devoted John Thurloe. By April 5th a peace treaty with the Dutch was signed and this was followed by a series of commercial treaties with Sweden, Portugal, Denmark and France which gradually put an end to the chaotic state of maritime trade and brought a burst of prosperity to commerce. At home Cromwell made efforts to pacify and conciliate both Royalists and Republicans. In January of the same year, 1654 he repealed the old tyrannical ordinance by which persons who refused for conscience' sake to take the engagement to be faithful to the Commonwealth were denied access to the Courts of Justice, and henceforward no one was obliged to take an oath to be a good citizen as an alternative to suffering severe penalties. Cromwell's policy was learned with dismay by the Court of Charles II, now ekeing out a precarious existence in Cologne. 'Dark prospects' came on to their horizon as they heard of the Dutch peace. In March they were told: 'Cromwell proceeds with strange dexterity towards the reconciling all kinds of persons, and chooses those of all parties whose abilities are most eminent.' 'Petty plots', it was freely said by the Royal advisers, would 'never do the business' now.

Early in January Cromwell addressed the French Protestant ministers in London and begged them to pray for him that 'God would grant him the grace to keep his ark in these nations'. His path was no smooth one. He had to tread delicately. There were so many different sects and interests which, if offended, would kindle a spark of hope for the ever-watchful exiles across the water. On Ash Wednesday, for example, Cromwell set out in grand style to be feasted in the City. The London magnates, then as now, always made deep outward obeisance to the powers that were. During the Interregnum they solemnly dined each successive Council of State as it made its transitory appearance at Whitehall, but the moneyed men kept their own counsel and provided credit for the Treasury sparsely and unwillingly. But the City apprentices were always Royalist, and the Court at Cologne was rejoiced to hear that the pageant of Ash Wednesday was made up only of 'dirt and multitude', 'not one "God save" ' on the road from Whitehall to the Grocers Hall where the reception was arranged. 'The Mayor, for his bare-headed service and feast of 800 dishes, was dubbed Sir Thomas Vyner; the Recorder was also called for, but was too cunning to be found.'

On April 14th Cromwell moved with his family into Whitehall from the Cockpit and in May was fortunate in escaping, through Thurloe's watchfulness, a plot to assassinate him in the City. In June two of the would-be assassins were put to death, and another plot, in which a French ambassador foolishly allowed himself to be involved, was discovered and stamped out. In August a feeble Royalist invasion of Scotland was put down, so that by Sunday, September 3rd, the anniversary of Dunbar and Worcester, the Protector was fully prepared to meet his Parliament and unroll before them the long list of achievements of the new government. Cromwell's star seemed to shine brightly in the autumn sky. 'According to the opinion of all the world,' reported an impartial observer, 'the Crown is only wanting to this government to establish and confirm the authority upon the head of the Lord Protector.'

In 1651 the minor poet Edmund Waller, who eight years earlier had been concerned in a Royalist plot and banished for his complicity, ventured to return to England from abroad. He owed his permission to return to the influence of Cromwell, who was connected with his family. Waller's mother was the sister of John Hampden's father and therefore indirectly related to the Cromwells. She was an unrepentant Royalist, but nevertheless Oliver used occasionally to pay her visits at her home at Beaconsfield in Buckinghamshire. But he declared politics taboo as a subject of conversation and when she tried to speak of him in favour of the Royalist cause he would 'throw napkins at her and say he would not dispute with his "aunt" '. Edmund conceived it to be a tactful idea to dedicate his muse to the newly-appointed Protector and hastened to compose a 'Panegyric of Oliver Cromwell'. In this poem he compared Cromwell to the successful dictators of the past, to Julius Caesar — killed by 'mistaken Brutus' — and to Augustus Caesar, the men who had destroyed and trampled on the Roman Republic:

> As the vex'd world to find repose at last
> Itself into Augustus's arms did cast,
> So England now does, with like toil oppress'd,
> Her weary head upon your bosom rest.

The poem was written some time in 1654; although Oliver

213

modestly repudiated the magnificent character given to him, in 1655, 'his very loving friend' Edmund Waller was awarded a post as Commissioner of Trade.

§ 2

The Instrument of Government had redistributed the constituencies and altered the franchise in a way which was beneficial to the middle classes, the bulwark of conservatism. The 1654 election had reflected this distribution, for the Saints of the Nominated Parliament were wiped out and the irreconcilable Republican party only obtained a handful of representatives. For the most part the members were Presbyterians who might have been expected to be especially benevolent towards the mixed constitution. Business on 'the Lord's Day' was confined to hearing a sermon, electing a Speaker and a homily by Cromwell on the value of united work 'for the peace and tranquillity of all the Saints in Sion'. The real opening of Parliament was reserved for the morrow.

On the Monday the Lord Protector went in glorious cavalcade from Whitehall to Westminster. Hundreds of officers marched bareheaded before him and his coach was preceded by Life Guardsmen, pages and lackeys all richly clothed. In the Abbey another sermon was preached, and then with the same trappings Oliver went into the Painted Chamber and there delivered what Whitelocke termed a 'large and subtle speech' and Ludlow a 'tedious' one. In fact the speech was the best arranged and prepared of any he made during the Protectorate. He began by stressing the fact that he was speaking to representatives of England, Scotland and Ireland for the first time met together in Parliament. 'You are met here', he said, 'in the greatest occasion that, I believe, England ever saw, having upon your shoulders the interests of three great nations with the territories belonging to them.' Then he turned to justify the new reign as the guarantee of 'healing and settling'. What, he asked, had been the condition of the country since the close of the civil wars?

What was the face that was upon our affairs as to the interest of the nation; to the authority of the nation; to the magistracy; to the ranks and orders of men; — whereby England has been known for hundreds of years? A nobleman, a gentleman, a yeoman; that is a good interest of the nation and a great one! The [natural] magistracy of the nation, was it not almost trampled under foot, under despite and contempt, by men of Levelling principles? I beseech you, for the orders of men and ranks of men, did not that Levelling principle tend to the reducing all to an equality? Did it think to do so; or did it practise towards it for property and interest? What was the purpose of it but to make the tenant as liberal a fortune as the landlord? Which I think if obtained would not have lasted long!

Such a principle, he assured his audience, would inevitably have led to an attack on property, equally pleasing to all poor men and all bad men. Nowhere does Cromwell expound more plainly his function as the guardian of private property. He went on to criticize the Presbyterians for prohibiting liberty of conscience and 'the more refined error' of the Fifth Monarchy Men. To the Fifth Monarchy men he devoted especial attention, for to him they were the misguided master minds who had led astray the Parliamentary Saints. He could not understand by what right they had appointed themselves 'to determine of property and liberty and everything else'. Having defended his rule as the only alternative to anarchy he outlined the actual achievements of the Protectorate. In foreign affairs he showed his audience how by reason of wars with France, Portugal, Holland and Denmark their trade had been ruined and their budget overburdened; how the cloth industry, the great staple trade of the nation, had been hampered and how taxation had been unbearable. The long-desired Dutch treaty and the commercial agreements had opened the way to trade revival as well as to diplomatic peace.

At home he drew attention to his efforts to reform the law and the clergy and to reduce taxation. You are to-day, he told them, 'a people brought out of Egypt towards the land of Canaan' — towards it but not yet near to it — and Moses could not lay down his staff until in sight of the Promised Land. With this theological analogy Cromwell dismissed the Parliament to examine the Instrument of Government.

Here we come at once to the gravest difference in outlook between Cromwell and Parliament. The former regarded the Nominated Parliament — with all its faults — as having played the part of a Constituent Assembly, by allowing the Instrument to be produced (although it was not called upon to ratify it). But the new Parliament regarded itself as the Constituent Assembly, the Instrument being, in modern language, merely 'a basis of discussion'. As soon as they were left alone the Republican group, always the most vociferous in the House, began to stress this point and opened 'the eyes of many young members who had never before heard their interests so clearly stated and asserted'. Although the extreme Republicans made little headway, a middle party, which wished to affirm that ultimate sovereignty lay with Parliament and that the Protector was merely a shackled executive, soon formed a solid block and obtained support from the Presbyterian pulpits outside.

The Protector watched the conduct of the House with gloom and apprehension. It had certainly not been his intention to erect another Constituent Assembly which should undermine the basis of his own rule. The Ship of State to which, like many politicians before and since, he had glibly appealed in his opening speech, was assuredly not upon unruffled waters. When he learned that Parliament was threatening to pass a motion increasing its own powers at the expense of the Protector and of the Council, he sent for the House once more and addressed the members indignantly, this time again rattling the military sword in its sheath. 'It is', he began, 'necessary for me now a little to magnify my office.' He reminded them briefly in what manner he had arrived at his present eminence and explained the danger of Parliaments as well as Kings becoming arbitrary. He then brought forward a number of 'proofs' of his rights. The failure of the Nominated Parliament had shown that God had not wished him to lay down his office. The generalship was in 1653 the sole constituted power (the general's friends having conveniently destroyed all other constituted powers). The City, the Army, the judges and the sheriffs of the counties had explicitly or tacitly confirmed him in the Protectorate. This being so, the House must accept at last the four fundamentals of his rule, to wit, that the Government lay in a Single Person and a Parliament, that Parliament should not perpetuate itself, that liberty of conscience in religion should be recognized and that the power of the militia should be under the control of Protector, Parliament and Council as laid down in the Instrument. He concluded by reiterating the necessity for a national government to defend the country from foes at home and abroad, and instructed all the members to sign a 'recognition' accepting the fundamentals of his rule before resuming their seats in the House. Faced with this price to pay for their continued existence as a legislature all the members except the extreme Republicans signed. They then fell with a good will to tearing the remainder of the constitution to pieces.

On September 29th Oliver and John Thurloe set out together for a drive in Hyde Park in a coach harnessed by six horses recently presented to the Protector by the Duke of Oldenburg. But Oliver who chose to act as coachman pressed them so hard that he was thrown, a pistol exploding in his pocket as he fell. Both men escaped without injury but his enemies did not fail to draw the moral that Cromwell could not drive horses like he drove Parliament:

Foreign ill-tutored jades, had you but known
Whom you rebelled against, whom you have thrown,
You would have pined to nothing, loathed the day,
And left the crows a memorable prey.

217

O Life of three great realms; whose brains did hatch
Successful plots, which no past age could match,
Whose army braves the land, whose fleets the main,
And only beasts did think unfit to reign. . . .

But now Parliament had met, it was clear that the result of
Cromwell's becoming Protector had been to concentrate on
him the united resentment of every element in the opposition.
In October three colonels were arrested for comparing the
new government to the old monarchy. In November Parliament began a firm attempt to wrest the control of the militia
from the Protector so as to counterbalance the overwhelming
influence of the Army; at the same time a vain attempt was
made to reduce the size of the Army. In December some of his
personal supporters in the House alienated the Army by proposing that he should be made King. In January Parliament
declared itself against the new £200 property franchise and in
favour of the restoration of the vote to the forty-shilling frec-
holder, while another military intrigue was unravelled by
Thurloe in Scotland.

In these circumstances Cromwell's stock of patience was
gradually absorbed. His effort to await unmoved the outcome
of interminable constitutional debates which to his mind bore
no relation to political realities was nevertheless genuine.
'My exercise of that little faith and patience I have,' he told
a confidant, 'was never greater.' But he saw no prospect of the
'healing and settling' at which he had aimed being realized.
On the contrary he discovered that 'whosoever labours to walk
with an even foot between the several interests of the people of
God for healing and accommodating their differences is sure
to have reproaches and anger from some of all sorts'.

He was particularly disgusted at the delay shown by the
Commons in providing money for his Army. But for this he
himself was not entirely without responsibility. He had
treated coldly a sub-committee which had been sent to discuss
the reduction of the forces with him in accordance with the

terms of the Instrument of Government, and seemed indeed reluctant to consent to any retrenchment at all. Ought not the Army to be maintained at full garrison and out of it for police purposes? he asked. 'As to the forces in England,' he said, 'the numbers are but few — the condition of the people such as the major part are persons disaffected and engaged against us.' The Levellers and Royalists' plots uncovered by Thurloe and by 'that simple-hearted man honest George Monk' (whom Cromwell had left behind in Scotland) caused him to believe that Parliament's delay in providing for the Army was a direct provocation to rebellion. Instead of healing and settling the Commons had poisoned and unsettled the nation by their refusal to devote themselves to the urgent business of government. He decided therefore to rid himself of this turbulent assembly as soon as he dare.

A study of the Instrument of Government either by himself or his advisers found a method of reverting to personal rule towards the end of January 1655. The Instrument provided that Parliament must sit for five months and could not during that time be adjourned or dissolved without its consent, but did not say that the months need be calendar months; if they were lunar months Parliament need only sit for one hundred and forty days and its time was already up. On the other hand, the Instrument appeared to provide that the Protector might only raise money without Parliamentary consent until the meeting of the first Parliament. If, therefore, he now chose to dissolve it before it had granted supplies, he would have no legal right to levy taxes to carry on his administration. Hence the Commons were under the impression that though their time was nearly at an end they were safe from dissolution. They believed that Cromwell would capitulate to their terms for army reform rather than dismiss them. They were mistaken.

On Monday, January 22nd, when the members went to take their daily dose of constitutional investigation at Westminster — they had not yet passed a single piece of legislation —

they were stopped by soldiers who informed them that the Protector awaited them in the Painted Chamber. He addressed them long and sadly in terms of reproof and disillusionment. What had they done to fulfil the great task that had been entrusted to them? 'I do not know whether you have been alive or dead.' Their discussions had been a mighty incentment to Royalist plots — 'weeds and nettles, briars and thorns have thriven under your shadow!' Their distemper — to vary a metaphor — had produced 'a quinsy or pleurisy that had hazarded the life of the Commonwealth'. No mortal physician could have cured the distemper. The fault was all theirs. Had they not irritated the Army by withholding supplies? And had not the people been put into a bad humour because the Army was forced to quarter itself upon them? Nor had they made any progress towards the sound establishment of organized religion. If now, therefore, he resumed the supreme power the necessity had been created by them and not by him. Let it not be imagined it was to make himself and his family great that he took on the burden; nor let them 'prate of freedom'. What good had all their talk of liberty done? Indeed, what right had they to talk of liberty when the lives and properties of peaceful citizens were still in danger of Royalist attacks: 'If it be my liberty to walk abroad in the fields or to take a journey, yet it is not my wisdom to do so when my house is on fire!' And so justifying a return to despotism by the plea that it was the sole alternative to anarchy Oliver declared, with his eyes full of tears, 'I do dissolve this Parliament'.

So failed the experiment with Britain's 'first written constitution' — this attempt, in Cromwell's words, 'to avoid the extremes of monarchy on the one hand and of democracy on the other'. Perhaps Cromwell did not appreciate how foolish it was for a man dominated by a will to power (albeit power to do good) to allow constitutional impediments to be imposed upon his actions. But he himself had risen to fame as a Member of Parliament; he had fought and risked his life in the name of Parliament; and his conservative instincts pressed him to keep some simulacrum of a Parliament in being. He was not, however, sufficiently 'in advance of his time' to conceive the idea of a Parliament (a Reichstag, as we call it in 1937) as a talking shop in which he alone did the talking. He was willing enough that others should talk if he might act. But if they would not give him scope to act, he had to act alone or at least with the aid of his more manageable Council.

§ 3

The theoretic limitations of Cromwell's powers as Protector were nowhere more clearly defined than in the realm of foreign policy. He could not make peace or war without the consent of his Council, whose members all held strong and differing opinions on the best course for the Government to pursue. In the earlier part of 1654 the majority of the Council, led by Lambert, favoured an alliance with Spain. A minority including the bulk of the non-military members headed by Sir Gilbert Pickering, who acted as interpreter for the French ambassadors (none of them spoke a word of English), preferred a French alliance. John Thurloe is said to have adopted a middle position, although one of the French agents asserted that he was 'entirely in the interests of Spain'. To some extent the divisions in the Council of State may have enabled Cromwell to follow an independent line. We have seen, for example, how while the Long Parliament was still sitting, he had entered upon a secret negotiation with Cardinal Mazarin. But the necessity for conciliating the Council partly explains the extraordinary vacillations in 1654, when Gardiner describes him as 'constant only in his inconstancy'.

When Cromwell became Protector he found a naval war in progress between England and Holland, a war to which he had been consistently opposed. In 1651 his friend and cousin, Oliver St. John, had visited The Hague to propose an alliance with the Dutch Republic. The commercial clauses of the

treaty were suggested along the lines of the Magnus Inter-
cursus concluded by Henry VII, which was extremely advan-
tageous to the Dutch. The Dutch, however, were dissatisfied
with the English offers and in 1652 a variety of causes brought
about the war. The English Army was from the beginning
inimical to it; Cromwell did not like it and announced that
'the interests of both nations consisted in the welfare of commerce and navigation . . . the world was wide enough for both;
if the two people could only thoroughly well understand one
another, their countries would become the markets of the
world'.

As soon as Cromwell had got rid of the Long Parliament and
succeeded to supreme power he initiated and encouraged a
series of diplomatic negotiations with a view to making a
dramatic and constructive peace with the Dutch. Sir Cornelius
Vermuyden, a Dutch engineer resident in England, acted as
his first intermediary with a proposal for an alliance between
the two countries, which all the Protestant powers should be
invited to join, for a 'general conquest of the world in trade and
religion'. A later proposal submitted to the Dutch ambassadors
was to include France in the Protestant union for the sake of
her Huguenots. A third offer, endorsed by Cromwell, was the
formation of a confederation against the persecutors of the
'reformed religion'. An English historian has claimed that
these three documents exemplified 'the magnificence and
grandeur of Cromwell's foreign policy'. This view is perhaps
a little unbalanced, but there is no doubt that Cromwell
reverted to very similar suggestions in 1656-7 and that the
scheme of a great Protestant union based on the two Republics
formed a regular part of his diplomatic outlook. But these
paper schemes came to nothing either then or later.

In the end the actual treaty of April 1654 obtained compensation for damages done to English commerce and a settlement of maritime and trading disputes in a way most displeasing
to the Dutch merchants. The Prince of Orange, related to the
Stuarts by marriage, was excluded upon Cromwell's insistence

from the high Dutch office of Stadtholder and the evangelical cantons of Switzerland together with the Protestant towns of Oldenburg and the Hanseatic League became parties to the Treaty. The Dutch were profoundly dissatisfied and directed their future efforts without success to the conclusion of a 'marine' treaty more favourable to their commerce.

Cromwell was immensely gratified that peace had been attained: on one occasion when a Dutch ambassador brought satisfactory instructions back from The Hague, he turned to the Swiss agent in London and exclaimed, 'God be blessed!' Finally he told the Commons in 1654 that this peace was as desirable and as acceptable to the spirit of the nations as anything he could lay before it, and that such a peace brought not only security but 'honour and assurance to the Protestant interest abroad'. The lengths to which he was prepared to go in pursuit of these two ends were shown by one of the proposals he made which was to add three Dutchmen to the English Council of State if three English statesmen were admitted into the government of the Netherlands.

Treaties were also made in 1654 with Denmark, the ally of Holland in the war, with Sweden on the eve of her Queen Christina's dramatic abdication on account of her conversion to Catholicism, and with Portugal which had sheltered Prince Rupert during his piratical raids on English merchantmen. The Portuguese Treaty, besides throwing open the Portuguese colonies to English trade in a way most unusual for those times, gave complete freedom of worship to all Englishmen in Portuguese dominions. According to Portuguese experts it marked the zenith of the English influence in Portugal and paved the way for bringing port wine to England. Once these settlements had been made, Cromwell was in a position to choose between the alliance of Spain or of France, who still waged a desultory war against each other. Both States, impressed by the strength and apparent stability of England, sought his friendship and active support. But the situation was complicated. In France a civil war, set in motion (like the English) by a revolt of the middle classes against taxation, was being waged, in which the Huguenots were fighting against the Regent, whose policy was directed by Cardinal Mazarin, and were aided by the forces of Spain. Between Bourbon France and Habsburg Spain a traditional rivalry endured and this was acerbated by the French desire to gain Spanish territory to round off her southern frontiers. For a long while Cromwell hesitated, whilst puzzled ambassadors scratched their heads and wrote lengthy dispatches home. On the one hand, he saw 'the need of a strong foreign power to keep the Huguenots from bartering themselves away and to things detrimental'; on the other, there were possibilities of obtaining a channel port in the Spanish Netherlands (Belgium) by French aid and at the same time exacting concessions for the French Protestants by peaceful means. Some of the reasons why he decided for the French alliance are given by Thurloe: firstly because it would drive Charles II into the arms of Spain which would prove, what had long been rumoured, that he was a Catholic and thus alienate his Protestant supporters in England; secondly, because of the dangers of the traditional Franco-Scottish friendship; thirdly, because he could insist upon better treatment for the Huguenots 'and thus draw them into a dependence on England'. It should also be added that Cromwell's spies who scoured the Protestant districts of France reported home that these showed a singular reluctance to rise in favour of 'the true reformed religion'.

The Anglo-French negotiations were temporarily interrupted by a massacre of Protestants in the Savoyan Alps (said by one writer to be partly in retaliation for Cromwell's massacre of Catholics at Drogheda) which he believed to have been carried out with the connivance of the French. Oliver headed a subscription list for the survivors with a gift of £2000, but that was a mere by-product of his indignation. He at once suspended all other schemes in order to procure joint intervention with the Duke of Savoy by all the Protestant States to obtain liberty of worship for the Piedmontese Protestants on whose behalf John Milton wrote dignified state letters and a celebrated sonnet. But the French promptly agreed to offer their services as mediators, and to Cromwell's irritation his own envoys actually arrived too late to participate in the treaty signed between the Duke of Savoy and his subjects through the mediation of the French and Swiss. But no further obstacle now remained to the Anglo-French alliance which was concluded in November 1655. Among other subjects the Treaty provided for the appointment of arbitrators over the question of three French Canadian forts which had been seized by Cromwell's orders in order to bring Mazarin to terms; and a secret clause prohibited Charles II from living in France. Meanwhile the English and the Spaniards had become involved in a war in the New World.

In the autumn of 1654, about the time that Parliament met, Cromwell had sent out two naval expeditions to assert the might of his country. One under Blake cruised in the Mediterranean and gave short shift to folk like the Dey of Tunis who did not properly respect the English flag. The other was unwisely put under the command of a committee including a quarrelsome general and equally quarrelsome admiral and dispatched to the West Indies. The West Indies were at that time thought to be the most valuable of all the English colonies on account of their sugar and tobacco industries, which were better organized and more profitable than any industries in New England. The comparative value set upon our two principal colonies is shown by Cromwell's one-time project of transporting the entire population of New England to the West Indies. Another reason why Cromwell regarded the West Indies as valuable was that they were thought to be a post admirably suited strategically both for attacking Spain and intercepting her treasure fleets and for further expansion. It was for the same reason that Cromwell later counselled Blake, if possible, to take and fortify Gibraltar.

Undoubtedly a primary consideration which induced Cromwell to favour the attack upon the Spanish West Indies in 1654 was his recollections of the profitable successes of the Elizabethan privateers and of the teaching of Sir Walter Ralegh that effective occupation constituted colonial rights. But in one respect the expedition organized by Cromwell was an entirely new departure in colonial policy. It was a departure because, whereas previously plantations had been established either by individual adventurers or by trading companies under royal charter, this expedition represented an elaborately planned effort on the part of the Government, as such, deliberately to acquire and colonize new territory. The latest historian of the expedition holds that 'according to all evidence the predominant reasons were purely economic, which inspired Cromwell to engage himself on a plan so radically different from everything that had been done until that date in the annals of English colonial history'. Although this view may be oversimplified it is at least certain that there were strong mercantile interests favourable to this attack upon the wealthiest and most populous of the Spanish islands — San Domingo, then called Hispaniola. Martin Noell, the contractor for the expedition, who was a friend of the Cromwell family and a brother-in-law of Thurloe, had a very considerable interest in the islands, and Cromwell undoubtedly hoped to use San Domingo as a profitable new source of income. But this by no means proves that his motives were entirely economic. For example, if one tries to read Thomas Gage's *New Survey of the West Indies* in the kind of spirit in which one imagines Cromwell read it, one realizes how tremendously its arguments must have appealed to the Protestant and nationalist elements in his mind. The first three chapters of this book are devoted to an attack on the Pope as 'a man of sin' whose agents, the Jesuits and the Friars, were hand-in-glove with the Spaniards. Roger Williams one of the earliest writers in favour of liberty of conscience, is said to have also urged an enterprise against the Spanish empire as a means of spreading abroad that liberty. It was thought, too, by many a letter writer of the day that it was Cromwell's intention to use Hispaniola as a stepping-stone to higher things, such as the religious duty of absorbing all the Spanish possessions in South America. Mazarin seems to have suggested the project to him as a bait for his own alliance.

But Cromwell was also influenced by the reports he had heard from various Englishmen about Spanish America. Thomas Gage visited him in person and assured him that the islands were easier to conquer than at any time since Cortez discovered them. One John Cotton had also urged upon Cromwell the religious necessity of cutting off the Spaniards from America. But owing to the quarrels and inefficiency of the commanders and also to the lack of care shown by Cromwell himself in organizing the expedition, the English only succeeded in capturing Jamaica, of which Gage had said that though 'filled with sweet and pleasant streams and fountains of water' it was inferior to the other islands in respect of wealth. Nor was Blake, who after his return from North Africa had been instructed in June 1655 to intercept the Plate Fleet from the East Indies, successful in his mission. Cromwell did not take his disappointments lightly; the military and naval commanders of the West Indian expedition were sent to the Tower as soon as they returned ignominiously home; the Protector retired to bed with an attack of bilious colic; and Thurloe had to console himself with the thought that Jamaica would make an excellent post 'for further designs' and should in any case have been attacked first. But the argument was scarcely convincing and the repulse was a distinct blow. As the Royalist poet Abraham Cowley justly observed, 'the ignominy' could not be hidden under 'the great name of the conquest of Jamaica: as if a defeated army should have the impudence to brag afterwards of the victory because though they had fled out of the field of battle yet they quartered that night in the village of the enemies.'

At the same time Cromwell discovered that he could not attack the Spaniards with impunity 'beyond the line' as Elizabeth had done of old. The Spanish king retaliated in October by laying an embargo on English goods, and in due course England was involved in a European war. War was actually declared the day after the signature of the French Treaty, but the Treaty was in substance merely commercial in character, and for the time being the war was only a maritime one.

§ 4

To sum up the position in western Europe during the early part of the Protectorate: in spite of the trade rivalry between England and Holland, of the refusal of the Dutch to enter into a close political alliance with us and of their continual demand for shipping concessions, the utmost efforts were made to keep on friendly terms with them. The French alliance, while mainly defensive in character, was largely determined by the considerable Protestant interest in that country. The Portuguese, in accepting English terms for freedom of trade and religion in their possessions, did as much as a Catholic country could be expected to do, while their enemies, the Spaniards, were henceforward subjected to English attacks throughout their vast empire. It is clear from Thurloe's own full accounts of Protectoral foreign policy that, except during the early period when Huguenot independence was believed to be in real danger, Cromwell never seriously contemplated an alliance with Spain. On the contrary, he was too much of a conservative to abandon so deeply ingrained a traditional enmity. Indeed a close study of Cromwell's foreign policy shows that it was dominated by the Elizabethan outlook towards Spain. The idea of fighting the Spaniards in the New World in the name of the Protestant religion was in direct imitation of the famous gentlemen pirates of three generations earlier. It is true that Oliver allowed himself to be persuaded in one respect into going even farther than Elizabeth. Whereas the Queen was content to provide a ship or two for the expeditions of Hawkins and Ralegh, Cromwell sent his own fleet to San Domingo.

JOHN THURLOE
' The little secretary '

But the principle was the same and his study of the writings of Sir Walter Ralegh suggest one source of his inspiration. Again his method of colonization, the shipment of the 'scum of the people' from Ireland or England to the colonies, a method which had been roundly condemned by Sir Francis Bacon, was also an imitation of Elizabethan procedure. Even the idea of sending spies and propagandists among the French Huguenots had its precedent in the propaganda campaign organized by Queen Elizabeth's Ministers in the Spanish Netherlands.

One explanation of the reliance placed by Cromwell on historical precedent at least in regard to foreign policy may be found in his conviction that the teachings of history as well as immediate events were part of the divine dispensation. 'What are all our stories and traditions of deeds of earlier times other than God revealing himself?' he once asked. Together with the Word of the Bible and the prompting of his own conscience the voice of God speaking through historical manifestations afforded a third form of guidance, a guidance which was demonstrated to him in particular through the writings of Sir Walter Ralegh and Dr. Thomas Beard. Above all, recent history as handed down by oral tradition in inns and at the family hearth had taught him that the Spaniard was the predestined antagonist of England. Was he not the author of the 'bloody inquisition' and the first of the Jesuits? Had not that great and good Protestant Queen Elizabeth 'of famous memory' contended with him for thirty years? 'Why truly', he was to tell his Parliament, 'your great enemy is the Spaniard.' He was their 'natural enemy'. This 'head of the papal interest and of the anti-Christian interest' had been, Cromwell was certain, destined by God for many years to be the enemy of England. His iniquities were enough to justify the seizure of any number of profitable colonies and loaded treasure fleets. Far from Cromwell's conception was any doctrine of a western European balance of power. He had no idea that the military power which was in a few years' time to dominate Europe, crush the French Protestants, imperil the Dutch Protestants and even menace the independence of England was not Spain but France, his chosen ally. He preferred to cling to ancient enmities just as he maintained the old traditional gulf between the property owners and propertyless. Spain, then, was the great enemy, the perfidious State whose promises could not be trusted and who together with the Pope and Habsburg Austria plotted the destruction of Protestantism throughout the world. So far as in him lay this should not be!

In the North of Europe Charles X had succeeded the abdicated Queen Christina and was a fighting representative of the great family of Vasa Kings. In 1655 a war broke out between Sweden and Poland. At first Cromwell rejoiced, for Charles's successful invasion of his enemy's country appeared a magnificent victory for Protestantism. But soon Charles became embroiled with his customary opponents, the Danes, who were encouraged and assisted by the Dutch, whilst a Swedish ambassador was dispatched to England to invoke Cromwell's aid. The Protector now was angry and hurt to see good Protestant countries flying at each other, and the principal object of his Northern policy was to mediate between the Swedes and the Danes, and to form a coalition of Protestant forces against Poland, Spain and the Empire. Among suggestions made on his side was that Charles should hand over to him the German port of Bremen which was to be used, like Dunkirk, as an outpost of English commerce and Christianity. Charles was not responsive but proposed a joint partition of Denmark and North Germany. Cromwell feared that the conquest of Denmark — apart from other considerations — would convert the Baltic into a Swedish lake and endanger English trade and timber supplies. This more practical consideration seems to have been urged upon him by the Dutch ambassador and by the more worldly members of his own Council of State. Though he heard their advice he continued to spin dreams and he preferred to revert to his hopeless plans for Protestant unity.

During the Dutch war Cromwell showed great zeal for the

realization of the scheme of close political alliance between the two Republics as the core around which other Protestant states might crystallize into world-wide union. This, presumably, was an alternative scheme after the rejection of Vermuyden's more comprehensive proposals. It is true that we have no direct proof that Cromwell thought well of Vermuyden's proposals, but there is the evidence in July 1654, of one of Mazarin's emissaries who wrote to him: 'the Protector proposes to assemble a council of all the Protestant communions, in order to unite them in one body by the common confession of one faith', and went on to say that it was Cromwell's obvious intention to put himself at the head of a league which would wage a war of religion adverse to the interests of France. Further, there is a later story based on the recollections of one of Cromwell's secret agents — which probably belongs to 1656 — that at that time also the Protector had in mind the formation of an international council of Protestant states that would act as a counterblast to the Roman Catholic Council *de propaganda fide*. Finally, on the outbreak of the Swedo-Danish war Milton was instructed to write a letter to the King of Denmark deploring the dissensions between co-religionists and advocating a wide Protestant alliance.

In the opening speech which Cromwell was to make to his last Parliament he announced (ignoring the profitable friendship with Portugal), 'We have not [now] to do with any Popish state except France: and that they do not think themselves under such a tie to the Pope' as to violate their promises at his bidding. In fact up to the end of 1656 Cromwell actively concerned himself in all directions for a union of Protestant Christendom, and excused his alliances with Catholic states on the ground of some indirect benefit to that interest. The conception of a close Protestant union found a significant place among his political ideas, but clearly, as with the great Napoleon, there mingled in his mind among the strains of a grandiose political dreamer the common sense of the realist politician.

CHAPTER XI

THE HIGH CONSTABLE

§ 1

The domestic policy of the Protectorate does not bear the distinct stamp of Oliver's personality in anything like the same way as its foreign policy. On the whole he and his Council were content to carry out and strengthen the programme of the Long Parliament. In Scotland and Ireland, for example, their aim was to draw close the bonds with England. The Instrument of Government had foreshadowed the absorption of Scotland and Ireland and the centralization of the legislatures of the three nations at Westminster. There was, however, administrative decentralization at Edinburgh and Dublin. The provisions of the franchise were such that the representatives sent from Scotland and Ireland in 1654 were known supporters of the Government and these sixty seats have been compared to the eighteenth-century 'pocket boroughs' which were represented according to the wishes of the landlord. But as in England, so in Scotland and Ireland, Cromwell made a real if useless effort to transform the military into a civic sword. After the suppression of Middleton's Royalist invasion of Scotland General Monk and others tried to fulfil the objects of the Act of Union, which Cromwell promulgated in April on lines thought out by the Long Parliament, namely, to reconcile the Scots to an alien government by trading and other privileges. In Ireland, after Cromwell's son-in-law, Fleetwood, had made a determined effort to induce the native Irish to go to 'hell or Connaught' in order that English investors and soldiers might settle on the best lands, Cromwell decided to modify this outrageous policy by gently superseding Fleetwood in favour of his second son, Henry, who went over in April 1655 and remained the effective ruler of Ireland until after his father's death. But the profound hatreds roused both in Ireland and Scotland by Cromwell's invasions of 1649 and 1650 ensured that the time was unripe for a successful imperialism.

The upkeep of armies of occupation in Scotland and Ireland, the large police forces necessary in England, the huge navies employed in maintaining English prestige abroad combined to make Cromwell's budgets the heaviest England had ever known. Discontented Republicans and post-Restoration scribblers attributed the size of his expenditure to personal extravagance, but such an accusation does not bear examination. His main difficulty was, as he himself stated, that when he accepted the Protectorate all the 'extraordinary' methods of raising revenue practised by the Long Parliament had been exhausted. The sales of royal lands and property, Church lands and Irish lands had been completed and the proceeds spent. The Dutch war which had cost two and a half million pounds had exhausted all the special reserves at the disposal of the Government, and in 1653 Cromwell himself had offered to set an example of voluntary subscription by giving £6000 to the Exchequer. But now the country looked to him, as it does invariably when a peace-time Conservative Government is formed, to reduce taxation. Finally, although in modern terms it is true that the State was solvent when the Rump was dismissed there was outstanding a considerable amount of debt, including most of the loans that were raised during the opening stages of the civil war.

According to the Instrument of Government, Cromwell was empowered to levy taxes until Parliament met. A merchant named George Cony resisted the customs officers in the performance of their duties, and was brought before the High Court for his offence. With the assistance of three of the ablest members of the Bar he fought the case on the ground that Cromwell had no legal right to levy taxes without the consent of the people in Parliament assembled — the same accusation which had been made against James I and Charles I. In fact this case raised the whole question of the validity of the

Instrument, which since it had been presented to Cromwell merely by the Council of Army officers, had no legal basis in the usual sense of the term. To enforce the Government's case Cromwell was reduced to throwing the three lawyers into prison, somehow (it is not known how) persuading Cony privately to give way, and afterwards dismissing the Lord Chief Justice who tried the case. But this incident warned Cromwell of the danger of arbitrarily exercising his taxing power. Thenceforward he saw that all customs and excise ordinances were confirmed by parliamentary Act, and he reluctantly acquiesced in the reductions made in the amounts of the property taxes. A newsletter writer in February 1655 noted that in publishing an ordinance for three months' taxes, instead of an Act 'his Highness hath modestly denied to assume the Legislature of the Nation', and two years later Thurloe wrote to tell Henry Cromwell that an Act of Assessment had been passed by the Parliament and that to the vote had been added 'that in the act to be passed for this money, the right of the people should be asserted, viz. that no money was to be levied but by consent of Parliament'. In those days when much of the taxable wealth of the country took the form of rents, when knowledge of public finance was weak and communications were poor, it was virtually impossible to exact taxation without the willing consent of the landed gentry who were represented in Parliament.

With the tight control which public opinion exercised over the imposition of taxation, the annual deficits and the extra expenditure of the Spanish war, it was natural that the national debt accumulated and all treasury payments fell behindhand. The smaller lenders who had invested their savings in the national debt complained bitterly against the Government. A widespread conspiracy during 1654 to forge bills issued on 'the public faith' further debased their credit. The richer lenders were generally able to obtain some security by a process known as 'doubling', whereby a state creditor who was prepared to advance a sum equal to that already owed to him was given a mortgage on some form of national property. But the poorer lenders could not afford to do this and, just as in the Army the rates of pay had become comparatively high for the officers and low for the common soldiers, so too with the national creditors, there was a differentiation between the treatment meted out to the rich and poor. Cromwell was not responsible for this, as it was forced upon him by the general condition of indebtedness. The Navy — to a greater extent than the Army — was regularly in arrears with its pay, and contractors and pensioners of the Government had to make long and emphatic petitions before they could obtain a Treasury order for sums due to them, and then often the treasurers were in doubt as to where the money could come from.

How did this state of stringency arise? There was plenty of money in the country; there were many London merchants and country landlords who were exceptionally wealthy even by modern standards. The customs and excise revenues, taking into account the rates at which they were levied, indicated a steady level of prosperity. The real reasons for the financial difficulties of the Government were two: first that no satisfactory means was found for anticipating the revenue, and secondly that the credit of the Government was never thought sound. Cromwell's credit was only a life-credit. He was a rapidly ageing man after 1654, and not a very healthy man either. Moreover, fanatical Royalists were constantly plotting to assassinate him, and it was obvious that if a restoration occurred, the debts made in his name would be promptly repudiated. Thus it was not so much that there were no banking methods or bankers that could be used by Cromwell to lend him money, nor was the rate of interest at which he would have to borrow unduly high for those days — the legal rate after 1651 was six per cent — but simply that the stability of the Government was not such as would enable him to obtain long-term credits. One final consideration may be urged in this connection. The City of London lent no money to Cromwell as a corporation, although we know he harangued them on more than one occasion on the necessity for their patriotic support. But the difficulties experienced by the City Chamber in obtaining repayment of the loans it advanced to the parliamentary forces before the King's execution explain their reluctance to attempt the novel experiment of City-floated loans again so soon. Yet Paris had been accustomed for some years back to float loans for the Government, and the explanation of the City's unwillingness to help Cromwell may have been political. The City was never Republican and hated the Army. Possibly if he had become King his difficulties might have been eased.

The principal source from which expenditure on the Army itself was met was the 'monthly assessment'. This was in fact a land tax, although it also fell in some places — certainly in London — on other forms of property, and was a fixed amount payable each month to receivers-general set up under the supervision of local committees in the various counties and towns throughout the land. Cromwell was, until his Protectorate, a member of the assessment committee both at Ely and in Cambridgeshire. The administrative method for raising this tax was a compromise between that of ship money and forced loans, the two obnoxious taxes of Charles I's reign. It combined the most efficient methods of central and local taxation and proved so successful that even after all deductions were made for the costs of raising the tax, a regular average of over ninety per cent of the sum asked for by the Government reached the Army. The receivers-general paid their money either directly to the regiments concerned or to the Army treasurers at Whitehall. Their transactions were therefore not liable to the ordinary Exchequer control and audit. The novelty, efficiency and frequency of the assessments made them of course a prolific source of grievance with the propertied classes, a fact which Cromwell readily saw. Hence when he became Protector he at once reduced the rate from £120,000 to £90,000 a month, and decreased the size of the Army and lessened the pay of the common soldiers in order to do so; but this was not good enough for a Parliament of landed proprietors who, when they met under the Protector, further reduced the rate by £30,000 a month, a reduction accepted by Cromwell with marked reluctance, although one for which he afterwards claimed credit.

Together with the expansion of the standing Army the period of the civil wars witnessed a rapid expansion in the size of the national Navy. In earlier times the fund out of which the Navy was paid was the customs revenue, but since, even at high rates, it only raised some £300,000 a year net and the Navy cost from about £450,000 to £1,500,000 a year, this did not prove sufficient and another expedient was used by the Long Parliament to meet this expense, namely, the excise, a tax on home manufactures as well as an extra tax on foreign imports paid by the first buyer from the importer. A large percentage of its produce came from beer and it is therefore the father of the modern beer duty. Like the monthly assessment, it proved prolific, even more so than the customs, and out of it contributions were made to the Army as well as to the Navy. The Army and Navy on the one side and the assessments, customs and excise on the other comprised the main items on Cromwell's balance sheet; this may be illustrated by the position during the first year of his son's Protectorate when, according to the report presented to the House of Commons, out of £2,201,520, £1,346,706 was spent on the Army and £453,986 on the Navy, and out of a net revenue of £1,868,717 the assessments were £404,721, the customs £358,916 and the excise £556,491. The civil expenditure was very moderate, for out of the £250,000 odd which it cost on an average not only the upkeep of the Protectoral Court and the expenses of Thurloe's famous spy system were paid but all the costs of the administration of justice, of the home civil service and of the diplomatic service, as well as military hospitals and State pensions. The stories of Cromwellian extravagance were therefore the grossest exaggerations; but the Army clung to his back like the old man of the sea.

Of the smaller sources of revenue only two were at all novel. The first was that of prize money, obtained by capture of foreign ships during the naval war with Spain; but the only large sum which accrued to the Treasury from it was the £200,000 obtained by Blake's fleet which was sent back to Cadiz in 1656. The other was the tax on new buildings which was an ingenious fine introduced, when money was becoming very scarce, in 1657. Throughout the century complaints had been made of the rate at which the City of London was growing and the overcrowding which ensued — a complaint that has been heard throughout the last three hundred years. Political considerations supplemented these complaints, for a powerful capital city was believed to be a menace to absolute government. James I and Charles I had produced measures to check this growth, but had been forced to suspend them on account of the outcry raised in the City. Cromwell demanded a kind of capital levy of a year's rent from every house built since 1622 without four acres of land attached to it, and a prohibitive fine on any further houses so built after the date of the Act. Great expectations were held of the yield from this levy, like those raised by the captures of prize ships; £400,000 — about one-fifth of the annual budget — was the yield anticipated. But the actual result of the collection of the fines was only one-tenth of that amount, and Cromwell had to tell the Commons in 1658 that certain supplies 'had not come in as expected'.

The old and almost universal system of collecting taxes was by means of tax farmers, who paid an agreed sum in advance into the exchequer and in return were allowed to pocket all the proceeds from the taxes they collected at the fixed rates. During the Interregnum the monthly assessments, as we have seen, were levied directly by the Government. The excise, likewise a new tax, was also originally levied by Government commissioners with the assistance of customs officers and local collectors. Gradually the excise slipped back under Cromwell into the old-fashioned sectional farming method, which was believed, not without reason, to be more profitable than the commission system. The customs were, however, only partially farmed during this period.

On the establishment of the Protectorate Cromwell carried out a plan which had long been meditated, namely the restoration of the old exchequer system. On the outbreak of the civil war the Exchequer had been carried off by Charles to Oxford, and the parliamentary finances had been managed by innumerable committees each with separate treasuries, audits, officers and offices. Cromwell ordered that all these committees should wind up their accounts and pay their money and arrears to the exchequer 'tellers' at Westminster, and the whole of the old course was re-established except that English was substituted for Latin in the documents. Treasury commissioners were appointed at a salary of £1000 a year and they all quickly learned the ancient procedure. The treasury of the Army which contained the assessments significantly remained, however, outside Exchequer control. The existence of a special fund for the Army was indeed almost the only original part of Cromwell's financial administration. The assessments and excise had been invented or adapted by the Long Parliament and maintained by the Protector for want of anything better. Prize money was an Elizabethan expedient and building taxes were tried by the Stuarts. The restoration of the Royal Exchequer was typical of Cromwell's conservative methods. Only where the Army was concerned did he venture to depart from the usage of the past hundred years.

But no degree of reliance upon the novel expedients of the Long Parliament and no amount of conservatism in his Exchequer methods could conceal from Cromwell's financial advisers the fact that his idealistic but expensive schemes of foreign aggrandizement could only be realized by the willing concurrence of the City magnates and the country gentlemen. He was obliged, just as Charles I had been obliged, to summon Parliaments to find money. If he limited to that extent the scope of his military dictatorship it was not so much because he disapproved of dictatorial methods as because without money he could not depend upon the military.

§ 2

Cromwell does not seem to have taken much interest in the internal economic activities of the community. Nevertheless, he was himself a landlord and had married the daughter of a tradesman, while at Whitehall he was in constant touch with mercantile opinion. He therefore appreciated the importance both of agriculture and of industry. As Protector it was his function to protect the new class of landlords created by the revolution who had bought up real property on a falling market as either a business proposition or a means of acquiring social prestige. He was anxious that his officers and soldiers should be in a position peacefully to cultivate the estates won from their enemies in England and Ireland. He also sanctioned the draining of the Fens to which he had been opposed as a young man. But there is no parallel between the benevolent despotism of Charles I and his advisers and of Cromwell and his Council. Cromwell's officials consisted of a different class of property owners from those who had worked for the King. They were in fact the very men who had suffered at the hands of monarchical reformers. During the Interregnum the official resistance to the enclosure movement which injured the agricultural labourer and the smallholder by converting arable land into pasture gradually waned (except for one or two spasmodic efforts by the Major-Generals to enforce the anti-enclosure laws), and the whole tone of the controversy turned in favour of the enclosers. Richard Baxter was among the last to raise his voice against the consequences of what he thought a soulless movement injurious to the English peasantry. When in 1656 a Bill to prevent enclosures was introduced into the House of Commons the Master of the Rolls observed that 'he never liked any Bill that touched upon property', and it was duly rejected. The protective administrative machinery of Royalist governments was either weakened or swept away, and however much Cromwell may have sympathized with the rights of the commoners, he was unable to do anything to withstand the prevailing tendency.

In industrial matters Cromwell was on the whole content to let well alone. He did not, like the Levellers, have a theoretical objection to all forms of monopoly. He drew a distinguishing line between a 'desirable patent' like the Post Office (then of course in private hands) and other forms of exclusive trading. Sir Matthew Hale in pronouncing judgment on the incorporation of the Soapmakers' Company in the Court of Exchequer in 1656 made the same sort of distinction, which no doubt represented the official view during the Protectorate. He said that 'a grant of the sole making of playing cards to one man was a void grant because injurious to the public', but 'an incorporation consisting of many persons' using a trade and allowing other persons to come into it subject to apprenticeship was 'quite another' and justifiable thing. But even with regard to the individual monopolies there were exceptions and Cromwell acquiesced in the Government Printer enjoying an exclusive and highly profitable monopoly in the sale of Bibles.

There are few or no signs of any new Government interferences during the Protectorate with the internal organization of industry. The traditional forms of control which were in some cases temporarily relaxed during the confusion of the civil wars are to be discovered in full force when Cromwell was supreme. Medieval methods of fixing wages and attempting to fix prices, the enforcement of apprenticeship laws and the maintenance of certain standards of quality in manufactured goods — all these were pursued as before and indeed encouraged during the Protectorate.

Cromwell likewise did little to alter or modify the customary attitude to the poor and unemployed. To the Puritan idleness was a sin, and consequently the poor man was lacking in the highest forms of virtue. A preacher before the Lord Mayor and aldermen of London in 1655 remarked that 'A diamond in a dirty rag is a Diamond, but in a gilt ring it sparkles and is more illustrious. So grace in a poor man is grace, and 'tis beautiful, but grace in a rich man is more conspicuous, more useful.' Hence the medieval teaching, exemplified in the preambles to the 'sumptuary' laws, that the poor should be encouraged to be abstemious and not indulge in luxuries was well approved, and one writer of the period suggested that all persons should be compelled to dress according to their stations in life in order that 'we shall know how to give honour to whom honour is due'. An Act confirmed by the Protector in 1657 engraved these ideas on the statute book; it bore the title 'An act for punishing of such persons as live at high rates and have no visible estate, profession or calling answerable thereunto'. (This Act was enforced at Petty and Quarter Sessions.) In conformity with the theory that idleness was sinful the Cromwellian Parliament and officials did their utmost to ensure the fullest punishment for the able-bodied vagrant. Another Act of 1657 ordered that all idle, dissolute persons who were found wandering away from their abodes were to be treated as rogues and punished accordingly. During the Interregnum there were signs in many places throughout the country of an increasingly severe attitude to vagrancy. Cromwell's Major-Generals were especially active in rounding up beggars. Beyond the whip and the stocks the Government did not achieve any new way of dealing with the problem and it was left to private enterprises such as the London Poor Corporation to experiment in new methods. In some localities, however, the procedure of providing work for the able-bodied unemployed, as laid down in an Act of 1601, was still followed, a few work-houses were built and there were abortive Parliamentary discussions as to creating public works schemes. Cromwell detested idlers and ne'er-do-wells as heartily as did any of his fellow-Puritans. He had kept them out of his Model Army, but his only solution to the problem of unemployment appears to have been to relieve the burden on the parishes of maintaining the out-of-work by shipping them off, together with political prisoners and dissolute women, to lay the foundations of the British Empire in the West Indies. But on the whole, if we may judge by the high wage-rates, the increased size of the Army and Navy and the outcries against under-population, there were comparatively few unemployed under Cromwell, although such as there were probably shared in what a Radical historian has called the seventeenth-century 'perpetuation of the misery of the poor'.

In foreign commerce Cromwell seems generally to have supported the established companies against their 'interloping' rivals. He ratified the charters of the Merchant Adventurers, of the Greenland Whaling Company and of the East India Company, although circumstances forced him to allow some degree of encouragement to independent trading. He limited the import carrying trade to British ships by upholding the exclusive Navigation Act of 1651 despite the anxiety of the Dutch, the principal European shippers, to have it rescinded. In war-time he instituted a system of convoys for merchant vessels, and in peace-time he saw that the Mediterranean and Channel were cleared of pirates. The customs figures available for the Protectorate suggest that there was a considerable improvement in foreign trade owing to the economic and foreign policy of the Government.

Only in questions of law reform is there clear proof that Cromwell took a personal interest in domestic policy. After his breaking of the Little Parliament that had tried so hard to improve the administration of the law, by way of compensation Cromwell called together a number of his legal advisers and announced 'that the Government hath desired to reform the laws'. There was certainly no shortage of ideas available, but apart from an unwillingness of the established lawyers to co-operate with the Government the bulk both of the Government's and of Parliament's time was too occupied with repressive legislation against enemies of the regime to permit much progress to be made. Hence although in theory Cromwell was a conservative reformer and had the wisdom to see the stupidity of laws that 'hang for a trifle and acquit murder' in practice his ordinances and his behaviour tended to be despotic.

His conduct over the Cony case was typical. A new high treason ordinance was passed and a somewhat arbitrary High Court of Justice was erected in the first year of the Protectorate. The prerogative jurisdiction of the County Palatine was restored. It is true that a crude attempt was made in 1654 to reform the Court of Chancery, but the refusal of leading lawyers to help rendered it ineffective. Two military gentlemen were, however, invited to determine all cases on the same day that they were brought forward, an obvious impracticability, even for military gentlemen, and three years later Cromwell's Chancery reform was allowed to lapse. In 1654 also a series of ordinances were passed in a Puritan sense against cockfighting, duelling, drunkenness, swearing and horse-racing. Secular music, and smoking, however, had official approval. Finally, the Protector took a personal interest in higher education. He promulgated an ordinance in support of the Scottish universities and another dealing with university visitation, while, in the words of an eighteenth-century historian of the Puritan movement, 'if there was a man in England who excelled in any faculty or science, the Protector would find him out and reward him according to his merit'.

§ 3

During the twenty-one months that followed the dissolution of the first Protectorate Parliament the control of foreign and domestic policy was entirely in the hands of Cromwell and his Council, and in practice a complete dictatorship grew up. The counties were policed with soldiers and honeycombed with spies and stool-pigeons; judges were intimidated; juries were suppressed; newspapers were gagged; municipal corporations were 'purged'; suspected conspirators were imprisoned without trial. The justification for this Terror had been made by Cromwell in dismissing Parliament — internal peace must be bought at any price.

Naturally, now that a Government so reminiscent of Tudor monarchy at its most despotic had been set up, the Stuart partisans renewed their hopes of an imminent restoration and sighed for the death of Cromwell. Feverish activity radiated from the royal circle. As was ever the history in the Stuart movement, there were plots within plots; desperate men and cautious men, men who aimed first and foremost at the assassination of the Great Usurper, and men who worked steadfastly for a comprehensive insurrection. At the beginning of 1654 a new Royalist secret council known as the Sealed Knot had been established in London with Charles II's benediction. Its existence soon became known to the watchful Thurloe, but its membership was shrouded in a secrecy so deep that not even he was able to penetrate it. But he was always hopeful of completer knowledge. One by one Royalist plots had been revealed to, and nipped in the bud by, him or his agents. A succession of two-faced spies communicated information to both sides, selling the truth and falsehood inextricably mixed. In the circumstances it is remarkable how many of the Royalist schemes awoke into the realm of action.

But Cromwell had created many of his own difficulties. The dictatorship drove the Levellers and other advocates of democratic and representative government straight into the arms of his enemies, who were prepared to promise all things to all parties. On January 10th, 1655, Colonel Overton, whose Leveller opinions were notorious, was arrested in Scotland on a charge of mutiny and was thrown into prison without a trial, and a month later Major John Wildman was caught in the act of dictating a 'Declaration of the free and well-affected people of England, now in arms against the tyrant Oliver Cromwell'. About the same time a letter written by Charles II to the Sealed Knot was intercepted and the Protector was therefore not afraid to present himself to the City and give them details of a 'new intended war'. Officers were ordered to their posts, the guards around the City tripled, many leading Royalists were arrested in the counties, horse-races were prohibited for six months and a new militia ordinance drafted to be put into immediate effect.

The exiled Royalists — not the Sealed Knot, who knew exactly what the Government was doing — remained sanguine. At the end of February, although orders had been given to secure the ports, the Earl of Rochester with other conspirators had got into the country, apparently with the connivance of customs officers, and despite warnings that the movement was inopportune, made preparations with the full authority and encouragement of Charles II for an immediate rising. The reason for this persistence has been a subject of controversy among historians. One side has maintained that since Charles II had sanctioned the rising against the advice of the Sealed Knot the faithful Cavaliers had no alternative but to obey. The other side has suggested that the insurrection was incited by *agents provocateurs* of the Government in order to give Oliver an excuse for tightening up his dictatorship. The weight of available evidence leans to the first view, although it is to be noted that both the French and the Venetian ambassadors believed Cromwell fully capable of adopting the second course and, as Guizot wrote, 'whether from accident or design Cromwell took no effective means to prevent the insurrection'. Nor did the Government afterwards hesitate in the interests of military despotism to exploit the rising to its uttermost extent.

On March 11th the only serious outbreak, under Colonel John Penruddock, a Wiltshire Royalist who succeeded in seizing Salisbury, was crushed. Elsewhere the Royalist military efforts were negligible. Cromwell's victory was easy and complete. At first the affair was made light of officially. It was thought unwise to lend weight to the notion that dissatisfaction against the Government was at all widespread. Later, however, a different plan was followed. The rising was described as 'a bold and dangerous insurrection' and was made the excuse for the introduction of a system of military government under eleven Major-Generals.

The establishment of the Major-Generals is best described first in Cromwell's own words:

When the Insurrection was, and we saw it in all the roots and grounds of it, we did find out a little, poor Invention. . . . I say, there was a little thing invented, which was . . . the erecting of your Major-Generals. To have a little inspection upon the People thus divided, thus discontented, thus dissatisfied. . . . And upon such a Rising as that was, — truly I think if ever anything was justifiable as to Necessity and honest in every respect, this was. And I could as soon venture my life with it as anything I ever undertook!

The vehemence of their defence and the minimizing of their importance are an index to the new institution's unpopularity. The English people have never acquiesced gladly in being dragooned in time of peace. And the Major-Generals dragooned with a vengeance. Their duties were the strict enforcement of the Puritan and anti-Royalist penal code. They were instructed not only to suppress all unlawful assemblies and disarm all 'Royalists and Papists', but to round up highwaymen, to eject 'scandalous ministers', to permit no horse-races, cockfights, idling, profanity, drunkenness, blasphemy or ungodliness. In effect, they replaced the old Lords-Lieutenant and partially superseded the local Justices of the Peace, who were accused of slackness in their work. They were ordered to keep a close watch on all inns and taverns. Generally, as Cromwell expressed it, they were to promote virtue and discourage vice. To pay for the militia who were to carry out their orders the Major-Generals were permitted to exact a special ten per cent property tax, known as the 'decimation', over and above the ordinary taxes on all those who at any time had supported the Royalist side.

It is not perhaps too much to say that the primary object of the system of Major-Generals was fiscal. Cromwell had been forced by the landowning classes to agree to a scaling down of taxation at the expense of a reduced Army establishment. His hopes of relieving his embarrassed finances by a capture of

Spanish treasure were blasted by the summer of 1655. So the Protector ventured on his one original financial experiment. The scheme of imposing a special tax on Royalists (although it contravened the Act of Indemnity) to pay for the police that their plotting rendered necessary had a superficial fairness that at first disarmed the middle-class supporters of the Government. This satisfaction did not endure. The system of Major-Generals was seventeenth-century dictatorship at its zenith, comparable with the centralized administration of contemporary France. It had no possible legal justification and its minute interferences with private lives were a complete exposure of the failure of the Protectorate to win the spontaneous loyalty of the people. To Cromwell himself the system seemed morally and politically defensible especially after the enforced reduction of his army, because it appeared to be the only practical method of keeping order and the best insurance against the gnawing fear of a Stuart Restoration. The conception that dominated his mind in these years was that he was the old local police constable writ large and projected upon a national screen: 'I am as a constable', he told a Fifth Monarchy preacher in February 1655, 'to part the godly of several judgments and keep them in peace'. 'I was forced', he said again later, 'to take upon me the office of High Constable'; and in a speech of 1657 he confessed frankly:

For truly I have as before God thought it often that I could not tell what my business was, nor what I was in the place I stood in save comparing myself to a good Constable to keep the peace of the Parish.

But he made himself an unpopular constable. If it is true that in 1655 the average English citizen was neither a partisan of Cromwell nor of Charles II, the activities of the Major-Generals were precisely calculated to alienate him permanently from Cromwell. The encouragement the system gave to some of the local gentry to lord it over others of the local gentry and the fears and hates that were engendered by local spies and by the opening of private letters can all be discerned even to-day in much of the correspondence of the period which survives. Outside the personal rancours of the inmates of country houses the closing of inns, the banning of horse-races and the shutting down of the sporting centres of the times, although these measures might please some Puritans, could scarcely do other than offend the ordinary villager who was neither Calvinist nor Catholic, neither Cromwellian nor Cavalier. Again, the imposition of the discriminatory tax against Royalists, many of them harmless and law-abiding people, was to recreate the divisions in the civil war which, if Oliver could have fully realized the despairing feelings of his opponents, it should have been his one object to consign to oblivion. His conviction that the maintenance of order was an unanswerable justification for his measures — however much it may have appealed to the orderly instincts of later historians — was hardly likely to be shared by more than a minority of his contemporaries who suffered from the well-meaning and therefore irritating dragooning of the Major-Generals.

Cromwell's brother-in-law, John Desborough, had been created Major-General of the six south-western counties in May 1655, the only area where the Royalist rising had been at all dangerous. On July 26th the new Army establishment with fewer numbers and lower pay was confirmed by the Protector. In August ten other Major-Generals like Desborough were set up to cover the whole of England. In September all newspapers except a dull official organ were suppressed. In October the Government published a proclamation in defence of the system, to which the Royalist Hyde replied with a stirring defence of liberty: 'If you have reason to believe that we have evil intentions against the Government, we are without any right or title to anything we enjoy, and are at your mercy to dispose of as you please — which is the lowest condition of traitors. If this be liberty, what nation in Europe is in servitude?' In 1656, however, this system was continued and indeed extended. In January Oliver wrote to Desborough to be careful to pack juries who would give verdicts favourable to the Government. It was in fact notorious that London juries would not give verdicts in the sense required of them. Moreover, in March Cromwell was obliged to make a two hours' speech to the Lord Mayor and the City Council in defence of the Major-Generals and asserting that the City was becoming a refuge for loose and vagrant persons who fled from the counties through fear of the wrath of these godly soldiers.

But London, long nurtured in a tradition of self-government, did not take willingly to the overriding powers conferred on the goldsmith who was now created their Major-General. There was, furthermore, a considerable volume of discontent among the rich City exporters at the embargo imposed by the King of Spain on English trade. Of all our foreign trade at this time the Spanish was the most valuable, and merchants besought the Protector not to insist on 'liberty of conscience' for their agents. They could do quite a profitable business without it. But since the failure at Hispaniola Oliver had turned his face more relentlessly than ever against Spain. He was nevertheless aware that his policy was unpopular in many quarters. At the same time the decimations had failed to rescue the Exchequer from its embarrassments. Indeed, they had not even met the cost of the new militia which had to be supplemented out of central funds. Without additional taxation, which he dare not increase on his own responsibility, an enormous debt loomed in front of him. The lack of money to pay the militia and the existence of outstanding debts still owing to the Regular Army provoked a considerable outcry among the soldiers. On one occasion a number of troopers in their desperation invaded the Whitehall kitchen and carried off the Protector's dinner. There were some officers who openly demanded that a man 'who was not involved in affairs' should be put at the head of the Army. According to the not very well-informed secretary to the Venetian embassy there was in June a rumour that Cromwell was thinking of appointing his son-in-law Fleetwood as General. But he would not have

Lambert, the Army favourite, at any price. Nor would he entertain the suggestions urged upon him for doubling the assessments or for forced loans, which proposals, it was believed, 'might easily lead to a disturbance'. The only solution left to him was to call Parliament, explain to it the grounds of the Spanish war and appeal to it for financial assistance. Instructions were therefore sent to the Major-Generals to set a general election in motion and to procure members of Parliament who would be sympathetic to the Government's point of view.

The decision to summon a new Parliament was announced on June 26th, 1656. Cromwell had only agreed to this course with the gravest misgivings. He was quite content to continue the repressive rule of his godly agents and to extend the special taxes on Royalists to everybody to pay for the war. But both his military and civilian advisers resisted him and after prolonged consultations he yielded. The Major-Generals therefore exerted themselves to pack Parliament. They assured the electors that the contest was between 'honest' party and the rest — presumably the dishonest parties. If the Government candidates were not returned, they asserted, a new war was bound to arise. By 'such arts' they strove — but with incomplete success — to do their master's will.

One method employed to try and obtain a favourable Parliament was to interfere with borough charters. Early in 1656 a Committee for Municipal Charters was established and the Major-Generals exerted their influence in parts of the country whose loyalty to Cromwell was in doubt to induce the minority to seek new charters. Where in a town there was a minority well-affected to the Government the Major-Generals, 'by indicating to the traders of a district or town the advantages likely to accrue from the acquisition of privileges from the Protector or even, it may be, by coercion in some localities', often engineered an application for a new municipal charter. By obtaining the surrender of the charter it was possible for Cromwell to adjust the terms of local government so that they benefited the party in the town which supported him. The tendency was for boroughs to become less democratic. Broadly such Cromwellian charters as survive, in so far as they contained the customary reaffirmation of rights of monopoly and trade regulation, are a testimony to the conservative character of his influence on local government.

The opposition to Cromwell in the boroughs and counties was not directed, at any rate openly, by the Royalists. The old oligarchical Republicans, led by men like Sir Henry Vane and Colonel Edmund Ludlow, were active in anti-Cromwellian propaganda. The Levellers also tried to awaken democratic yearnings. A certain Venner wrote an able pamphlet called 'England's Remembrancers' by means of which he hoped to unite the interests of all the elements of the opposition. This was a general attack on the Government's policy: offence, it was realized, was better at election time than constructive ideas. It claimed that the national treasure had been wasted, trade endangered and liberty menaced. The tears of widows and orphans were said to bedew the ground.

Cromwell bestirred himself to conciliate or muzzle his enemies. In August he sent for his old friend, Sir Henry Vane, and asked him if he had written an anti-Government pamphlet called 'The Healing Question'. Vane admitted he had, but refused to give security for his good conduct. He was therefore clapped into Carisbrooke Castle whence Charles I had been brought to his death. Later Cromwell sent for Ludlow. 'What I do', he told him, 'proceeds not from any motion of fear, but from a timely prudence to foresee and prevent danger.' 'What do you want?' he asked. 'That which we fought for,' replied the stern Republican, 'that the nation might be governed by its own consent.' 'But where shall we find that consent,' asked Cromwell, 'among the Church of England Royalists, perhaps?' At which Ludlow was forced to admit that it could only be found among the 'honest' party. And honesty is a question of definition; Ludlow was no democrat. The interview ended with Cromwell commending his own rule and boasting of the protection and quiet the people enjoyed. He was resolved, he said, 'to keep the nation from being imbrued with blood. . . . In respect to my outward condition [foreign policy],' he concluded, 'have I not much improved it? — as these gentlemen [and he turned to his Council] well know.' Ludlow was then ordered to leave Town.

In spite of all precautions a large number of members who were known enemies of the Protector were returned. A few days before he met Parliament Cromwell called the officers of the Army to him and explaining to them how Charles II, with Spanish and Popish auxiliaries, was waiting to fall on England as soon as signs of national disunity were discernible, begged them to stand behind him. He then prepared to meet his Parliament. On September 17th he went in half-military pageant to the Abbey where four hundred members were gathered. John Owen, the founder of the existing State Church, preached the sermon from a suitable text in Isaiah: 'What shall one answer to the Messengers of the Nation? That the Lord hath found Zion, and the Poor of His people shall trust in it.'

Before we study the last phase of Cromwell's life, we shall turn aside to consider Owen's State Church and Cromwell's theory of religious toleration, which is so much the most valuable of his political ideas as to deserve a chapter to itself.

CHAPTER XII

LIBERTY OF CONSCIENCE

§ I

THE seventeenth century was an age in which there emerged a theory of religious toleration advocated not merely as an expedient or as an ideal of obscure pamphleteers but on the basis of justice and of reason; its practice was recommended by the philosophers Descartes, Leibnitz, Locke and Bayle, and in England the first Toleration Act, although a very incomplete one, found its way into the statute book in 1689. This Act heralded an age of reasonableness and lack of enthusiasm in matters of religion, for it was not until the later years of the seventeenth century that the fires of religious fervour began to burn less fiercely; the Huguenot persecution in France in the sixteen-eighties and the stringent penal code enforced against Nonconformists in England are two indications of this fact. Hence, if Oliver Cromwell was the protagonist of 'liberty of conscience' in the fourth decade of the century, the reason is clear why that has been generally considered the most original, advanced and striking of his political ideas. What is perhaps even more remarkable than this early advocacy of a doctrine which had already appeared in the writings of political philosophers and of some advanced theological writers, is that it should have been put into practice by a man who was himself deeply imbued with the Puritan spirit which neither in its nature nor its manifestations had shown itself particularly tolerant.

It has been said of the Middle Ages that from the point of view of political theory the Church was then the State. The followers of John Calvin, who in many ways were essentially medieval in their political thought, were most anxious that the complete subordination of the State to the Church should continue, save that in place of the doctrinal teaching and hierarchical organization of the Roman Catholic Church they wished to substitute their own. This programme had been successfully carried out in Geneva under Calvin himself and in Scotland under John Knox, and nothing was farther from the mind of the average Calvinist than the toleration of religions other than his own. At the opening of the English civil wars he hoped to impose the Presbyterian organization of religion in its completest form on England, and it is well known that in bidding for Scottish assistance the parliamentary party promised, and later the King half-promised, that this should be done, while in the years 1646-7 beginnings were actually made, by the election of 'elders' and the formation of 'classes' in various parts of the country, to organize a Presbyterian system to supersede the old English episcopacy.

The Westminster Assembly of divines which had been given the task in 1643 of working out a new religious system for England soon found difficulties in the way of any completely symmetrical plan. For they discovered an opinion was gathering strength that individual Christian congregations, so far from being subjected to an elaborate central control, ought to be left completely free to manage their own affairs. This view of the 'Independents' or 'Congregationalists' had found negligible support in Parliament but was represented most strongly in the Army and especially in the regiments raised by Cromwell in the Eastern counties. On September 6th, 1644, Cromwell wrote from Lincolnshire to London emphasizing the fact that the Army were not fighting to maintain their opinions in religion by force, and on his return to London he procured an appointment of a committee

to take into consideration the differences in opinion of the members of the Assembly of Divines in point of Church government, and to endeavour a union if it be possible; and in case that cannot be done, to endeavour the finding out some way, how far tender consciences, who cannot in all things submit to the common rule which shall be established, may be borne with according to the Word, and as may stand with the public peace.

This order has been quoted at length because it summarizes very exactly the character of Cromwell's theory of toleration, its basis and its limitations, and also because it marked the divergence between the opinions of Cromwell and those of the then prevailing Puritan party. Writing of this order the Presbyterian, Baillie, remarked: 'The great shot of Cromwell and Vane is to have a liberty for all religions without any exceptions. Many a time we are put to great trouble of mind: we must make the best of an ill game we can . . . God help us.'

How is this order an adequate summary of Cromwell's theory of toleration? Cromwell favoured liberty of conscience for two principal reasons. Firstly, because he had a genuine belief that the persecution of those who differed minutely from himself on religious questions was contrary to the true spirit of Christianity and that they should be 'borne with according to the Word', and secondly, because he saw that if a new political regime were to be established in England in affirmation of what was in fact, however much the fact might be disguised in the language of law and precedent, a constitutional revolution, that regime could thrive only by means of the maximum of unanimity among the citizens, which could never be achieved if one sect were allowed to persecute another. It would be absurd to try and judge on the basis of documentary evidence which consideration was foremost in Cromwell's mind. Some would say that the factor of personal ambition was determinate, and that the knowledge that he himself was destined to be a leader in any new political order was the motive power in forcing upon his mind the necessity for toleration. Others would point out that his actions, long before there was any likelihood of royalty being overthrown, suffice to show that political expediency played a very minor part in the question. He himself affirmed in 1655 that while he had not at first thought that religious liberty was the cause of the civil wars,

God had at length shown him that the real issue was that 'all species of Protestants' might obtain liberty 'to worship God according to their own light and consciences', for want of which liberty the Puritan Fathers had been forced to flee to the 'howling wilderness of New England'. The problem is nicely balanced, but as Horace Walpole suggested somewhere, it is a matter of temperament whether we choose to attribute a man's actions to motives which we deem ourselves to be 'higher' or 'lower' in nature. It will be sufficient to try to analyse a little further and to fit together the two grounds which Cromwell gave for his belief in the practice of liberty of conscience.

It would be foolish to imagine that the idea of religious toleration was a sudden intellectual discovery of Cromwell's and that there were no Englishmen ready to advocate it before him. The comprehensive researches of Dr. W. K. Jordan of Harvard University have indeed unearthed an extremely impressive list of names of men who in one degree or another wrote in favour of toleration during the reigns of Queen Elizabeth, of James I and of Charles I. But even so Dr. Jordan admits that these were strange gusts of wind in the normal religious atmosphere before the civil wars. 'Toleration was not possible in England,' he writes, 'so long as the various religious parties were growing more rigid and more hostile to each other and, in particular, so long as the extreme groups laid claim to an exclusive truth. Toleration had little to expect from the Puritans and even less from the Anglo-Catholics.' But these two latter parties were the main religious protagonists when the Long Parliament met. Nevertheless, there were in each party some men whose thoughts, or one aspect of whose thoughts, were directed towards the development of toleration. Even Archbishop Laud was in theory anxious to find a comprehensive basis of doctrinal truth, nor should one forget that his party alone adhered to the doctrine of free will which surely implies the right to make a choice. (Some of the great Arminians, the Dutch believers in free will, with whom Laud's followers were commonly confounded, were the most outspoken advocates of toleration.)

On the contrary the Puritans — including Cromwell — who maintained that some were predestined to be saved and others to be damned had to confess in the last resort that only the chosen few had the right to lay down the law both in State and Church. For them to permit Christians outside the fold to teach and preach without impediment would have been a radical departure from the orthodox point of view. Some Puritans, however, notably Leonard Busher a Baptist, were convinced that if only complete freedom of thought were allowed to prevail truth would be certain to triumph and God's own people find their appointed level.

It was natural enough that advocates of liberty of conscience should be more numerous among the smaller groups who had less hopes of becoming the ruling power in the State. Many of the seventeenth-century pleas for toleration were not based upon solid philosophical premises but upon the desires of a particular sect that it should not suffer persecution by the Government of the day. But there were a few men, especially among the Independents, who stuck firmly to the idea as good in itself. Robert Browne's *Life and Manner of all true Christians* is indeed said by some to be the earliest book in English to suggest a full measure of religious liberty; but Dr. Jordan points out that on the whole the Congregationalists did not make a great contribution towards the doctrine of religious toleration as a 'positive virtue' as distinct from a 'protective cloak for the development of their own faith'. In so far as Cromwell derived any of his ideas on this question from the Independents we may assume it was his intolerant attitude to the Anglicans, which this party displayed in a marked degree, rather than his tolerant attitude to the rival sects.

But quite apart from the Puritans, Anglo-Catholics, moderate churchmen and relatively uninfluential thinkers like Sir Thomas Browne and John Selden, it is not always sufficiently recalled that throughout the seventeenth century and almost from the Elizabethan reformation of the English Church there had been a small but influential section of rigidly orthodox thinkers who, perceiving the subversive character of the Puritan movement, had argued that the Church of England should attempt to reconcile the ideal of comprehension with the existing diversity of views by means of tolerance and a narrowing of the number of its fundamental dogmas. These thinkers were not named 'latitudinarians' till after the Restoration but in the writings of William Chillingworth, John Hales and Jeremy Taylor they appear well before the outbreak of the civil war. These three taught that everything 'fundamental', that is, necessary to salvation, could be found by the instrument of reason in the inspired scriptures: and if men sought honestly after these fundamental truths, when they erred they were not damned. The Church of England should embrace all those who loved their neighbour, strove to understand God's will and accepted Christ and the creed: 'it is the unity of the Spirit in the bond of peace, and not identity of conceit which the Holy Ghost requires at the hands of Christians'. During the Interregnum and the years immediately preceding it there grew up at Cambridge a school of divines which attempted to formulate this latitudinarian teaching on a more philosophical basis. We have definite proof of Cromwell's knowledge of and connection with this Cambridge group. One of its members, John Worthington, was made Vice-Chancellor of the University by him as Lord Protector; another, Ralph Cudworth, Fellow of Christ's, frequently communicated with Cromwell and was consulted by him on preferments; a third, John Wilkins, originally Warden of Wadham College, Oxford, but later Master of Trinity, Cambridge, in 1656 married Robina Cromwell as his second wife and thus became Oliver's brother-in-law. (Cromwell granted Wilkins a dispensation to continue his Wardenship though it was not supposed to be held by a married man.) This group of latitudinarians, generally though not accurately called the Cambridge Platonists, differed to some extent in their writings and preaching (Wilkins, for example, had affinities with the Puritans), but apart from the mathematical methods and pseudoplatonic approach in their works, which did not perhaps simplify their views, they had in common a belief in a kind of Christianity, similar to that taught earlier by Chillingworth and his fellows, insisting on the primary importance of the moral life; their aim was to introduce a moral and rational Christianity which could comprehend all within its scheme: 'In Christ Jesus neither circumcision nor uncircumcision availeth anything, but the keeping of the commandments of God.' During the Interregnum the Cambridge school of Christian philosophers was content to concentrate on the purely theoretical side of its teaching, but both before and after it urged that the solution to the political problem raised by the increasing number of Puritans was to tolerate and treat as fellow-Christians all those who lived righteously and accepted Christ and the creed. They shared this view with such lay thinkers as Sir Francis Bacon and Sir Thomas Browne, and with a great poet, John Donne. We have only to read one passage out of several similar passages in Cromwell's speeches to observe how closely he agreed with them:

That men that believe in Jesus Christ — that's the form that gives the being to true religion, faith in Christ and walking in a profession answerable to that faith. . . . Whoever hath this faith, let his form be what it will; he walking peaceably, without the prejudicing of others under another form: — it is a debt due to God and Christ; and He will require it, if he [that Christian] may not enjoy this liberty.

Thomas Carlyle summed up Cromwell's attitude as one of 'liberty in non-essentials'.

Beyond Oliver Cromwell's connections and affinities with the latitudinarians we have proof of his patronage of three other men who in their various ways were believers in toleration. The Reverend John Dury, the son of a Scottish minister, was educated at Sedan, Leyden and Oxford and for a time was minister to the Leyden company in Prussia. His cosmopolitan experience convinced him of the wrongfulness of Protestant disunity and he devoted his life to trying to effect a conciliation between the followers of John Calvin and of Martin Luther. He enlisted among others the support of King Gustavus Adolphus of Sweden and during the Protectorate he laboured in the Netherlands and in Switzerland to that end. In 1654 he succeeded in interesting Cromwell in his plans, which were in tune with Cromwell's more militaristic schemes for Protestant unity, and a correspondence which exists among Thurloe's papers bears witness to the hopes he held of the Protector's encouragement and support. The second man whose tolerant views received some measure of recognition during the Protectorate was the poet George Wither. Wither condemned as factious and self-interested the division of England into innumerable sects. He urged that the clergy would only do their true work of preaching faith, repentance and charity and the good life if they

> From bitter words and sharp invective cease;
> Invoke for grace and then provoke to peace;
> From all your pulpits banning partaking
> In factions . . .

Whereas during the reigns of James I and Charles II he was cast into prison, under the Protectorate Wither was given a minor clerkship. Thirdly there was Nathaniel Fiennes, the lawyer whose pamphlet on the battle of Edgehill shed such obscure light upon Cromwell's own part in the fight. Fiennes was a moderate Calvinist but he also was an Erastian, that is to say he believed the State should rule the Church, unlike the Presbyterians who thought that the Church should rule the State. The Government, he believed, should 'clip the wings' of the clergy, itself order the administration of Church affairs and limit narrowly the meaning of heresy. Nathaniel Fiennes was a member of Cromwell's Council of State and Commissioner of the Great Seal, and we shall see that because of Cromwell's receptiveness to the idea of broad fundamentals of belief he also supported the organization of the Church by State committees which determined the reliability of ministers, and thereby the Protector put into practice, at least in part, the views of his political associate.

When we turn from studying Cromwell's relations with advanced thinkers to see how far political expediency affected his attitude to the Churches and sects we come to the limits of his toleration. On September 17th, 1656, in an earlier part of the speech in which he described the basis of true religion Cromwell explained the policy of the Protectorate on the question of these limits:

I will tell you the truth: Our practice since the last Parliament hath been — To let all this nation see that whatever pretensions to religion would continue quiet and peaceable, they should enjoy conscience and liberty to themselves and not make their religion a pretence for arms and blood, truly we have suffered them, and that cheerfully, so to enjoy their liberties. Whatsoever is contrary, let the pretence be never so specious, — if it tend to combination, to interests and factions, we shall not care, by the grace of God, whom we meet withal, though never so specious, though never so quiet! And truly I am against all liberty of conscience repugnant to this.

Cromwell is here arguing that if a citizen does not disturb the public peace or plot against the Government he shall be allowed a full measure of liberty to practise his own form of Christianity. But it was the duty of the magistrate, he said in 1654, to make sure that liberty of conscience was not abused for 'the patronizing of villains'. Earlier at the beginning of his public career Cromwell put this argument in a rather different way: he said that if a man be prepared actively to serve the Government then no religious peccadilloes must be allowed to intervene. 'Sir,' he sternly informed an inferior officer, 'the State, in choosing men to serve them, takes no notice of their opinions, if they be willing faithfully to serve them, that satisfies.' In this policy of tolerating all Christians who did not act as enemies to his Government and of enlisting them in its service, Cromwell was following quite naturally the example set by Cardinal Richelieu in France and not finally abandoned by the French

Government till 1685. But how are we to reconcile this comparatively wide toleration with the belief that only a certain number are chosen of God from the beginning of time to be His children, to obey His will on earth and to attain to a life of eternal felicity afterwards? The explanation lies probably in the growth of the Erastian movement which was always implicit in Independency. As the Independents wished to rule their religious life in perfect freedom from outside interference in their individual congregations, equally they were prepared to leave the determination of matters of purely secular concernment in the hands of the Government. The Presbyterian also when he found that he was not after all to dominate the new Government acquiesced reluctantly in the existence of other religious organizations besides his own, and looked forward to the ultimate restoration of the monarchy when he hoped to have a controlling voice in secular administration once again. There was also a secular party among the politicians of the day, men like Henry Marten and Algernon Sidney, who accepted John Selden's teaching on the subjection of the Church to the State and were glad to support a policy which persecuted only, as did Queen Elizabeth, for reasons of State.

It is difficult to say whether the principal reason for the exception of Roman Catholics from Cromwell's theory of toleration was political or religious in character. Puritanism is of course at the opposite end of the Christian religion scale of values from Roman Catholicism, and what appeared to the Puritans to be the extremely superstitious use of the sacraments by the Roman Catholics was undoubtedly particularly offensive to Cromwell. In Thomas Gage's book on his travels in the New World, which was one of the few books besides the Bible that Cromwell read, we can see the extraordinary virulence and contempt the converted Protestant poured upon the delusive sacramental practices of the followers of the Pope. Moreover, one may recall that Dr. Thomas Beard, Oliver's old schoolmaster, had taken some trouble to prove in 1625 the identity of the Pope with Antichrist. The Mass was of course the central feature of Catholic worship, and we seem to read a hatred of superstition rather than any political reason into Cromwell's famous utterance to the Governor of Ross, (October 1649):

For what you mention concerning liberty of conscience, I meddle not with any man's conscience. But if by liberty of conscience you mean a liberty to exercise the Mass, I judge it best to use plain dealing, and to let you know, where the Parliament of England have power, that will be not allowed of.

So he told the confederate Irish (a part of Antichrist he named these) who that very same year had been offered by the Marquess of Ormond on behalf of Charles I peace terms which promised complete toleration for their religion and freedom for their parliament.

But although Cromwell was utterly opposed to the Roman Catholic religion, one may still argue that his exclusion of its adherents from his scheme of toleration was mainly determined by what he thought reasons of State. He had been led to believe, and with full justification, that large numbers of Roman Catholics had fought in the armies and had opposed the parliamentary forces in England. It was always recognized that the priests were the political leaders of the Irish and it was no doubt true, as Cromwell declared at Kilkenny, that the English had invariably treated the practice of Roman Catholicism as subversive to law and order. Moreover, like John Pym in the reign of Charles I but with far better reason, he felt that the English Catholics bore among them the seeds of sedition. The bulk of them had been Cavaliers; they had good cause to show gratitude to the early Stuarts; and it was certain that they would be among the first to join any hopeful plots towards a Stuart restoration. Again, Cromwell knew that some of the leading supporters of Charles I, of whom Laud was the most famous, were Anglo-Catholics, but he may well have been unable to distinguish, as throughout the last three hundred years a great many well-meaning people have been unable to distinguish, between English and Roman Catholics. Finally, it may be remembered that the large number of Protestants whom Queen Mary I had burnt in the last three years of her reign stamped an ineradicable memory into the English religious tradition and it was always felt that if the exponents of that religion were once allowed a foothold upon the State all the dangers of the Spanish Inquisition might be brought in with them. If the English in 1654 themselves adopted the methods of the Inquisition and put to death a Roman Catholic priest for no other reason than because he was a priest there is good reason to believe that it was against Cromwell's wishes. And although he ordered the hanging of Irish priests in 1650, probably the fact that they were attached to the enemies' army was a real justification. But to the Irish generally he was less intolerant, provided of course that they did not practise the Mass and kept their opinions to themselves:

'As for the people [said Cromwell at Kilkenny] what thoughts they have in matters of religion in their own breasts I cannot reach; but think it my duty, if they walk honestly and peaceably, not to cause them in the least to suffer for the same, but shall endeavour to walk patiently and in love towards them, to see if at any time it shall please God to give them another or a better mind.'

In September 1656 the French ambassador was able to report from London that 'even the Catholics find their position better than under the recent kings who dared not allow them such a free exercise of their religion'. He went on to point out that it was useless for foreign Powers to intercede with the Protector because the Government was obliged to profess an enmity towards the Roman Church. But professions apart, non-political Catholics had no complaints sufficient to justify their seeking outside support and they were not ungrateful to Cromwell. The Parliament of 1656, it is true, revived the old Elizabethan laws against the Catholics in a more stringent form, but the Protector wrote to Cardinal Mazarin to assure him that although he could not guarantee toleration 'at this juncture of time and as my affairs now stand', his Government would continue to show as much leniency as it dared to members of the Catholic Church. Undoubtedly English public opinion would no more have tolerated open Catholic worship under Cromwell than it was to do under Charles II. At least neither in England nor in Ireland were the Roman Catholics fined for not attending Protestant Churches as they were to be under Charles II.

Another exception to Oliver's rule of toleration for Christians was the Society of Friends, nicknamed the Quakers, and their case is probably the best example of the 'political' character of Cromwell's practice on this question. The famous interview between George Fox, the founder of the sect, and the Lord Protector in 1655, when Cromwell listened with deep interest to what Fox had to say makes it clear that, although there was some kind of an attempt to prosecute them under the Blasphemy Act of 1650, it was not really the religious opinions of the Quakers which were offensive to him. It might, however, be asked with reason how a sect which preached passive resistance and abhorred the 'carnal sword' could be deemed dangerous to the State. Surely the refusal of Quakers to doff their hats to magistrates was not the cause of their numerous imprisonments? Surely their objection to taking oaths was an equally trivial affair? The explanation of Cromwell's fear of the Quakers is to be found in a number of converging lines of thought. Firstly it must be remembered that passive resistance is not identical with non-resistance. The doctrine of the 'inner light', the cardinal fact in the Quaker teaching, did not permit toleration of other people's worship; and if in the course of a religious meeting a Quaker was seized with the command to prophesy he did not hesitate to interrupt and to create riot and confusion. We know that hundreds of meetings were interrupted in this way, including two at Canterbury and York, the citadels of State religion. Secondly, some confusion may well have existed in the Protector's mind between the followers of Fox and the revolutionary sect of Levellers led by John Lilburne, who did not altogether disdain the use of the carnal sword. Lilburne declared himself a Quaker before he died in prison and we know of the existence of a sect of 'fighting' Quakers and other sects called by the same name, which was probably used of all those who actually went through a physical act of quaking in the course of conversion, and these may well have rendered the passive resisters suspect. The refusal to take oaths confirmed suspicions of seditious conduct, while the unfortunate incident which occurred at Bristol in 1656 when James Naylor, a Quaker, his head turned by an excess of popularity and by the enthusiasm of a small group of women, imagined himself to be Christ, directed public opinion violently against the sect, and in this year some hundred and twenty Quakers were imprisoned. Although Cromwell interfered in a vain attempt to protect Naylor from the fury of a pious Parliament (he had already saved the life of John Biddle, the Unitarian) he refused to release the Quakers who were in prison, and Thomas Aldan, a Quaker who came to remonstrate with him on the subject, finding the Protector determined to do nothing, took his cap from his head and rending it, exclaimed: 'So shall the government of this nation be rent from thee and thy house.' There is evidence that after this several Quakers openly advocated the restoration of the monarchy; and despite Fox's declaration that 'they which you in scorn calls Quakers hath no seditious books or papers, but their books are against sedition and seditious men and seditious teachers and seditious ways', it was not entirely without reason that Cromwell considered the Quaker movement a force disruptive both within Church and State. Equally his attitude to the Fifth Monarchy Men, against whom he had a grievance on account of their incursion into politics in 1653, was determined largely by considerations of law and order. Since Cromwell recognized that within these limits men had the right to choose their own religious opinions and since at the same time he made no call upon English citizens to fall down and worship the Government or himself as an inspired prophet he had no occasion to interfere with doctrines. So long as they behaved with restraint and decorum the fervent sectarians of the Interregnum did not have to make the choice between serving Christ or Caesar.

Cromwell's wish to bring the Jews back to England is often considered a notable instance of his anxiety to ensure general liberty of conscience. If it were so, it would have been a remarkable departure from contemporary thought. It is true that a certain John Weemse, writing in 1636, argued that the Jews should be permitted to live in a Christian Commonwealth so long as they did not attempt to make converts. But there is no reason to suppose that Cromwell studied the voluminous and obscure writings of Weemse or that it was because he trusted the power of the Spirit to work miracles that he re-admitted the Jews to England. On the contrary it seems quite clear that the motives that determined him to negotiate with their spokesman, Manasseh Ben Israel, were as definitely political as those which decided him not to tolerate Roman Catholics and Quakers. Here, too, Puritan public opinion militated against toleration. There were already in England a number of 'crypto' or nominally converted Jews. One of these, Caravajal, was a rich and powerful merchant, a government corn contractor, who did useful work in supplying the Council of State with foreign news. Another of this community was of special assistance to Cromwell in the colonization of Jamaica, while others who dealt in merchandise and bullion-smuggling from Spain are said to have helped him out of his financial difficulties by lending money. Yet another is said to have dropped a valuable hint about enemy shipping at the time of the Spanish war. Cromwell may well have had a kindly regard for the original Chosen People, but their special services to him greatly influenced his decision. Though the divines opposed the project of their readmission and a conference consulted by Cromwell proved hostile, by taking the question into his own hands and after fortification by a judicial opinion that there was no law forbidding the return of the Jews, from the middle of the Protectorate Cromwell was able to connive at their resettlement.

The subject of the Jews leads on to the general question of the connection between trade development and the expediency of religious toleration. The Dutch Republic was generally regarded, not merely by the Press but by merchants and civil servants as well, as the most successful country of the day in organizing and profiting from the pursuit of commerce; one pamphleteer went so far as to say that the aim of the Dutch was to engross universal trade, as the Spaniards in the past had aimed at universal monarchy. Many explanations were offered of the Dutch economic success and prosperity, and one of these was its encouragement of traders and manufacturers to come from abroad and settle in the Netherlands. By throwing open their ports to all traders the Dutch made their country a commercial entrepôt for Northern Europe, and by granting full religious toleration they induced skilled artisans to migrate especially from Catholic countries and settle with them.

The first part of the Dutch practice was not imitated fully by the Commonwealth Governments, but the second, the encouragement of specialists to come to England (even as post-war Soviet Russia called over expert advisers from capitalist America) was frequently copied. Two examples will suffice. Captain Joachim Hane, a subject of the Elector of Brandenburg, was a greatly trusted officer in Cromwell's army and his use of the mortar-piece played no mean part in the victory of the parliamentary forces, especially as English country towns were in no way used to being attacked by shells. M. Peter Blondeau was especially brought over from France to advise the Council of State how to avoid losses to their coinage by the counterfeiting and cutting down of coins of the realm. He claimed to have invented and first demonstrated in England a machine designed to mill the edges of silver and gold coins.

Apart from the need for such experts who could only be obtained from abroad, there were other reasons for encouraging the settlement of industrious foreigners. It seems to have been generally held by economic writers at this date, in contra-distinction to the physiocratic view of the eighteenth century, that industry was a more valuable form of wealth than agriculture. Thomas Mun, an East Indian merchant, whose opinions were much admired in the seventeenth century, said that:

forasmuch as the people which live by the arts are far more in number than they who are masters of the fruits, we ought the more carefully to maintain these endeavours of the multitude, in whom doth consist the greatest strength and riches both of King and kingdom: for where the people are many, and the arts good, there the traffic must be great, and the country rich.

Another pamphleteer in whose writings an even more direct connection may be traced between the idea of toleration and the progress of trade was Henry Robinson, who produced books on a vast range of subjects which were mainly a popularization of the thoughts of other people. To him is attributed one of the earliest tracts on 'Liberty of Conscience'; he was an advocate of labour exchanges and held various important financial posts under Cromwell. He produced three pamphlets, explaining how he personally would improve the trade of the country, in 1641, 1649 and 1652. In one of these pamphlets he parti-cularly stated that, while 'some form of Government is necessary but all forms are good' (a thought probably approved of by Cromwell himself), whatever government is set up must be certain 'to proclaim absolute liberty of conscience'.

It is (or was) the view of Professor Sombart, the eminent German economic historian, that a primary reason for the economic prosperity of bodies like the Jews and Huguenots who were shut out from political work was this very exclusion which caused them to concentrate on other fields of activity. But in England it is generally held that the business ability

of the Puritans was exemplified well before they were out-
lawed from Church and State and became Nonconformists
during the reign of Charles II; and writers of that time, such as
Josiah Child and Andrew Yarranton, pleaded for liberty of
conscience on the ground that this would bring back into the
orbit of the national community an element of extraordinary
value to its economic development. We can discern another
hint of the interconnection of the ideas of tolerance and commercial development in the writings of the reign of Charles
II, and that is in the plea for the repeal of the acts against
naturalization on the ground that the country was underpopulated. The idea that England was underpopulated, despite
the grave unemployment difficulties which occurred from
time to time, seems to have been one that prevailed throughout almost the whole of English history up till the date when
Malthus produced the opposite thesis. It was true that there
were held to be a number of 'unproductive' trades, such as the
law, but on the whole it was maintained that men beget wealth
and not that wealth begets men, as the moderns might say.
Roger Coke, grandson of the great Sir Edward and a highly
respected writer of the Restoration era, produced the dictum
that 'Scarcity of People Diminisheth Trade', condemned colonization and argued for naturalization of industrious foreigners.
In sum, Cromwell's theory of liberty of conscience within
limits fitted in more exactly with the economic than with the
religious ideas of his age.

How did Cromwell put his conception of religious toleration
into effect in the Church of the Commonwealth? Dr. Shaw,
who investigated this subject exhaustively, reached 'the unexpected conclusion that the Commonwealth never either
declaratively or legislatively annulled Presbytery or established
Independency in its place, and that the actual enactment of
toleration was not achieved till 1653 or 1657', and his view
has been generally accepted. In other words, legislation intro-
ducing some measure of toleration coincided with the calling
of Cromwell to supreme power. We have recorded that in

1646 a Presbyterian system was established and in the confused period of civil warfare which followed during the next five years these local 'classes' were allowed to develop as best they could. But with the triumph of the predominantly Independent Army and of Cromwell its leader, it was plain that the funds and organization of the Church would have to be arranged in such a way that they would benefit as large a number of Christians as possible. This, as we have seen, was the theory of the latitudinarians and, despite the diversity of the sects, the great majority of people still believed in the necessity of a unified Christendom; but difference of opinion arose as to whether each sect should endeavour to convert the other and achieve ecclesiastical comprehension in that way or whether the Church should make its conditions of membership so wide as to leave very few outside its fold — to be tolerated until they were converted. The latter was the attitude taken in the 'Instrument of Government', and in 1654 Cromwell began to build up a Church establishment on this basis. He took as his model a scheme that had been invented by one of his chaplains, the Welsh Independent, John Owen. Oliver had first been attracted to Owen when he heard him preach in 1649. 'Sir,' he said to him then, 'you are the person I must be acquainted with.' 'That,' replied Owen politely, 'will be much more to my advantage than yours.' Owen's plan, which he first put forward in 1652, was for the continuance of an Established Church but without bishops or the old hierarchy. The Government was to set up two central committees, the first to examine the credentials of all new incumbents, the second to ascertain that no ministers or schoolmasters actually in office were unworthy of their positions. All ministers must accept a certain number of fundamentals if they wished to remain in the existing churches, but preachers of other sects who were unable to do so, such as Unitarians, were to be allowed to hold meetings if they notified the local magistrates and did not disturb the public peace.

Limitations were imposed upon the wide toleration

envisaged in Owen's plan by the 'Instrument', the thirty-seventh clause of which declared:

That such as profess faith in God by Jesus Christ (though differing in judgment from the doctrine, worship or discipline publicly held forth) shall not be restrained from, but shall be protected in, the profession of the faith and exercise of their religion; so as they abuse not this liberty to the civil injury of others and to the actual disturbance of the public peace on their parts: provided this liberty be not extended to Popery or Prelacy, nor to such as under the profession of Christ hold forth and practise licentiousness.

Members of the Church of England, that is to say, those who abided by the Book of Common Prayer, and Roman Catholics were not deemed Christians worthy of toleration. The system created by Cromwell in 1654 had perforce to accept this point of view. On March 25th he instituted by ordinance a general Commission of Triers for England and Wales to examine the credentials of candidates for the ministry, and on August 28th he added a Commission of Ejectors who were instructed to see that no minister lived an immoral life, blasphemed, used the Common Prayer Book or encouraged such loose practices as Morris dancing or play-acting. The rights of lay patrons were left untouched so long as those whom they appointed to their livings were fit persons. Tithes were likewise unaltered, although Cromwell is supposed to have favoured a change in the method of paying the clergy. The attack launched by the Nominated Parliament on the rights of patronage and of tithe-owners had struck such deep fear into the hearts of all property owners that Cromwell — whose self-chosen function it was to protect property — would not have been allowed even if he had wished to do anything in this direction.

It only remained now for a committee to define fundamentals. This was appointed by the Parliament that met in September 1654, and a committee of divines, including John Owen and Richard Baxter, sat down with good zest to discuss exactly who were Christians. The theologians soon fell out among themselves and wide differences of opinion arose between Owen and Baxter; for Baxter considered that Owen put unnecessary obstacles in the way of salvation; and by the time they were ready to present their report to Parliament it was dissolved. A few days later Cromwell sent for Baxter to ask him his opinions about liberty of conscience. The interview was not a success: Baxter sent him a paper containing his opinions on the subject, but he 'saw that what he [Cromwell] learned must be from himself, being more disposed to speak many hours than to hear one and little heeding what another said when he had spoken himself'. Nevertheless, the mere fact that Cromwell sent for Baxter seems to indicate some sympathy with the breadth of his tolerance, and even the narrower views of Owen were generous compared with the attitude to Christianity of the hitherto prevalent Presbyterianism. Moreover, the real reason why Cromwell refused to expedite the recommendations of the Committee was probably just as Baxter said, namely that he desired himself to determine the limits of toleration, and in his speech to the second Protectorate Parliament he reiterated his belief in the justice and efficacy of the ordinances which he had framed in 1654, as a basis for the constitution of a comprehensive Church. Under these ordinances the commissioners who appointed ministers and schoolmasters were instructed to select them indifferently from among the Presbyterians, Independents and Baptists, easily the three largest sects, and although these 'Triers and Ejectors' seem to have met with much criticism Cromwell defended them vehemently as having produced a ministry filled with the grace of God. 'There hath not been,' he said, 'such a service to England since the Christian religion was perfect in England.'

The final position with regard to liberty of conscience reached by the Cromwellian Government was summarized in the eleventh clause of the 'Humble Petition and Advice' of May 1657. This clause laid down that a Confession of Faith summarizing the true Protestant Christian religion and based on the Scriptures should be recommended to the people by the Protector and Parliament. But such who professed faith in the Trinity and the inspiration of the Testaments should be convinced only by 'sound doctrine and the example of good conversation' and not forced to conform by penalties and punishments. This insistence on belief in the Trinity was an additional requirement as compared with the Instrument of Government of 1654 and went much farther than Cromwell himself would have liked in broadening necessary religious 'fundamentals' — a plain proof that on this question Cromwell was in advance of his contemporaries. Moreover, it was again made clear that liberty of conscience was not to extend to 'Popery or Prelacy' or to the countenancing of 'horrible blasphemies, licentiousness or profanities'. In the last year of Cromwell's reign there really began at last a promising movement for conciliation between Presbyterians and Independents, with the Protector's approval if not at his request. A correspondent of Henry Cromwell, writing in July 1658, even spoke of 'a uniting spirit breathed forth' among the hitherto rigid Presbyterians, and that year the ubiquitous John Dury reached Lancashire in his world tour with his proposals for Protestant unity. Under the benevolent rule of the Protector — benevolent, that is, so far as Christian practices were concerned — 'moderation' was actually becoming the order of the day. But it came too late.

In the first instance, unfortunately, Cromwell's plan of a Church permitting the maximum of toleration within it and allowing at the same time toleration for all who 'do profess faith in God by Jesus Christ' outside it had to contend with the dogmatic enthusiasm of many of the sects themselves. His scheme in its broader aspects was that of a statesman and pointed the kind of path along which very slowly the Church of England was to go in the future. The Reformation was the mother of dissension as well as dissent; and for that reason it may be doubted whether Cromwell's plan for a State Church which would include Presbyterians, Independents and Baptists reconciled together but would exclude Episcopalians (whom Richard Baxter had wished to include) was at all practical. At least Cromwell's conception of liberty of conscience, with all its limitations and shortcomings, was a noble one, and was his most valuable contribution to political ideas.

CHAPTER XIII

HIS HIGHNESS

§ I

THE alliance between the Levellers and the Royalists that had been formed in mutual opposition to Cromwell's dictatorship now began to yield some doubtful fruits. Colonel Sexby, a desperate Leveller leader, confessed to one of Mr. Secretary Thurloe's spies that his agents in London would become significantly active in September. Sexby did not, however, specify their exact plans, probably because he was unaware of them. Thus three conspirators, headed by ex-Quartermaster Miles Sindercombe, were able, unmolested, to hire a room over a tailor's in King Street, Westminster, from which to shoot the Protector on his way to meet Parliament. But they found the shop had no back door. So they shifted their quarters to a better-furnished house with several back doors near to the Abbey, and after Owen's sermon was finished carried their blunderbusses thither. At the last moment their courage deserted them, and Cromwell passed into Westminster Hall unscathed and unconscious of his danger.

Nevertheless, he did not fail to point out in the three-hour speech which he then delivered that the country was still threatened with every kind of peril both at home and from abroad. He would deal, he said, with Things not Words, and launched upon a long inventory of the national enemies. First there were the Spaniards, 'your natural enemy', as had been proved since the days of Queen Elizabeth of famous memory. The King of Spain was allied with Royalists and with English Catholics who were in fact 'Spaniolized'. Beyond them were black Levellers and irrepressible Fifth Monarchy Men. Penruddock's rising had demonstrated the lengths to which their domestic foes would go. Only the institution of the Major-Generals, which he defended energetically and in detail, had prevented a renewal of the civil wars. What, he asked, were the remedies for this state of affairs? Above all they must have security, by which he meant the continuation of the Major-Generals and of their special taxes. Additional money was needed for the Spanish war — 'Our Nation is overwhelmed with debts.' Liberty of conscience would reconcile the sects to the Government; reformation of manners would unite the people in virtue; university students must be encouraged to study their own hearts instead of books. Another general grievance of the nation could be met by a reform of the law. Oliver wound up his speech by a triple appeal. He begged Parliament to vote a good supply of money to pay the national debt. He urged them not to attack the Major-Generals who had been singularly 'effectual for the preservation of peace'. Admittedly they were an illegal creation, but 'if nothing should be done but what is according to law, the throat of the nation may be cut while we send for some to make a law'. Lastly he pleaded for unity and an 'active instead of a lukewarm spirit'. Then neither Pope nor Spaniard nor the Devil himself could destroy them.

The members of Parliament must have been exhausted as Cromwell's lengthy oration reached its close, for the hall was packed and the weather unbearably hot. But they trooped off excitedly to their House convinced that the main objects for which they had been summoned were to vote money and to confirm the military rule of the Major-Generals. At the door of the House they were brought to a halt by a body of soldiers under three colonels who demanded of each whether he had received a certificate of election from the Chancery clerk. Oliver, warned by experience, had decided to take no chances. By a gross perversion of a clause in the Instrument of Government which permitted the Council to determine whether persons elected were of 'known integrity, fearing God and of good conversation' certificates were withheld from all members known to be opposed to the Court, by which means about a hundred members were excluded. The middle-class representatives from the boroughs who could be counted upon to regard 'security' as their chief interest were admitted and welcomed. In effect Parliament, like the Press, was muzzled.

The Commons at first protested at the violation of their privileges but quickly subsided and soon showed a becoming subservience to the Protector. On September 26th an Act annulling the title of Charles II was passed and on October 9th an Act for the security of the Protector followed. These two Acts drew up the penalties and created the machinery for the punishment of High Treason against the Protectorate. The House also turned to the reformation of manners and took into consideration a motion 'against black patches used by women on their faces and all indecency in apparel'. On October 2nd they were cheered by the news of a naval victory over Spain and of the capture of a large Spanish treasure. This stimulated them to discuss the provision of money, but they thought it wise to postpone a final vote until they knew to how much the captured treasure amounted. If, as some said, it were worth three million pounds, perhaps all the national financial embarrassments would be at an end.

But the real problem that faced Parliament was harder even than the raising of money. It was how to establish 'security' or 'a settlement', the two objects which in Cromwell's mind justified his Protectorate, without the perpetuation of a military dictatorship. The problem opened up the dilemma that confronted Cromwell through the last years of his life. He claimed that his rule guarded the nation against the warlike plots of the extremist on either side. Yet he had to stress the continued existence and repetition of such plots as the justification for the despotic methods he employed. But he was blind if he thought that either of these self-contradictory arguments would convince the middle-classes, who formed the basis of 'consent' to his Government, that the military dictatorship was necessary. If the country was at peace, why use extraordinary methods? they asked. If it is not at peace, then these methods are not effectual and better ones could be devised. In any case they wondered why they had set up a Protector against revolutionary Levellers and revengeful Cavaliers in order to have their every private action spied upon and interfered with by the military agents (however pious) of the central government. These Parliamentarians saw, or thought they saw, an alternative to the Major-Generals in a restoration of the monarchy. If Cromwell became King, the old order would be re-established, the old laws would hold good and extraordinary military modes of rule might be abolished. The hatred of the standing army, which was to colour the whole of English history during the next two centuries, is sufficient evidence of a civilian Parliament's determination to acquiesce in any form of constitution rather than the reign of the military. Hence this Parliament of 1656 had a twofold aim before it: the destruction of the Major-Generals, and the restoration of monarchy.

Cromwell at first stood by the Major-Generals. But he was never 'wedded or glued' to forms of government. If the House was willing spontaneously to offer him a Crown, he was ready to see if it were a feasible solution to the national problems. There was nothing new or startling in the proposal itself. It had been put forward when Oliver first accepted the Instrument of Government. A motion to this effect had also been made in his first Parliament. He had been petitioned to become King again in the summer of 1655, whilst a product of the reaction against the Major-Generals had been a pamphlet in favour of his Kingship in 1656. As soon as the present Parliament met, a rumour spread that monarchical ideas were being favourably if secretly examined, and they were crystallized in a definite proposal put forward by an Irish Major Jephson on October 28th. No record of debates or parliamentary diary has yet been unearthed for this month and consequently we do not know exactly what reception the proposal obtained. To the Republican (who had been shut out of the House) it was 'sudden and unexpected', but it was greeted with enthusiasm by the lawyers and civilians who were 'very bitter' against the Major-Generals. The Army interest was antagonistic — there were hot discussions among the officers in the smoking-room of the House of Commons — and Cromwell seems to have given little indication of his views. Still, four independent witnesses assert that he thought well of the suggestion, although he believed it better to dissemble his opinions until he saw how events shaped themselves.

Jephson's motion was never put to the vote. A sudden interruption in the shape of a mad Quaker put a stop upon the discussion. This Quaker, James Naylor by name, had at Bristol parodied Christ's entry into Jerusalem, his inner voice telling him that he was himself the Messiah. It was a momentary lapse that Naylor never ceased to regret, but it sufficed to stem the course of Cromwell's history. A shocked Parliament decided that there was no extant law capable of punishing such outrageous blasphemy. It therefore converted itself into a court and, after examining Naylor at the bar of the House, interminably debated an adequate penalty.

Meanwhile the normal work of the Commons went on. Social legislation and the Scottish Union were discussed. An official report stating that the Spanish treasure was worth only £200,000 recalled attention to the financial problem. On the whole the Protector was pleased with his new House; packed and purged, it was the friendliest assembly he ever knew. On November 27th he told the Speaker, 'though you have sat but a little time, you have made many good laws'. He withheld his hand and closely followed proceedings.

But by Christmas little had been settled. The Council of State, presumably with Cromwell's tacit approval, now thought it time to obtain legal sanction for the Major-Generals. On Christmas Day therefore, Desborough, the first of the Major-Generals, rose in a languid and half-empty House and offered 'a short bill for continuance of a tax upon some people, for the maintenance of the militia'. But no 'snap vote' was possible; there was indeed an immediate protest. Jephson, sponsor of monarchy, doubted the honesty of a partial tax, and although leave was given to bring in the Bill by 86 votes to 63, it must have been clear to Cromwell that in a full House it would be defeated.

To clear the way for a settlement that very Christmas Day Oliver sat down and wrote a letter to the Speaker in effect desiring to know the reasons why the Commons had proceeded against Naylor without his consent. This letter did nothing to save the unhappy fanatic from the cruel punishments of flogging and branding that awaited him. But it spurred the House on to action and drew the attention of the Army and of the City to the fact that a Parliament itself could be as arbitrary as any single person. It was an advertisement for monarchy.

Although the letter did not in fact help Naylor there is every reason to suppose that Cromwell's humanitarian and tolerant outlook was offended by the conduct of the Commons. It confirmed his belief in the virtues of autocracy and antagonized him as a violation of his own rights; for had not the Commons by sentencing Naylor arrogated to themselves judicial power instead of proceeding against their victim by means of a Bill which would have needed his consent as Protector? Moreover, he always consistently adhered to his theory of a limited liberty of conscience. On December 18th he had written to the Mayor of Newcastle urging him to give equal treatment to Presbyterians and Independents in his town. But on the very day when his letter about Naylor was read in the Commons, he was writing to Cardinal Mazarin that he could by no means permit open toleration for Roman Catholics.

Cromwell did not press the matter of Naylor any further. He had decided to abide by this congenial House. Furthermore, he had need of its help, for it alone could give the customary legal basis to his rule. It alone — now that the seizure of Spanish treasure and decimations on Royalists had both proved uneconomic methods of raising revenue — could supply him with provision for his Spanish war. But he saw that if he supported the House he must throw over the Army. He did so. On January 7th his son-in-law, John Claypole, M.P., husband of his favourite daughter, who seldom spoke in the Commons and whose speech was obviously inspired, rose to move the rejection of the Militia Bill. The Major-Generals, all of whom were members of the House of Commons, furious with the Protector, fought a gallant rearguard action, but were finally beaten by thirty-six votes.

It is possible that one reason for Cromwell's desertion of the Army was that he was jealous of the growing power of the Major-Generals, as dictators always tend to become suspicious of their powerful subordinates. It may well be that it was Lambert and Desborough who prevailed upon Cromwell to allow them the attempt to obtain the renewal of the decimation tax by a snap vote and that Cromwell was opposed to this method as detrimental to his chances of obtaining wider powers from this friendly Parliament. It is known that throughout the Protectorate John Lambert, a gloomy, irreligious and ambitious man, gorged with offices of State, led a sort of opposition to Cromwell on the Council. Oliver may easily have resented the increasing influence possessed by the Major-Generals, whose very creation had been the inspiration of Lambert, and been glad of the excuse offered by the failure of their parliamentary manœuvre to get rid of them. Looking at the question through the spectacles of Italian statecraft the Venetian ambassador in England so interpreted the Protector's action.

Ten days before the defeat of the Major-Generals, Thurloe unravelled Sindercombe's assassination plot. It was a long tale of unbelievably incompetent conspiracy; on one occasion Sindercombe offered £1500 to one of the Protector's body-guard to tell him 'at which end of the coach his Highness sat' when passing through Hammersmith on his way to Hampton Court; but unfortunately at that time Cromwell ceased going down to Hampton Court. On another occasion one of the conspirators plotted to kill Cromwell in Hyde Park but by bad luck the horse on which he planned to make his escape 'had a cold'. Their last effort, which was betrayed, was to deposit a box of fireworks with slow-matches attached near the Whitehall chapel. But no sooner had the would-be incendiaries gone than the officer of the guard smelt the fire and put the matches out. Their plan was said to aim at inducing the Protector 'who likes to take a hand personally in everything' to hasten to extinguish the fire in the hope that he would be blown up in the confusion. The whole series of plots, as described by Thurloe to Parliament, were so improbable that it was no wonder that 'knowing ones' declared the whole thing an elaborate pretence designed to strengthen the Court against the King and the Cavaliers.

But true or false, and the tales as reported at the subsequent trial of Sindercombe were no doubt a mixture of both, they convinced the Commons. A wave of enthusiasm swept over the House for the Protector who stood between them and the murderous envoys of the Stuart King. A member at once rose to beg His Highness to take up 'the government according to the ancient constitution' for 'the preservation of himself and us'. The proposal for the restoration of monarchy was shelved as too important for hasty discussion, and a vote of thanks was accorded Cromwell, who came and thanked them all in a gracious speech at once patriotic and paternal. The Major-Generals optimistically hoped that the exposure of the plot would heighten the chances of getting their Bill passed. John Thurloe spoke and voted in its favour in the belief that Army rule was the safest protection for his master. But Cromwell preferred to balance Parliamentary claims against Army ambition, thus securing a stalemate which left untouched his own supremacy. When the Major-Generals came to complain to him about the behaviour of the Commons he replied blandly that he hoped for better things. And his hopes were realized. For after the Militia Bill had been rejected, the following day to prove their loyalty the Commons voted £400,000 especially for the cost of the Spanish war, a far more useful sum than anything the Major-Generals could have produced. Then after a pause of less than a month they reverted to the question of kingship.

§ 2

On February 23rd, 1657, Sir Christopher Packe, Master of the Merchant Adventurers' Company, which at that date was seeking a renewal of its charter and therefore wished to be in the good graces of the Government, rose in the Commons holding in his hand a paper 'tending to the settlement of the nation and of liberty and of property'. It was an 'address' and a 'remonstrance' and it proposed a radical reform of the constitution. In a sense it was a proposal to return to the old constitution of the land which should henceforward cease to be 'unwritten' but should be writ plain for every man to read. Under the new law Cromwell would be the first King of Britain and would choose his own House of Lords. Cromwell, Thurloe and the majority of the Commons expressed their astonishment at the sudden introduction of the scheme, but in fact it was generally known ever since the discovery of Sindercombe's plot and the suppression of the Major-Generals that monarchical ideas were gaining favour among influential party leaders. But the re-introduction of monarchy was not the most significant point in the plan, the history of which deserves the closest attention.

The address, the contents of which were almost unknown to Packe, had been drawn up by a small committee of lawyers and ex-Royalists who sought a return to the rule of law. The undefined character of the Protectorate had not merely shocked their legal minds but had appeared to them a real danger to their interests. For if the Protector could by his mere motion set up a new system of local and military govern-ment and levy taxes without consultation with the taxed, it seemed clear to them that the country was little better off than

it had been under Charles I. On the other hand, they certainly
did not want to restore the Stuart monarchy. If they did that,
the vast landed properties that had been bought by them at
bargain prices might easily be confiscated without compensation; their offices would be equally forfeit, their very heads in
peril. Finally the Calvinist religion now dominant in the land
would, they felt sure, be proscribed. Hence they evolved this
scheme. They knew that Cromwell was not averse from
becoming King — he had hinted as much to Whitelocke on
more than one occasion — and they knew that he had friends,
relations and associates who would be only too glad to form
the basis of a new aristocracy, especially if some of the older
aristocrats could be persuaded to mix with them. These two
clauses, on which historians have tended to dwell, were, however, only the baits dangled before Oliver in order to buy his
consent to the rest of the plan. Two much more important
clauses were that which would have established a Presbyterian
Church of England and at the same time perceptibly narrowed
the area of liberty of conscience (no more Naylors should
flourish), and that which readmitted the hundred excluded
Left Wing members into the House of Commons.

The Commons allowed Packe to bring in his petition by
144 votes to 54 and for three excited weeks debated its clauses,
reshaping them into the final form known as the 'Humble
Petition and Advice'. Among significant clauses agreed to by
the Commons were those which limited Cromwell's revenue
to £1,300,000 a year, a sum that precluded a revival of
military rule, and forbade the levying of a land tax, the bane
of the country gentlemen who made up the major part of the
House; on the other hand, the Church clauses were made more
liberal; Cromwell was asked to name his successor, and on
March 25th it was carried by 123 votes to 63 that he should
also be asked to assume the title of King.

The opposition inside and outside the House came mainly
from the leaders of the Army, who feared their powers and
rights would be endangered by a settled constitution. They

plainly understood, just as Cromwell himself understood, exactly what it was the lawyers and landed proprietors had in mind. The Protector, it was known, was to be asked to accept the whole constitution or to refuse it. He was not to be made King and then upheld in the almost unlimited powers he wielded as Protector. This was pointed out to him by the lawyers in the course of their ensuing discussions: 'As for the new Title that of Protector was not known to the Law; that of King is, and has been, for many hundreds of years. . . .' 'The title of Protector is not limited by any rule of Law, the title of King is.' Nevertheless, Cromwell was tempted by the bait. Not so the Army. They did not object to the House of Lords which as a reward for their faithful services to Oliver they might hope to control and would moreover act as check on the Commons; but they could not permit a return to the monarchy that they once fought and now feared.

As early as four days after Packe had introduced his proposal, and whilst the Commons were fasting to clear their heads, a hundred officers presented themselves to Cromwell and prayed him not to 'hearken to the title [King] because it was not pleasing to his army and matter of scandal to the people of God [and] of great rejoicing to the enemy; that it was hazardous to his own person and of great danger to the three nations, such an assumption making way for Charles Stuart to come in again'. Although some of the leading officers may have been concerned for their own position undoubtedly there were many zealous Republicans in the Army who wholeheartedly believed that God disapproved of kingship. Oliver was furious at the presumption of their petition and for once lost his temper in public. He asserted that they had not always boggled at the word King and that in any case he loved the title, 'a feather in his hat', as little as they. But, he went on, they should not make him their drudge again as they had done before when they forced him to dissolve the Long Parliament and the Little Parliament, accept the Instrument and set up the Major-Generals. No doubt they would like to retain their power to kick him out. But this time he would decide for himself. Did not the case of James Naylor prove the need for a check or balancing power upon the proceedings of the Commons? If he wanted to be King, he would be King. The question was: did he want to be King?

During the next month there followed a series of fascinating manœuvres between Cromwell and the Commons. One writer has described them as a 'comedy' played to please the public outside Whitehall; but this view cannot be sustained, for the classes represented in the Commons and by the Army were the only public that counted. The fact was that each side wanted something that the other was unwilling to concede. Oliver himself was sincerely anxious for a settlement, but he did not intend to bind himself to a constitution that would limit his sphere of activity or menace beliefs, such as liberty of conscience, which he held dear. Above all, he decided, after he had recovered his temper, the best way to win over or at least counteract the Army was to insist that the offer of the Crown was made to him by the majority in the Commons almost against his own will.

On March 31st, therefore, Cromwell asked time to seek the counsel of God, and three days later in a short speech delivered to a committee appointed to receive his reply he stressed the fact that, as they demanded a categorical answer, the acceptance or rejection of the whole petition, he must reject it; but he did so with marked and obvious reluctance. They therefore reaffirmed their entire petition. Cromwell then came out into the open and asked for satisfaction on certain points. Would they agree to a free conference? In such a conference Cromwell clearly hoped that the Parliamentarians would persist with the offer of the Crown and modify the obnoxious clauses in the petition. The next day the Fifth Monarchy Men, who wanted no King but Christ, signified their displeasure by a feeble rising which only strengthened the desire of both sides to reach an agreement, and on April 11th the free conference opened. Cromwell began by trying to lay upon the representatives of Parliament the burden of persuading him to be King. Whitelocke and his fellow-lawyers cleverly parried this move by simply expanding the arguments for kingship which had first brought the Commons to their decision, above all the argument that people were used to the title of King and the name and the idea were bound up with the statute and common law. Whitelocke also pointed out that as the existing constitution, the Instrument of Government, had been merely the product of a clique, it would be none the worse for emendation and for the approval of the supreme authority.

Cromwell heard the arguments carefully and was half-convinced. Speaking on April 13th to the lawyers he confessed that their arguments for his assuming the title were convincing but not conclusive; they were arguments from conveniency but not from expediency. The problem he had to determine was — was the thing really necessary? If so, like a good pre-destinarian then 'what must be, must be'. But he had some doubts even about their legal reasoning. Was the title really so interwoven with the nation's laws as they suggested? Surely they would not dare to imply (as they certainly did imply) that law and order were worse administered under his Protectorate than in the so-called 'halcyon days of peace' under earlier Kings? In truth there was double as much justice done to-day as then. Moreover, he had to consider whether the arguments from 'necessity' were strong enough to induce him to offend the Ironside soldiers. 'I cannot think God would bless me if I should unjustly and without cause grieve them.' But truly the times were 'fickle and unsettled'. If the lawyers could persuade him that the divine dispensation demanded the change he was open to conviction. Above all he was willing to accept a title freely conferred by Parliament. In other words his inclination to acceptance would be, he repeated, determined by the amount of enthusiasm with which Parliament begged him for it.

And so the conference dragged on in a watchful but friendly spirit. 'The Protector', wrote Whitelocke, 'often advised about this and other great businesses with Lord Broghill, Pierrepoint, myself, Sir Charles Wolseley, and Thurloe, and would be shut up three or four hours together in private discourse, and none were admitted to come to him. He would sometimes be very cheerful with us, and laying aside his greatness, he would be exceeding familiar with us, and, by way of diversion, would make verses with us, and every one must try his fancy. He commonly called for tobacco, pipes and a candle, and would now and then take tobacco himself. Then he would fall again to his serious and great business, and advise with us in those affairs: and this he did often with us.'

Meanwhile the Army leaders were not idle; but some of them were persuaded to withdraw their opposition and others offered a compromise whereby Cromwell should refuse the Crown but agree to the remainder of the Constitution. This was the solution to which Cromwell was ultimately driven, but at first he decided to separate the two questions. On April 21st he asked permission to lay aside the question of kingship and examine the other claims. 'I am hugely taken with the word settlement,' he announced, and in an important speech he cast his thoughts back over the whole course of his public career since the summoning of the Long Parliament, and showed how they had twice failed to reach a settlement, first in the Long Parliament, which had tried to make itself an arbitrary power, then in the Little Parliament — 'a story of my own weakness and folly'. Therefore 'I must needs be in love with this Paper'. Broadly he approved the new arrangements suggested. 'I think you have provided for the liberty of the people of God and of the nation.' He then described the modifications he wanted in it, most of which were aimed at keeping the Stuart supporters out of politics and at guaranteeing the existing property arrangements. He pointed out that 'the security of property and religion and the titles of private men to their estates all depended upon the confirmation of the acts made under the Protectorate'. He also asked for an increase in his revenue, a securer toleration outside and a wider comprehension within the State Church. To most but not to all of his requests the Commons consented.

Cromwell thus won a decisive tactical victory over the lawyers, but the officers were still dissatisfied. While the Commons were discussing the amended Petition and Advice and Cromwell's friends were concluding that he would now certainly become King, the Army leaders were preparing a final defensive stroke. On May 5th Cromwell invited himself to dine with Desborough and Fleetwood and joked about kingship, saying, 'it was but a feather in a man's cap, and he therefore wondered that men would not please the children and permit them to enjoy their rattle'. But his listeners were not convinced and he chided them for 'a couple of scrupulous fellows'. The next evening he met Desborough in St. James's Park and gave him to understand that he had decided to take the Crown. Desborough warned him that if he did so, he, Lambert and Fleetwood, would all resign. Moreover, a group of colonels in the Army headed by Thomas Pride, the ex-drayman, and a certain Colonel Mason drew up a petition to Parliament merely begging the House not to insist on kingship as Cromwell had already explained his unwillingness to accept it. The three Generals had nothing to do with the petition and Fleetwood told Cromwell about it, who vainly tried to get it suppressed. Although the Commons took no notice of it, there is little doubt that the action of the Army was decisive on Cromwell. The following day he finally refused the Crown.

The manœuvres, hesitations and final, sudden and devastating decision were, as we have seen before, all usual parts of Cromwell's political conduct. His decision to execute the King, to destroy the Long Parliament, to ally himself with France against Spain, were all arrived at in exactly the same way. They do not imply insincerity; they are rather the principles of generalship applied to the field of politics. The ground is examined, the possibilities weighed and balanced, the appropriate attack discovered and the element of surprise applied. In this case he had known all along that the 'three great ones' — Lambert, Fleetwood and Desborough — were against him. He hoped to neutralize them through Parliament. He had expressed his anxiety not to undertake anything, 'kingship or whatever else', that would grieve the Ironsides. The arguments put forward at the conferences had failed to disturb enough of the Army Republicans. Hence while he had yielded to much of what the lawyers asked, to achieve a constitutional settlement, he had not gained the feather in his cap as his reward. In the contest with his friendly Parliament he had been out-generalled.

For two and a half weeks, from May 8th to May 25th, the Commons occupied themselves in putting the final touches to their Petition, but with the rejection of the title the life went out of the debates, the attendance diminished, and the members were confident that Cromwell dared not show his displeasure by dissolving them until further money bills were passed. On the 25th, therefore, the Protector accepted the Petition in the Painted Chamber. Cromwell showed himself disappointed and ended his speech of acceptance:

I confess there are other things that tend to reformation, to the discountenancing of vice, to the encouragement of good men and virtue, and the completing of those things also, — concerning some of which you have not yet resolved anything . . . but I do earnestly and heartily desire, to the end God may crown your work and bless you and this Government, that in your own time, and with what speed you judge fit, these things may be provided for.

Three days later Thurloe described the proceedings in the following words:[1]

This Parliament have now finished the Advice that they have thought necessary to give His Highness concerning the

---

[1] This and the following letter from Thurloe quoted on page 304 have not previously been published. Exact and complete copies of the originals will be found in Appendix A.

Government of these nations, and seeing His Highness hath scrupled and indeed refused to take on him the title of King, they have done the same thing under the title of Protector, and His Highness gave his assent thereunto upon Monday last [May 25] so that there is a full agreement between His Highness and the Parliament which I hope will increase every day. And this morning we have received the news of a great victory that it pleased God to give our fleet under the conduct of General Blake at the Canaries. . . . It is a very great mercy and an action as honourable as hath been done at sea in Europe these many years.

His modified rapture paled into nothing compared with his rejoicings that day in Court over Blake's great victory over the Spaniards at Santa Cruz. It was a consolation, and a justification for the Protector's rule.

The session now drew to its close. Such members of Parliament as remained in London announced their anxiety to return to their homes in the country as a warm summer approached. Pleased at Blake's success they hastened to put through the additional grant of taxation to pay for the Spanish war, together with a number of small well-meaning Acts such as that abolishing 'purveyance', the last relic of prerogative revenue powers, that licensing the export of fish, and that settling the postage of England. On June 26th Cromwell was solemnly installed Protector under the new constitution. He was dressed in a purple robe and presented by the Speaker with a sword, sceptre and a Bible richly gilt and bossed. The Speaker spoke, a chaplain prayed, heralds blew their trumpets and the people outside Westminster Hall cried huzza. Parliament then adjourned until January.

But before the end of the session one other thing had been done. General John Lambert, he who had been so much Cromwell's right-hand man that men doubted whether 'John' or 'Richard' (Cromwell) would be appointed his successor, was dismissed. He had refused to take the required oath under the Petition, and Cromwell, as was only human, gratified his wrath against the known leader of the opposition to kingship by demanding his commissions. Lambert retired to Wimbledon and employed himself painting flowers on canvas and cultivating his garden until better days should come for him, when a weaker man ascended the Protectoral throne.

CHAPTER XIV

CROMWELL AND HIS PARLIAMENTS

§ 1

CROMWELL was growing old and weary. Indeed, the burden of the Protectorate had made him an old man before his time. Whereas the military excitement of the civil wars, the swift rides from town to town, the organization of armies and of campaigns, the need for rapid decision amid the smoke of battlefields had conferred a second youth upon the middle-aged farmer, political power and the embarrassment of problems that could not be solved by the sword imposed upon him a wearisome and scarcely bearable strain. As early as January 1654, just after the establishment of the Protectorate, a neutral observer had noted that 'since this new accession of dignity Cromwell has looked utterly careworn'. Two years later in 1656 the Venetian ambassador extraordinary reported in his *Relazione*:

I have found Cromwell somewhat haggard in appearance and looking in not quite good health . . . the hand holding his hat was trembling. He is a man of fifty-six with a scanty beard, of sanguine countenance, middle height, robust and of a martial aspect. . . .

A comparison of his signature in 1648 with his signature less than ten years later clearly indicates how a strong man had become prematurely weak and old.[1]

Cromwell was convinced perhaps through self-deception but certainly in all honesty that the possession of supreme power by himself was the only means of assuring the 'liberties' of the people. But these left-wing Parliamentarians, these rabid Republicans in the Army and outside it, these fanatic Leveller believers in equality and other newfangled ideas

[1] See illustration facing page 296.

would never see his point. Yet (like all other politicians) he only retained office for the general good. In his speech finally refusing the Crown he had dilated upon 'this insupportable burden to flesh and blood — the carrying on the government of these nations'. And again, a little earlier, he had said in a speech delivered after he had recovered from one of the periodic indispositions from which he suffered throughout the Protectorate, 'any man may give me leave to die; and anybody may give me leave to be as a dead man — when God takes away the spirit and life and activity' necessary to a ruler. In truth although flashes of his old decisive will-power occasionally lighted the last months of his reign his mind grew less capable of adjusting itself to novel problems, and he preferred either to depend upon the advice of others or to give himself over to his emotions and to try to crush opposition with a simple display of force. It was not of course that he had ever been an even-tempered man. But in those busy days before Charles I was executed he was always trying to conciliate opponents, to arrange compromises, to exercise tact. Now dictatorial power offered the temptation either to show magnanimity by yielding completely to others or to 'solve' his problems by a mere outburst of bad temper.

But for a time after his rejection of the Crown there was an era of comparative peace at home and of freedom from troublesome domestic questions. The energies of the Protector were devoted to organizing the war which was being waged on the other side of the Channel. In March 1657 an offensive treaty had at last been signed by Cromwell and Mazarin, by which England promised to loan France 6000 Roundhead soldiers in return for the possession of Mardyke and Dunkirk, two fortified ports, when they had been captured from Spain. Mazarin had defended this treaty in France as the only means available to him of preventing an Anglo-Spanish alliance with Calais or some other French port as its price. Cromwell, who found the maritime war against Spain dragging on inconclusively, since Spanish shipping was small and Spanish

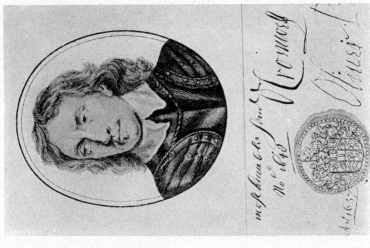

ELIZABETH CROMWELL AND HER HUSBAND OLIVER

treasure elusive, decided, as he later explained, that the English could neither keep their 'Ditch [the Channel] nor their shipping — unless they turned their ships and shipping into troops of horse and companies of foot; and fought to defend themselves on terra firma'. In May, therefore, Sir John Reynolds, an able commander, and 6000 soldiers, a mixture of recruits and veterans, landed at Boulogne, while Cromwell continued to press on his admirals the importance of intercepting the Spanish fleet.

But his most famous admiral had fought his last battle. After his victory at Santa Cruz Blake was taken ill. He received Cromwell's congratulations and the gift of a jewel from Parliament, and made his way home; but when in sight of Portsmouth this untamed Republican died, having faithfully served the man who would have been King.

Edward Montague, the other admiral in the Mediterranean, was now ordered to enter the Channel and support the Army from the sea. Henceforward the main effort in the war was to be concentrated on Flanders. The French King, Louis XIV, and the French Commander-in-Chief, Turenne, had both declared their satisfaction with the English troops but both proved equally reluctant to fulfil the treaty. Politically they were not enthusiastic over attacking Mardyke and Dunkirk merely to hand them over to the English. Militarily Turenne maintained it was not the best way of bringing the Spaniards to battle. Cromwell was extremely indignant and instructed his ambassador at Paris not to be put off with promises of inland garrisons:

To talk of giving us garrisons which are inland, as caution for future action; to talk of what will be done next campaign, are but parcels of words for children. If they will give us garrisons, let them give us Calais, Dieppe and Boulogne; which I think they will do as soon as be honest to their words in giving us any one Spanish garrison upon the coast into our hands! I positively think, which I say to you, they are afraid we should have any footing on that side, though Spanish.

The view put forward in the last sentence was no doubt correct, but a threat to withdraw his troops brought the French to heel and on September 13th Mardyke was besieged. The fortress fell on September 23rd and was handed over to the English. Cromwell sent out a Dutch engineer to fortify it, instructing Montague to co-operate. But a day later other considerations brought Montague orders to sail to the Baltic.

The position in Northern Europe was that King Charles X of Sweden, the 'poor prince', as Cromwell called him, had been confronted by a big coalition of Protestant and Catholic enemies. Throughout the summer of 1657 he had pleaded for English aid, promising a share of the spoils from a joint offensive against Denmark or Poland. Cromwell replied with a scheme for a joint attack on the House of Habsburg, Charles to attack the Austrian branch while he himself dealt, or continued to deal, with the Spanish. He also asked Charles that the town of Bremen, then a Swedish possession, should be ceded to England as security for any money lent to Sweden. For Bremen, he thought, would be a suitable centre from which to rally the German Protestant Princes to a Protestant Crusade. Oliver saw the Habsburgs preparing in their capacities as Emperor of the Holy Roman Empire and Catholic King of the Spanish Empire, united by the Pope, to destroy the entire Protestant world, and he planned to withstand this dreadful (but non-existent) design. His plan for a Protestant union to overcome a Catholic conspiracy was, however, out of tune with the realities of the European situation. The Swedes and the Danes hated each other, while the Dutch besides hating the English were the allies of Denmark. Moreover, because we then depended on the Baltic for our naval supplies we could not allow either the Danes or the Swedes to create a monopoly. Cromwell therefore sent envoys to Denmark and to Sweden to try to persuade them to come to terms with each other; and when there was a rumour that the Dutch would assist the Danes he ordered Montague to sail to the help of Sweden. But neither fleet sailed, and Cromwell continued his attempts at mediation. But without foreign aid Charles X split the coalition against him and in the autumn of 1657 he at last offered Cromwell Bremen if he would help him to further his conquests. Cromwell now refused — he had in any case tied up his military resources in Flanders — and to his joy, after long-drawn-out negotiations, the English mediators succeeded in patching up a treaty between Sweden and Denmark (Roskild, February 27th, 1658).

The hostile attitude of the Dutch towards Sweden had merely been one of the causes of increasingly strained relations between the English and Dutch Republics. It was common knowledge that the Dutch had profited from the Anglo-Spanish war to carry merchandise for both combatants. Cromwell suspected that the Dutch smuggled gold for Spain, without which that country could not subsist, but the Dutch resisted as far as they could his claim to search neutral vessels carrying enemy goods. There was also nearly a naval clash between the English and Dutch fleets outside Lisbon; for the English were allied with the Portuguese against Spain, whereas the Dutch were in conflict with Portugal over a dispute about Brazil. The official English view of the Dutch at this time was revealed by Thurloe in a paper compiled by him on foreign policy. Dutch policy, he declared, had no other purpose than the increase of their trade. They aimed at an 'open' sea and would only acknowledge a superior fleet; they demanded freedom to fish anywhere and denied the right of search. They sought to monopolize the colonial trade and objected to the English Navigation Acts. They expected 'liberty of having free trade and commerce with all kingdoms and States in amity and neutrality with them, though the declared enemy of other States'. They concealed Spanish goods under Dutch names and allowed the Spaniards to pursue their trade in security. 'And therefore,' concluded Thurloe, 'though this State was very desirous of a near and intimate conjunction with them ... the considerations of preserving

the commerce and navigation [of England] were applied to . . .
lest the English should be wholly eaten out by the people of
the United Netherlands.' Cromwell laid deeper stress on the
religious side of the Dutch misconduct, explaining how
shocked he was that a good Protestant people should stoop
to do trade with Roman Catholics — 'God will find them out!'

The Dutch point of view and the Northern war which (said
Thurloe) 'whilst it lasted discomposed affairs so much as they
could never be composed again' were the death-blows to
Cromwell's plan of an anti-Habsburg league. Indeed, the
only ripe fruit of his diplomacy was the alliance with France
with whom he acted in concert towards both Spain and
Sweden.

In domestic affairs there is little to record in the last six
months of 1657. The distribution of an ingenious Royalist
pamphlet entitled 'Killing No Murder', in which Cromwell
was invited to die for his country's good, caused so much
fluttering in the Protectoral cotes that at least three Royalists
laid claim to its authorship. The one who certainly did not
write it was the William Allen whose name appeared on the
title-page. Cromwell sent for Allen and demanded if he was
indeed the author. Allen asked to see the book and Cromwell
lent him a copy to read. After he had read it Allen said that
he did not possess the ability to write it but that if he could
have written it he would gladly have done so. Although the
poet Dryden wrote of Cromwell that ''tis true his countenance
did imprint an awe', a dictator to whom men could speak as
Allen did was assuredly not a very frightening figure, at any
rate at that time. In fact we know that at this period of his life
Cromwell was a singularly human figure craving for praise
for his work, for companionship and for encouragement. He
sought out friendly Royalists and vainly tried to reconcile
Republicans to the new order.

On one occasion about this time he sent for Roger Boyle,
Lord Broghill, an Irish ex-Royalist whom he had successfully
employed in his Irish campaigns, and asked him the news of

the town. 'It was strange news', was the reply, 'it was said he was going to marry his daughter Frances to the King.' 'And what do the fools think of it?' asked Oliver lightly. 'All like it and think it the wisest thing you can do if you can accomplish it.' Then Cromwell stood up, looked steadfastly in Broghill's face and asked: 'And do you believe so, too?' 'Yes,' replied Broghill, 'it is the best thing you can do to secure yourself.' But Cromwell saw that like kingship the idea, though ingenious, was not politically practical. And on November 11th his youngest daughter, who had been designed by the gossips for the embraces of Charles II, was married with much pomp to her lover, Robert Rich.

Cromwell amused himself by choosing his House of Lords that winter, and was less amused when in January 1658 he was forced to summon it to meet together with the House of Commons in order that he might have the backing of Parliament for the levying of new taxation to pay for his expensive experiments in foreign policy.

§ 2

When Christmas Day, 1657, dawned preparations were well advanced for the meeting of Parliament under the constitution known as the Humble Petition and Advice. The work planned for it was to raise money for the war. 'Mardyke', announced one M.P., 'will cost blood and money to maintain. Sweden and Portugal must have money to help them.' Money would also be needed, he thought, 'to buy a Crown for home'. A fortnight before Christmas Cromwell published his list of peers, the nominated life members of the Other House. They were a mixed bunch including some of the abler supporters of the Government from the Commons, a number of lawyers and soldiers and a handful of the old nobility. But most peers would have nothing to do with it; even the Earl of Warwick, recently connected with Cromwell by his grandson's marriage, refused to sit; and it has been calculated that over a third of the House consisted of Cromwell's own relatives. One curious choice was that of Sir Arthur Haselrig, the Republican leader and sole survivor of the Five Members Charles I had vainly tried to arrest, who had been shut out from the last session of the House of Commons. But on Christmas Day he again presented himself to the Commons, insisting upon his right under the Humble Petition and Advice to take his oath and his seat. 'I like your company well, gentlemen; and I do not aspire higher than to be a commoner of England.' This honour was not denied him.

At the other end of the political scale from Haselrig there were signs of activity. The Royalists were said to be 'certainly conspiring'. 'Divers of the old clergymen' insisted on holding 'a superstitious observance of Christmas' contrary to the ordinance of Parliament and the express orders of Cromwell. Very few or no shops opened. According to a Royalist present in London 'our great one at Whitehall hath a world of fears and jealousies in his breast, for on Christmas Day and the day following he hath caused at least five or six persons to be apprehended and sent to places of security', and unbiased reports spoke of men arrested for attending Christmas Church services because the Government feared they were covers for political plots. Such were the preliminaries to the assembling of the two Houses in January.

The result of the clause in the constitution which allowed the readmittance of the excluded members was to bring to the House a hundred acknowledged and embittered opponents of Cromwell led by Haselrig and Thomas Scott who promptly began 'to call into question all that had been done in the former sessions'. Apart from that the Commons showed themselves very touchy over their privileges. For example, the first news that reached the House when it met was that their clerk had gone to the Lords and another one was appointed by the Government in his place. 'There is one Mr. Smythe waiting

at the door, that was appointed,' announced the Speaker.
'I move first to clear our privilege,' came the reply, 'whether
we shall name or approve a clerk or both.'

That same day Oliver came down and addressed his Lords
and gentlemen of the House of Commons in the speech of an
old, weary and sick man who did not appear to recognize the
changed character of his audience. He pleaded his ill-health as
an excuse for a short oration; it was almost a sermon based on
the eighty-fifth Psalm. His principal argument was that the
revolution had now been completed; there was nothing left
to do but to stabilize its results. They had fought for their
civil liberties as men, their spiritual liberties as Christians;
these now had been gained and God had given them peace.
'The generations that come will bless us. You shall be
"the repairers of the breaches, and the restorers of the paths to
dwell in".' His speech was followed by one from Nathaniel
Fiennes, the Chief Commissioner of the Great Seal, which was
described by one present as 'such stuff as is scarce imaginable
by us who have heard the Beast himself speaking . . . a Hocus,
a Cabal, mysterious and Jewish throughout but demanding
money for the Spanish war'.

Two days later the Commons returned to the question of
their privileges. The new House of Lords sent a message
proposing a joint fast. This was considered by the Commons to
be a simple trap to get them to acknowledge the members of
the other House were Lords—and were they? Led by Haselrig
and Scott the Commons settled down to a serious investigation.
Cromwell was furious at the delay in getting to business and
called the Houses to the Banqueting Hall where, addressing
them again as 'My Lords and Gentlemen of the Two Houses
of Parliament', he rated them severely. In substance his
speech, which was made, according to impartial report, 'with
eloquence and digressions', was a repetition of the arguments
as to a national crisis that he had used in 1654. 'Your dangers,'
he began, 'for that is the head of my speech.' He outlined the
situation abroad and pointed out how while the Protestant

cause was 'struck at and quite under foot trodden down' the
Catholics were ready to unite under a new Emperor. He
blamed the Dutch and the Danes, although he diplomatically
hid their names, for this lack of Protestant cohesion and
repeated his previous attack on the Spaniards. Why would not
the Dutch join in the war against Spain? he inquired plain-
tively. Had not the Spaniards fought Queen Elizabeth and
had not Queen Elizabeth assisted the Dutch? But instead of
proceeding in brotherly unity the Dutch had even 'hired
sloops — I think they call them or some other name' to
transport an army on behalf of Charles II. There was, he said
in effect, no Protestant collective security and therefore they
must furnish the Government with money 'to defend ourselves'. As to the state of affairs at home he asserted almost,
in contradiction with his speech of three days earlier, there was
still much discontent and plotting. 'It were a happy thing if
the nation could be content with rule ... because misrule is
better than no rule and an ill Government better than none.' But
order at home and peace abroad could not be assured without
the help of his Army which was at least six months behindhand
with its pay. The Army had given them peace at home and glory
abroad; and so he begged them to supply the means for its continuance. Thus after a long speech he returned in the end to
his theme: 'My business to you is to prove the verity of the
designs from abroad and [the] still unsatisfied spirit of Cavaliers
at home.' In these circumstances unity and submission were
essential. The sequence of events is thus described by Thurloe:

His [Cromwell's] speech was specially to set forth the state of
the Protestant cause abroad and the necessity of finding money
at home. Both Houses (though hitherto they have not met
otherwise together since the first) yet were equally affected
with what he said in so much that the House of Commons
yesterday do desire a copy of the speech to be printed and a
state of the revenue that they might provide better . . . the
general rise and inclination of the House is right and tends to
all things of sobriety and settlement.

Thurloe's optimism was too high. The very day he wrote two independent members were laying down the rule, so frequently asserted and approved by Cromwell and his friends under Charles I, that redress of grievances must precede the voting of money. On February 2nd Haselrig reverted strongly and passionately to the subject of the House of Lords. 'Well for Pym, Stroud and Hampden, my fellow traitors, impeached by the King, they are dead; yet I am glad I am alive to see this day.'

Cromwell, the contemporary of Pym and Hampden, indeed their third in command, could not bear with this flood of reminiscence and soon lost patience. Undoubtedly Thurloe was right that after their susceptibilities had been smoothed the Commons would have settled down to a sober and useful life. Many reform bills, including provision for orphans, debtors and hospitals, were being prepared, and an understanding between Cromwell and Parliament was the best insurance against Royalist plots. But the Republican Opposition in the House unwisely decided not to confine their attacks on the Government to mere debating. They took part in the drawing up of a petition calculated to please the sectarians outside the new National Church, that is to say Fifth Monarchy Men, Unitarians and the like, the discontented Army officers and the enemies of the new semi-monarchical constitution. The petition advocated the restoration of government by one House, the transfer of the control of the militia to 'trustworthy hands', liberty of worship for all Christians indifferently and the right of the Army officers to be tried by court martial before dismissal: in sum an advanced and radical programme but a definite infringement of the dictatorial powers of the Protector. The petition was circulated in the City for signature. The attempt to incite an agitation against the whole basis of his rule infuriated Cromwell beyond measure. He refused to wait to discover whether the petition was likely to carry weight or whether it was a mere display of spleen by a group of malcontents. There is in fact small evidence that it made any serious impression on the Army.

On the night of February 3rd, however, Cromwell was awoken with a vague story of a plot against him. Next morning he went to see Thurloe, who was ill in bed, but said nothing to him of his intentions. After he had had dinner at nine o'clock in the morning without consulting a soul he suddenly rushed out of the palace, hailed a hackney cab and with a few soldiers drove to Westminster. He entered a private room where his son-in-law Fleetwood came to him and vainly tried to dissuade him from rash action. 'You are a milksop,' he retorted. 'By the living God I must and shall dissolve them.' He went to the House of Lords, summoned the judges and sent Black Rod to call the recalcitrant Commons to his presence.

He spoke to them a short speech of anger mingled with sorrow. He had, he said, only accepted the present constitution for their own good and at their own request. Personally he would rather have kept sheep under a hedge. But they had made oaths to abide by the 'Humble Petition and Advice'. Instead of keeping faith they had questioned the validity of his House of Lords and plotted to revise the constitution again. It was common knowledge that a conspiracy was on foot to seduce the Army and to raise a rebellion in the City of London while Charles II had an army waiting at the waterside ready to be shipped to England. It was no time for quarrelling. 'The enemy is ready to invade us . . . blood and confusion is present.' They were threatened with 'an incredible army to be landed within these three months'. 'I do dissolve this Parliament', he wound up, 'and let God judge between you and me.' 'Amen!' answered the unrepentant Republicans. Thus Cromwell's last Parliament was broken by force 'without the least disturbance among the City or among the soldiers' — a fact which proved incidentally that the rebellious plotting — if it existed at all — had scarcely reached an advanced stage.

§ 3

The last Parliament with which Oliver Cromwell was concerned came to its end not without dignity. To many modern writers it has seemed that the devotion of Cromwell to Parliaments proves his reluctance to be a dictator, and even disproves that he ever was a dictator. He was, it has been stated, a 'constitutional innovator', anxious to solve the problem of how to achieve checks and balances so that no factor in government should become 'arbitrary'. Actually it is difficult to point to any one of Cromwell's constitutions which was the product of his own initiative or imagination. The 'Little Parliament' was the conception of Major-General Harrison and other extreme Puritan political thinkers who believed that the Chosen People should rule, a conception to which, according to Cromwell, he weakly assented. The 'Instrument of Government' was derived by General Lambert from the idea of a written constitution put forward by Henry Ireton first as the 'Heads of the Proposals'. Cromwell was not concerned directly in its composition. The 'Humble Petition and Advice' was the product of leading lawyers, again reluctantly accepted by Cromwell as an alternative to the tyrannical administration of the Major-Generals. But the rule of the Major-Generals was more readily accepted by Cromwell (although it was again the idea of Lambert) and was most unwillingly abandoned by him.

It is true that Cromwell, being himself a Parliamentarian and having achieved political leadership from his position in the Long Parliament, had some lingering notion that Parliament had a function to fulfil. But when during the Civil War of 1648 — the turning-point in Cromwell's career — he found the Presbyterian majority of the Commons still negotiating with Charles I, the fomenter of the war, he turned against Parliament. Henceforward he regarded it as Charles I, himself, and many preceding Kings of England, had regarded it from its origination by Edward I, as a money-producing machine. When Cromwell found in 1653 that the Long Parliament was trying to disband the Army, the guarantee of law and order, without paying its arrears and was at the same time trying to perpetuate itself, he dissolved it. He accepted the Instrument of Government which obliged him to recall Parliament largely because it contained a clause providing for a regular and stable income out of which the Army could be paid. The failure of Parliament to vote an adequate revenue and its determination in cutting down the Army brought about its prorogation in 1655, and the new Parliament of 1656 was called for no other reason than because neither the decimations of Royalists by the Major-Generals nor the existing revenue sufficed to pay for the Cromwellian experiments in foreign policy.

So much for the practical side of Cromwell's attitude to his Parliaments. Intellectually it may be said that his difficulties arose because a dim struggle was going on in his mind between a theory of divided political powers each with its own sphere of action and a more modern theory of absolute undivided sovereignty. Cromwell wished to preserve 'liberty of conscience', by which he meant the right of the 'harmless' Puritan sects to practise their religion as they pleased, and also to protect the 'liberty of the subject', by which he meant the security of the property owner either from arbitrary interference or from the greed of levelling democrats. Charles I had been resisted by the Puritans and property owners in the Long Parliament because he encroached on those liberties. Cromwell therefore welcomed Ireton's conception of a written and unalterable constitution (no provision was made in the 'Heads of the Proposals' or in the 'Instrument of Government' for revision) because it would guarantee them. Likewise the Protector, his Council and his House of Commons should, according to Ireton's scheme, have acted as a check upon each other to prevent any arbitrary attack on the national 'liberties'. On the other side Parliament, representing the new classes of landed proprietors, the officers and officials who had bought up Royalist property at ludicrously low prices and the merchants who were increasingly investing in real property, naturally put forward a claim to have the ultimate voice of authority in the State. After all, was it not they who had beaten the King? A certain Captain Baynes speaking in Richard Cromwell's Parliament was to say frankly:

The people were too hard for the King in property; and then in arms too hard for him. We must either lay the foundation in property or else it [Government] will not stand. Property is now generally with the people; the Government must therefore be there.

But Captain Baynes's conception of the 'people' was shown by the revealing remark that all government must be built on property 'else the poor must rule it'.

Oliver Cromwell resented the claim of Parliament to rule as a dangerous departure from past practice. The Rump of the Long Parliament to his mind had usurped the authority of the Three Estates — executive, legislature and judiciary — as it had existed before, so that 'if any man would have come and said, "What are the rules you judge by?" the reply would have been, "Why! we have none! But we are supreme, we in legislature and judicature".' If therefore a Parliament must sit he welcomed in the end the restoration of a House of Lords as a check upon the Commons. But Cromwell's common sense brought him in practice to the conclusion that the country was better governed by power remaining in one hand, and that hand had naturally to be his own. He would abide by the ancient laws, protect property rights, ensure liberty of conscience, act as a benevolent constable of the realm. To him liberty was the totality of the recognized and customary privileges of Englishmen, liberties which they carried with them and occasionally demonstrated to ignorant foreigners. We come, he told the Irish in 1650, 'by the assistance of God to hold forth and maintain the lustre and glory of English liberty in a nation where we have an undoubted right to do it'. These liberties or privileges could only flourish within an orderly community, and since it was his duty to maintain law and secure privilege there was little left for Parliament to do except to support him with the means for carrying out his duties. He was indeed the real absolute sovereign of whom the philosopher Thomas Hobbes was at that date writing, who should create order where otherwise anarchy must reign. Yet Cromwell never wielded sovereign power as Hobbes would have wished. For, as Professor Laski has written, 'Sovereignty is historically conditioned always by the environment it encounters'. Cromwell could neither get on with or without Parliament. The need for money, the claims of an Army upon which his power was built modified his sovereignty as the sovereignty of modern dictators has been modified by their parties or armies without thereby making them any the less dictators. Increasingly the threads of government were concentrated in his hands during the Protectorate. The police system, through the Major-Generals established in the counties, the financial system through the restoration of the old Exchequer, the Church organization through the Committees of Triers and Ejectors, the legal system through the re-establishment of the prerogative courts, were all brought to centre in Whitehall. Gradually every enemy of his form of government was silenced by force or by persuasion. But such is the logic of dictatorship that even then he scarcely gained a victory for the causes to which he was attached. For if one remembers his tampering with the judges, the discriminatory taxes against Royalists, his attitude to Anglicans and to Catholics, it is hard to deny that even in terms of his own conception of liberty, comprising security of property and freedom of worship, there was little liberty in the empire over which he ruled.

CHAPTER XV

DEATH OF A DICTATOR

§ I

ONCE more Cromwell had been forced to fall back from the assistance of a Parliament upon the support of the Army. Two days after he had dissolved his last Parliament he called two hundred officers to Whitehall and addressed them in a lengthy speech in which he explained that he had called Parliament on the advice of his Council of State although he had not himself regarded it as an appropriate time to do so. Now for the public safety he had been obliged to dissolve it. He begged if any of them felt they could not conscientiously conform to the new Government in accordance with the 'Humble Petition and Advice' to deal plainly and freely with him. The results of this speech were variously reported. Afterwards 'he drank to them, and many bottles of wine were drunk', wrote one contemporary, 'but no reply made'. They made a fresh resolve, said another more friendly witness, 'to stand and fall, live and die, with my Lord Protector'. 'His rhetoric did not charm them all,' noted a third, for seventeen or eighteen laid down their commissions and six, including Major Packer, the commander of his own regiment of horse, were cashiered, because they refused to recognize the new House of Lords. One outspoken officer said that the price of a dictatorship was too high to pay for having liberty of conscience. But on the whole the Army undoubtedly acquiesced in his move. At the same time the usual proclamation was made for banishing Cavaliers and Catholics from the City as a precaution against a rising. The different parties waited expectantly for a declaration of the Government's next step. But for a few days Cromwell retired to bed with an abscess on his back.

As soon as Cromwell felt better he next invited the Lord Mayor, Aldermen and Common Council of the City of London to Whitehall where they were joined by many of the Army officers whom, wrote Thurloe, he took 'great pains to satisfy', and spoke to them for two hours of the mighty deliverances which God had vouchsafed to them in the past and of the imminent danger in which they stood in the present. He described how the Marquess of Ormond had recently been in London on Charles II's behalf to stir up a rising but had got away undetected (according to one account this was by Cromwell's own connivance), and that only the utmost vigilance and unity in the City could prevent a catastrophe. His appeals to the Army and to the City were indications that Cromwell hardly knew which way to turn, for the expedients of his diplomacy were exhausted. The inner Council of his advisers was left in complete ignorance as to what he would do next. Would he return to the Major-Generals and illegal taxes? Would he become King and defy the Army? Or would he revert to a packed or nominated Parliament? Charles Fleet-wood favoured the first course, but Cromwell may well have recalled that it had not proved the most economical or the most profitable way of raising a revenue.

Money was the urgent problem. Whereas in 1656 the budget had been as near to being balanced as at any time during the Protectorate, in 1657 the deficiency was £1,544,000, or more than a year's revenue, and still no means of borrowing were available. The supplies voted for the Spanish war had not realized what had been anticipated; the Army and Navy were both heavily in debt; the City refused succour. Immediately after Parliament had dissolved, Cromwell had sent privately for the Lord Mayor to ask for money and the Lord Mayor had replied on behalf of the City Fathers 'they were so poor they were forced to go from door to door for contributions'. Cromwell managed to borrow £200,000 from an individual merchant to satisfy the Army for the time being, but this was a mere palliative as compared with the general burden of debt. But he did not again importune the City, which probably for that reason became more cheerful in its expressions of loyalty and more willing to police London to check rioting and rebellion as it was requested.

The truth was that the Parliament of 1658 had been called to supply money and when Oliver got rid of it in a fit of hasty temper the Treasury was left without resources. After the refusal of the City an appeal to some new form of Parliament seemed to be the only solution. Within three weeks of the dissolution there was a rumour that another Parliament would have to be called. Towards the end of March the Protector's Council reached the conclusion that another Parliament ought to be summoned, but could not decide what to seek from the members apart from money. 'Parliaments are so casual', wrote Henry Cromwell from Ireland, 'that one would not profane them by overfrequency and yet, on the other side, to raise money without them is a condition from which I pray God to keep us.' In April a new Royalist plot detected by Thurloe put a temporary stop to these rumours. In the beginning of June, however, Thurloe told Henry Cromwell of 'deep discourse' at Whitehall about a settlement and 'how to prepare for the coming of Parliament'. Oliver hesitated, shelved the matter and then appointed a special sub-committee to advise him as to what should be done about a new Parliament. But this committee, consisting half of soldiers and half of civilians, agreed in nothing except a vague dislike of hereditary monarchy. Finding that he could obtain no helpful advice, a puzzled dictator determined to make up his own mind. He decided to summon a Parliament of some sort in the autumn, probably in the conviction that it would now offer him a Crown which he need not refuse.

Meanwhile English affairs abroad prospered. In January Sir George Downing went to The Hague to clear up outstanding differences with the Dutch; in February the English mediators had succeeded in negotiating a peace treaty between Sweden and Denmark; and in March the offensive alliance with France against Spain was renewed. Dunkirk was invested soon after the opening of the campaign, and in June the English redcoats played a notable part in the battle of the Dunes when a Spanish relieving army was decisively repulsed. The campaign then marched on to a climax propitious for the allies. That same summer in Jamaica the Spaniards were finally driven off by the English colonists. The only cloud on the continental horizon was that the Swedo-Danish conflict broke out again in August and all the patient diplomacy of the previous year was wasted.

The sudden dissolution of the Parliament and the threat of a return to military dictatorship naturally caused discontent and unrest at home throughout the summer. Equally naturally there were men who questioned whether the cry of an imminent Royalist rising and the necessity for national unity whenever the Government was in difficulties might not be a cry of 'wolf'. Fleetwood asserted that it was essential to convince all men that the Government did not pretend a plot 'but that the thing was real'. Undoubtedly, as in 1655, there were genuine Royalist movements. Ormond's adventurous journey, for example, was a fact. At the same time the situation was little graver than usual. Hyde, indeed, had opposed Ormond's mission which he described as 'an unreasonable adventure upon an improbable design'. The French ambassador in London, referring to Cromwell's speech to the City, reported home 'as to the talk of a descent by the King of Scotland [Charles II] with eight thousand cavalry: since the Protector himself gave this alarm, there is reason to believe that it is intended (affectée) to reunite the spirits of the army and to draw money from the City of London'. Cromwell clearly exaggerated but it is also plain that there was fire behind the smoke. Thurloe's spies and traitors kept the Government well informed about all plots, and it learned that some kind of insurrection was planned for the middle of May. Already by the beginning of May Cromwell had constituted his *ad hoc* Court of Justice to try offenders, a court so arbitrary that although set up by Act of Parliament no judges and few lawyers would have anything to do with it. One lawyer advised Cromwell to proceed against conspirators by common law but found the Protector 'too much in love with the new way'. The new court condemned two men to death, Sir Henry Slingsby, a Yorkshire Cavalier, and Dr. John Hewitt, an Anglican priest. There had been so little evidence against Slingsby in the first instance that on Cromwell's personal instructions he was lured on by *agents provocateurs* until he had made sufficient treasonable utterances to justify arrest. Hewitt had likewise betrayed himself to one of Thurloe's spies. Despite the intervention of powerful friends at Whitehall, Cromwell insisted on upholding both the sentences. Hewitt was said to have secretly married Cromwell's daughter Mary to Lord Fauconberg, and there is no adequate reason for doubting Ludlow's story that Elizabeth Claypole 'laboured earnestly' with her father to save his life. Her sister Mary even went to the French ambassador to ask him to get the French King to plead with her father to spare Sir Henry Slingsby, who was her husband's uncle. It was all unavailing. All the evidences go to show that in this, the last year of his reign, Cromwell began slowly to lose his grip upon affairs. He grew melancholy and pensive, it was said, and a trifle afraid. Henry Cromwell's father-in-law, Sir Francis Russell, had written to him in July 1657 that the Council of State was unhelpful to his father and that the Protector was forced to rely upon his own judgment: 'he counsels himself', wrote Sir Francis, 'were it not so, lo, I well know what would become of things!' But now a year later with the Council still unhelpful, Oliver went far afield for advice and could not obtain it. The only practical recommendation offered to him was to nominate his successor so as to ensure the stability of the Government in the event of his death. But to the best-informed observers it was obvious that the strength of the dictatorship, in which neither Republicans nor Royalists could acquiesce, rested upon the life of the dictator. 'Have you after all', inquired Henry Cromwell of Thurloe, 'got any settlement for men to swear to? Does not your peace depend upon his Highness's life and upon his peculiar skill and faculty and personal interest in the Army as now modelled and commanded? ... If I know anything of the affairs of England there is no other reason why we are not in blood this day.' After the failure of the specially appointed sub-committee to agree as to what policy he ought to follow, Cromwell contemplated trying to reconcile the Republicans to his rule, but the negotiations, such as they were, were fruitless. He also had second thoughts after the executions of Slingsby and Hewitt about the usefulness of his Court of Justice and ordered proceedings to be held up and punishments not to be carried out. 'I have long wished', complained the faithful Thurloe, 'that his Highness would proceed according to his own satisfaction and not so much to consider others. . . .'

§ 2

It is possible that Cromwell's knowledge, that only his own influence and strength of will held the nation together, that he could not conciliate many of the men who had fought the civil wars on his side and that death loomed ahead caused him to wonder about the future and what his place in history — that record of the divine will — might be.

It is given to few men to read their own obituary notices, but if Oliver had been able to do so he might have been surprised to learn that his immediate posterity praised him not because he had established liberty of conscience or conserved ancient institutions but as the great nationalist and imperialist, the restorer of England's lost European prestige. The victory of the Dunes and the acquisition of Dunkirk by England were the two big scenes on which the curtain of his reign was to fall. John Dryden in his poem upon Cromwell's death was to write:

He made us Free men of the Continent
Whom Nations did like captives treat before;
To nobler prizes the English lion sent
And taught him first in Belgian walks to roar.

Even before his death Waller had written in similar strain, comparing him with Edward III, the Black Prince and Henry V, the heroes of the Hundred Years War who won England a temporary empire on the European continent.

But had Cromwell any concept of an 'overseas' empire? Did he envisage any general scheme of central political control or influence over the colonies established in the reigns of Elizabeth and James I? Most of the committees which were set up to look after the colonies during the Interregnum were also significantly boards of trade. Consequently they concerned themselves mainly with the immediate issues which affected merchants rather than with the internal political affairs of the 'plantations', as the colonies were then called. Moreover, throughout the entire Interregnum administrative confusion was caused by there being invariably two or three committees entrusted with the management of the colonies and of trade questions, and whose work to a great extent overlapped with incongruous results. Some of the committees were unwieldy in size, and a Council or Board of Trade and Navigation — 'a business', Whitelocke tell us, 'of much concern to the Commonwealth upon which the Protector was earnestly set' — contained no less than seventy members. Merchants and publicists who were interested in commercial policy perpetually urged upon Cromwell the creation of an advisory board consisting exclusively of merchants, and at length an 'American' committee and a West Indian committee were actually formed on these lines. Unfortunately, these committees run by business men for business men had small chance to prove their capabilities before the Protectorate came to an end.

Whatever the wishes of those at home, the plantations retained complete freedom in their local government; one known Royalist was left as Governor of Surinam throughout the Protectorate; and although colonists might complain of commercial and fiscal regulations imposed at Westminster, in fact save when a naval squadron was near at hand they had little difficulty in evading any rules that they disliked. It is true that the Governors in the West Indies were appointed by the central government, but they generally found it advisable to identify themselves with the interests of their subjects. On the American continent the only important function of the central government was to see that the colonies did not quarrel among themselves, and on one occasion Cromwell as Protector had to write letters to the Governors of Virginia and Maryland in an effort to smooth away a dispute between them. His sole intention, he wrote, was to prevent any violence being offered by one force of colonists to another during the settlement of a frontier dispute.

If partly owing to the conditions of the time the direct political control exercised by Cromwell was small his economic control was paramount. Here his mind was cast in an Elizabethan mould; he at first insisted that the Navigation Act of 1651, which restricted the export of colonial supplies to English ships, should be rigidly enforced in the colonies. The idea that the English merchant should not derive the fullest possible benefit from the English colonies would have appeared as absurd to him as it would to the contemporary Frenchmen, Dutchmen or Spaniards, all of whom maintained monopolies of their colonial trade. But the British Empire was not self-supporting in Cromwell's day; the West Indian Governors asserted that often English ships did not call on them for weeks on end, and hence they were compelled to violate with or without the home Government's permission the trade restrictions laid down by Parliament. Equally although industry in the plantations was beginning to develop, only a few commodities were supplied in sufficient quantity to meet the home demand. For example, the timber trade in the American colonies was at that time inadequate to meet the needs of

British shipping. Consequently England was still dependent on the Baltic for her naval supplies. It was on this account that Cromwell was so anxious that control of the Baltic Sound should not be in the hands of only one Power. In 1649 the Dutch obtained by a treaty with Sweden freedom from Sound dues, an immense advantage which it was the aim of British policy to counteract. Cromwell sent an ambassador to negotiate with Queen Christina of Sweden, who astutely inquired how the English expected to obtain freedom of commerce in the Baltic when they maintained a close monopoly in the Atlantic. Ultimately in 1656 Cromwell promised to grant licences exempting bona fide Swedish merchants from the penalties of the Navigation Act.

In 1653, at a time when England was not at war with France, an enterprising officer had captured Nova Scotia from the French and it remained a part of the empire throughout the Protectorate. Cromwell approved of this acquisition and also put forward persistent claims to Canada during the Anglo-French negotiations of 1654-5. His attitude towards India was in the main one of indifference. The East India Company which owned by royal charter the English trading settlements in India obtained compensations for damages done to it by the Dutch, then our great colonial rivals, and by the Anglo-Portuguese Treaty of the same year the Portuguese East Indies were thrown open to English merchants. But when the Company petitioned the Protector to renew the charter which gave it monopoly rights he long postponed doing anything about it. He was originally said to favour the trade being thrown open to free competition between Englishmen but at length referred the matter to the Council of State. Between 1654 and 1657 no definite policy towards India was adopted, and during that time merchants and groups of merchants were allowed to engage upon individual 'adventures' according to the Elizabethan tradition. Finally, in 1657, the original Company threatened to sell all its ships and forts and to close down; in face of this threat a charter was drawn up and approved by the Protector. It is difficult to believe that this charter really constituted, as has been claimed, the turning-point from the medieval to the modern history of India. Cromwell regarded the Company as a useful source of financial assistance and borrowed £64,000 from it in the course of the Protectorate, most of which was never repaid; in answer to its petitions he frequently took no notice or said he was too busy; but he did indicate that he looked upon the fortified trading-posts in India as national territories that must be managed for the good of the State. In Africa the basis of the growing English trade was the export of negroes as slaves to the West Indies. There is no proof that Cromwell had any views one way or the other about this trade.

On the whole it is difficult to see in Cromwell's piecemeal handling of the colonies the 'liberal' (or, more accurately, Tory) dream of empire which has been attributed to him by some of his modern admirers. To contemporaries at least the empire which he merited praise for building was not a collection of scattered trading-posts and independent settlements but the new English empire over Scotland and Ireland; and the patriotic zeal which he was held to have exhibited in foreign affairs was the very contrary of the traditional Tory idea of steering clear of European entanglements in order to preserve and cherish more fully our overseas dominions. In the last years of his life he concentrated his main resources and energies upon regaining an English foothold in Europe. The acquisition of Dunkirk was thought to wipe out the blot upon English prestige made by the Roman Catholic Queen Mary's loss of Calais. And certainly the fright given to European monarchs by the presence of English redcoats in the Netherlands was an enduring memory. Two English ambassadors retained from the Cromwellian age noted in the early part of the reign of Charles II that they were not treated with the respect they had received as Cromwell's agents, and in 1667 Samuel Pepys wrote in his diary: 'It is strange . . . everybody do nowadays reflect upon Oliver and commend him what brave things he did and made all the neighbour princes fear him'. It was not the last time that dictators were feared in Europe.

Apart from his establishment of a new English empire and his achievement of glory in Europe the other commendation that Cromwell might have discovered in an impartial obituary notice was, curiously enough, that while winning wars abroad he had maintained peace at home. Dryden, writing his elegy, could say:

> No civil broils have since his death arose
> But Fashion now by habit does obey . . .

But looking back down the years it seems to have been a precarious peace that was won, for anarchy speedily followed his death. It was a precarious peace, too, because it was based upon a host of policemen and spies and upon a dictatorial Court of Justice; upon a Government without a Parliament; upon the circumscribed loyalty of the Army to one man. And in the last year of the Protectorate Cromwell's advisers were, as we have seen, writing to each other vainly scheming for a national 'settlement' which was never attained.

If that settlement had been reached there is no reason to believe that it would have been a revolutionary settlement. The forces which brought about the Puritan Rebellion in England were powerful and irresistible and in economic and religious matters were to triumph by the end of the century. Cromwell made efforts, largely in vain, to harness these forces, but he did not create them. On the other hand, in questions of purely political organization he did effectively constitute himself the focus point of resistance to many progressive forces then prevailing. During his years of supreme power he was a sick, somewhat lonely and rapidly ageing man. Perhaps for this reason he allowed, indeed encouraged, the re-establishment of monarchical institutions and forms, and himself was a king with the powers of a dictator. Save in religious questions he was essentially the counter-revolutionary. And at the end of life he was not the daring and mighty destroyer, but a painful

x

rebuilder of ancient institutions and a steady believer in the orthodox political ideas of the class from which he emerged: a well-meaning, dictatorial and intensely irritable country gentleman, insecurely seated upon a well-guarded throne.

§ 3

During the last nine months of Oliver's life private troubles crowded in upon him. In February Robert Rich, the newly-wed husband of his youngest daughter, died suddenly of the 'King's Evil' (blood-poisoning perhaps). In April Sir Thomas Vyner, the rich merchant who came to his rescue in March by lending him some of the money he so badly needed to pay his troops and whom he regarded as a friend, also died. Early that summer the horses broke loose from Richard Cromwell's coach in which his father was sitting and it was smashed to pieces; Richard was injured and Oliver severely shaken. The spring had been a severe one and the signs were unpropitious. In June came the ominous news that 'a young whale about fifty foot long' had been killed near Greenwich and that 'many porpoises were seen to rise that day above the bridge'. At that very time Lady Elizabeth Claypole (her husband was now one of Cromwell's peers) fell sick. A curious letter of hers is extant (to Lady Henry Cromwell, June 12th, 1658):

I have bin so extreme sickly of late. . . . Truly the Lord has bin very gratius to us, in doeing for us abofe whot we could exspekt: and now has shod himself extraordinary in delevering my father out of the hands of his enymise, which wee have all reson to be sensible of in a very pertikeller manner: for sertingly not ondly his famely would have bin ruined but in all proba-billyti the hol nation would have bin invold in blod. . . .

She was indeed dying in agony of a disease no doctor could cure, cancer in the breast. Oliver deserted his cabals and

CROMWELL — A VICTORIAN CONCEPTION

committees and drove down to Hampton Court to watch by her bedside, the Court was removed from Whitehall and the Council of State also summoned to Hampton Court. But no decisions were taken and public business came to a stand-still whilst he prayed vainly to God to spare her life. She died on August 6th. He returned to Town for the funeral, with his gout and other ailments aggravated and with his mind half-deranged by the sufferings which he had seen her bear. Three days later he was reported 'well recovered' and he insisted on struggling out of doors for an hour. But George Fox, the Quaker, who saw him on August 20th, was convinced that the Protector was a dying man.

The doctors had ordered him to remain permanently at Whitehall and not to return to Hampton Court in the hope that the change of air would do him good. But then it was decided that the proximity of the palace to the river was bad for his health and St. James's Palace was prepared for him. The news of his serious state became public and a foreign observer reported to his government that 'if this chief should die . . . disturbance and dissension would undoubtedly arise. Neither of his sons is capable.'

'Truly, my lord', wrote Thurloe to Henry Cromwell, 'we have cause to fear that it may go ill with us if the Lord should take away his Highness at this conjuncture; not that I think Charles Stuart's interest is so great or his party so powerful in themselves; but I fear our own divisions which would be great enough.'

Just before George Fox saw him Cromwell developed a short and sharp tertian ague 'at an ill time of the year', of a kind that made men say his health 'ebbed and flowed'. His sleep was interrupted with restless pain. In another three days he began to sweat horribly — the doctors feared that he could not recover. On Saturday, August 28th, he fell into a double ague, having two fits in twenty-four hours. By Sunday he was beyond hope. On Monday as he lay dying in state he conveyed to Thurloe his desire that Richard, his eldest son, should succeed him. On the Tuesday there was a slight rally but it heralded the end. Finally on the Thursday he declared Richard his successor; but his fevered thoughts were engaged elsewhere in that great struggle between his belief in salvation and his consciousness of sin. He inquired anxiously of a chaplain whether it were possible to fall from grace, and when he was assured that it was not so fell back with a sigh, saying 'then I am saved for I know that once I was in grace'. 'Lord', he prayed, 'though I am a miserable and wretched creature I am in Covenant with Thee through grace. And I may, I will, come to Thee for Thy People. Thou hast made me, though very unworthy, a mean instrument to do Them some good and Thee service.' He clung to the Covenant made by God with His Chosen. 'Truly God is good; indeed He is, He will not . . .' 'forsake me' was unuttered. He made up his mind to die. A doctor offered him a drink and advised him to sleep, but he answered: 'It is not my design to drink or to sleep, but to make what haste I can to be gone.' As he was sinking, a terrific storm, uprooting trees and shaking houses, had broken, signifying, said some, 'the devil coming to fetch the regicide's soul'. He died on September 3rd, the anniversary of his victories of Dunbar and Worcester, at four in the afternoon. In Amsterdam they said it was the Devil himself that had passed on: 'As for this town', the exiled Court of Charles II was informed, 'they are mad with joy: no man is at leisure to buy or sell; the young fry dance in the streets at noon day . . . and the entertainment of the graver sort is only to contemplate the happy days now approaching'. No such feeling showed itself openly at Whitehall. The little Secretary left the weeping family and set himself to impart the news to its one member who was not present there but away in far off Dublin:

'I am not able to speak or write: the stroke is so sore, so unexpected, the providence of God in it so stupendous, the person that is fallen, the time and season wherein God took him away with other circumstances, I can do nothing but put my mouth in the dust, and say "It is the Lord".'

Cromwell's body had to be interred at once; it was apparently buried in Henry VII's Chapel at Westminster Abbey alongside the body of Elizabeth Claypole, his daughter; and figures of wax were prepared for the ceremonials of lying-in-state at Somerset House and for the public funeral. On November 23rd a standing effigy wearing an Imperial crown set with precious stones was taken in an open coach in royal procession from Somerset House to the Abbey, followed by nine thousand mourners. Abraham Cowley, the poet, who saw the funeral procession described it as consisting of 'much noise, much tumult, much expense, much magnificence, much vainglory — in brief, a great show', and went home to dream about the old Protector. So empty was the Treasury that his son Richard had to devote a large part of his short reign to finding money to pay for the funeral. Richard was indeed too weak and unassuming to tread the road to kingship opened for him by his father. An attempt to re-establish an oligarchic Army Republic failed to meet the conditions of the day, and early in 1660 General Monk marched from Scotland to restore the patient Charles II to the throne. Perhaps Oliver foresaw some such future. Certainly there is a contemporary report that in the last year of his life he could not take his natural sleep but cried out upon 'Monk, Monk, so that it seems there is something in Scotland that troubles him'.

On December 8th, 1660, an exuberant Royalist Parliament voted that Cromwell's carcass with others, 'whether buried in Westminster Abbey or elsewhere', should 'be with all expedition taken up and drawn upon a hurdle to Tyburn, and there hanged up in their coffins for some time; and after that buried under the said gallows'. On January 30th, 1661, three carcasses were at Tyburn pulled out of their coffins, hung up there for the day and then beheaded and interred. The heads were for a while on exhibition at the southern end of Westminster Hall. According to some accounts Cromwell's embalmed head remained there for twenty-five years until it was blown off one night in a storm and picked up by a sentry whence it came into the possession of an eighteenth-century comedian and still survives. But there was another story prevalent at the time, which is also by no means impossible, that the Restoration carcass was not the decomposed body of the great Protector at all, but that friends had spirited it away and that it lies deep in Naseby field or in some country churchyard for no man to desecrate or to deify.

JOHN THURLOE

HERE are two new letters of Mr. Secretary Thurloe (see Chapter XIII, p. 292, footnote). They belong to 1657-8, when Thurloe was an M.P. and member of the Council of State.

§ I

The first letter is written to Dr. John Pell, the British Agent in Switzerland. The history of this letter is known. Samuel Morland, another of Thurloe's agents, who had been deputed by him to correspond with Pell, had been away from London to attend his mother's funeral; he returned post-haste to London, wrote to Pell and went to bed. Thurloe sent a messenger to Morland's lodgings with an account of the battle of Santa Cruz and a covering letter for Pell; but as Morland was by this time asleep he was unable to forward it until the next post on June 1st, 1657. Pell acknowledged the account and covering letter on June 18th. The letter here is the covering letter. The account has been printed. (R. Vaughan, *The Protectorate of Oliver Cromwell*, II, 173-9):

John Thurloe to John Pell (Landsdowne MSS. 754, f. 195)

Sir,
    I have omitted the writeinge to you of late in respect of the great affairs wch have been agitated in parlement upon wch I was necessitated to attend, and therefore referred it to Mr. Morland to give you an Account of was [*sic*, what?] passed weekly here; The parlament have now finished the Advise wch they have thought necessary to give his Highness concerninge the Governmt of these nations, and seeinge H. H. hath scrupled and indeed refused to take upon hym the title of Kinge, they have done the same thing under the Title of Protector, and his Highnes gave his assent thereunto upon Munday last [25th], soe that there is a full Agreemt between H. H. and the Parliament wch I hope will encrease every day. And this morninge wee have received the news of a great victory that it pleased god to give o^r Fleet under the conduct of Genll

Blake, at the Canaries, the perticulars are conteyned in the enclosed Narrative, wch I received from the Generall in a Letter of his to me. He is returnd againe to Cadiz Bay, there to witnes the motions of the Spanish Fleet wch is preparinge in that Bay. The plate was landed before the attempt, but most of their rich goods were on board, and all burnt, beside what our sea men plunderd, before they fired the ships; It is a very great mercy, and an Action as honoᵇˡᵉ as hath been done at sea in Europe these many yeare. I suppose you have heard of his Highness sendinge 6000 men into France in assistance of that Kinge against the Spanyard, they are commanded by Sir John Reynolds that they are yet in noe Engagement.

I remeyne
your very affectionate friend & servant
Jo: Thurloe

Whitehall
  28 May 1657
  Mr. Pell.

§ 2

The second letter is written to George Downing, the English ambassador at The Hague. For Cromwell's speech, referred to therein and the circumstances surrounding it, see Burton's *Diary*, II, 346 *seq.*, and above, Chapter XIV, p. 304:

John Thurloe to George Downing (Add. MSS. 22919, *f.* 11)

Sir,
    I have been ever since you went so sick that I have not been able to set penn to paper but now God be praised pritty well recovered. So that having received your three Letters, concerning what you write I shall give you satisfaction by the next Post. The two Houses have not yet had any conference together. The house of Lords sent a message to that of the Commons by two judges concerning a fast to be kept [Jan. 22]. After some little debate they were admitted and returned that they would send answer by Messengers of their own. Since that his Hignesse writ to both houses distinctly Letters to meet him at the banketting house Which they did. His speech was especially to set forth the State of the protestant cause abroad and the necessity of finding mony at home [Jan. 25]. Both houses (though hitherto they have not met otherwise together since the first) yet were equally affected with what was said in so much that the house of Commons sent yesterday to desire a copy of the Speech to be printed and a State of the Revenue that they might provide better. His Highness

answerd that he could scarce give account of three lines together of his speech it being spoken upon the present; that there should be a State sent of the revenue;[1] that he expected it had been from both houses for they must conceive that it is himselfe and they two that must carry things on. When it came to make a Report in the House today your old great friend of the North[2] blusterd terribly that it was a violation of their privileges to Whom it onely belong to give order in Mony. As also they considering to returne their answer to that former message of the Lords he would have gott it into a grand Committee that the busynes might have hanged there. But in both he was slighted and could effect nothing. Also Mr. Scott spoke much today against the house of Lords as an house of Lords. But you may know that though hitherto some of us who would willingly and shall shortly, have not been able to be there, and though there be some among them who would not acknowledge the others as an house or not as an house of Lords yet neither the old Commonwealth Party nor any are so potent but that the general rise and inclination of the house is right and tends to all things of Sobriety and Settlement.

> I shall for the present say no more
> than that I am
> Your very loving friend
> (signed) Jo. Thurloe

Whitehall, Jan, 28 [29?], 1658

§ 3

I append a letter from Dr. Pell to Thurloe which throws some light on Thurloe's hobbies (see Chapter IX, p. 202). I do not think the letter from Thurloe to Morland referred to in it survives. Mathematics was a very popular hobby in the seventeenth century and Pell was himself a Professor of Mathematics:

John Pell to John Thurloe (Lansdowne MSS. 752, f. 264)

May it please your Honour to accept of a slight new-yeares gift, not ill agreeing with the letter which, no long since, M. M. [Morland] received from you; whence I gathered that French and Mathematicks took

---

[1] This is printed in Carlyle's *Letters and Speeches of Oliver Cromwell* (ed. Lomas), II, 493-4.

[2] This presumably refers to Sir Arthur Haselrig who was a Leicestershire man and to his speech given in Burton, II, 380. But that speech was made on January 29th, not January 28th, as was also a long speech of Scott on the House of Lords (*Ibid.*, 382). I therefore assume that Thurloe's letter is misdated and should be January 29th.

up part of your spare houres. Of French bookes I know none, that at this time I would desire your Honour to reade over before this. For Mathematicks, I cannot guesse at your progresse, or what kind of questions you desire. I have heere sent one, which, if it seems troublesome may be laid by for a weeke or two, till there come a solution from

Your Honours most faithfull servant

J. P.

Geneva

Decemb. 20/30 1655

§ 4

The following letter (see Chapter XV, p. 315) throws a little light on Cromwell, Thurloe, and his Council. The writer, Sir Francis Russell, was an M.P. and Henry Cromwell's father-in-law. Some of his other letters have been printed by Sir Charles Firth and Mr. R. W. Ramsey. This letter was written three weeks before Lambert's dismissal by Cromwell:

Sir Francis Russell to Henry Cromwell (Lansdowne MSS. 822, f. 132)

My Deare Lord,

I am told about this time of the yeare you are in your progresse, and I hope in time twill reach as far as Chippenham, for me thinks your Father should long as much as your other freinds to see you sometimes in England. We who know nothing of State affaires are deviseing you some other imployment for you besides that of Ireland, sometimes we will have you Generall of the English army than [then] Lord Admirall and so to viset us once a yeare, and keepe a good correspondency with all your freinds here. Something we have in our heads for you, and would not have you buryed in Ireland. You must not laugh at us because we are in good earnest. If I were of your good freind Olivers counsell, I should set his head a workeing more than the little Secretary [Thurloe] old Rouse or Skipon, for I think they are to grave and wise for this Mercuryall quick age; but the best of it is your father is a notable man, and he and all his counsell rides all but upon one horse, I meane he counsells himselfe, were it not, Lo, I well know what would become of things. My Lord Lambert lookes but sadly he puts me in mind of a saying of old Solomons, that there is an appointed time for all things under the sun to hate as well as to love, to be sad as well as merry. My lord Deputy [Fleetwood] and Generall Disbrow beginne to grow in request at Whitehall. Disbrow made a notable speech in the Parliment house in answer to one of my Lord Lamberts, twas very like him blunt and honest. My Lord if your inte-

330

grety and wisedom continues with you, you will see through all our clouds here, and it may be in time you may by your wisedome helpe to disperse them: my good opinion of you makes me to say anything, but to think much more. I wish you all happynes and true inward peace. My love to your wife. You know I am My Lord

Your lordships
Franc: Russell

Chip [penham]:
   July 4th, 1657

NOTES AND REFERENCES

THE biographer of Oliver Cromwell is excused a complete bibliography on account of the existence of Mr. Godfrey Davies's *Bibliography of British History*, 1603–1714 (Oxford University Press, 1928) and of Professor W. C. Abbott's *Bibliography of Oliver Cromwell* (Harvard University Press, 1929). Since 1929 there have been published a large number of secondary authorities, especially biographies dealing with the Cromwellian period, including biographies of Cromwell by Hilaire Belloc, John Buchan, F. H. Hayward and E. Momigliano; of John Hampden by H. R. Williamson and John Drinkwater; of Prince Rupert by C. Wilkinson and James Cleugh; of Charles I by Hilaire Belloc, F. M. G. Higham and Evan John; of Charles II by Arthur Bryant; and of Strafford by Lady Burghclere and Miss Wedgwood. There have also appeared by Mr. R. W. Ramsey lives of Henry Cromwell and Richard Cromwell, and *Cromwell and his Family Circle*, and a study of *Charles I and Cromwell* by Mr. G. M. Young. Lady Burghclere's, Signor Momigliano's and Mr. Ramsey's books contain some new material for the Cromwellian period.

Other secondary authorities based on new material include:

M. P. Ashley: *Financial and Commercial Policy under the Cromwellian Protectorate* (1934).

G. Davies: *The Early Stuarts* (1937).

M. James: *Social Policy during the Puritan Revolution* (1930).

W. K. Jordan: *The Development of Religious Toleration in England*, 1603–1640 (1936).

H. Oncken: *Cromwell, vier Essays* (1935).

K. Pearson and G. M. Morant: *The Portraiture of Oliver Cromwell* (1935).

F. J. Varley: *Cambridgeshire during the Civil War* (1935).

Editions of original authorities include:

F. Bamford (ed.): *The Commonplace Book of Sir John Oglander* (1936).

Calendar of State Papers (Clarendon), Vol. IV (1932).

Calendar of State Papers (Venetian), 1653-9, 3 vols. (1929-31).

I must acknowledge my indebtedness to the works of Professor Abbott and Pearson and Morant for information about Cromwell's portraits; cf. also S. R. Gardiner, *Cromwell* (Goupil limited edition, 1899).

REFERENCES

In the following notes I omit all references (1) where I have followed the invaluable standard works of Dr. S. R. Gardiner and Sir Charles Firth or Mrs. Lomas's indispensable edition of Thomas Carlyle's *Letters and Speeches of Oliver Cromwell* — books without which biographies like mine cannot be written; (2) where the source of my quotation is obvious from the text:

Chapter I, pp. 13-14: I owe my views of Wolsey and Thomas Cromwell especially to A. F. Pollard, *Wolsey*, and R. B. Merriman, *Life and Times of Thomas Cromwell*.

Pp. 24-7: For Cromwell as a farmer and encloser in Huntingdonshire during the sixteen-thirties see E. F. Gay: 'The Midland Revolt', *Transactions of the Royal Historical Society*, N.S. XVIII; E. M. Leonard: 'The Inclosure of the Common Fields in the Seventeenth Century', *Ibid.*, XIX, esp. 132, 136; E. C. K. Gonner: *Common Land and Enclosure*, 165-7; M. Noble: *Memoirs of the Protectoral House* (ed. 1787), I, 83, 96, 103-6; J. E. T. Rogers: *History of Agriculture and Prices in England*, Vols. V and VI; W. R. Scott: *History of Joint Stock Companies*, I, 167, 186, etc.

Pp. 27-32: For the rise of Puritanism see J. B. Black: *The Reign of Queen Elizabeth*; C. Burrage: *History of Dissent* (who stresses the importance of Henry Jacob); H. W. Clark: *History of English Noncon-formity*; J. D. Mackie: *Cavalier and Puritan*; R. G. Usher: *Early History of Presbyterianism*. The Robert Harley quotation is from *Portland Papers* (Historical MSS. Commission), III, 132-4.

Chapter II, p. 37: The quotations from James I come from C. H. McIlwain: *Works of James I*, XXXV, 63.

Pp. 41-2: The report of Cromwell's speech in the Commons is from Notestein and Relf: *The Commons Debates of 1629*, 192-3.

Pp. 43-4: The account of the Huntingdon charter dispute is derived from British Museum Add. MSS. 25302, ff. 48-50.

Pp. 45-6: On Beard's retirement see Add. MSS. 15615, f. 126.

Chapter III, pp. 50-1: I owe my character sketch of Charles I largely to Mrs. Higham's excellent biography.

P. 55: The tale of the oatmeal maker is in R. Williams: *Court and Times of Charles I*, II, 71.

Pp. 60-1: Lord Keeper Finch's letter is printed in J. L. Sandford: *Great Rebellion*, 263-4.

P. 63: For ship money in Cambridgeshire see A. Kingston: *East Anglia and the Great Civil War*, 21.

P. 66: The report of Cromwell's speech on the bishops is in *The*

APPENDIX B

Journal of Sir Simon D'Ewes (ed. Notestein), 339-40; I have also used in this chapter unpublished parts of D'Ewes from Harleian MSS. 162.

P. 73: The 'paper' 'To Your Tents, O Israel', was in fact a pamphlet by a journalist Henry Walker, for which he was put in the pillory.

Chapter IV, p. 75: The quotations from Sir John Oglander are in F. Bamford: *A Royalist Notebook*, 109, 117. The Marston Moor story is in Sandford, 590 note.

Pp. 76-7: Cromwell's activities at Cambridge are described in A. Kingston: *East Anglia and the Great Civil War*, 56 *seq.*; F. J. Varley: *Cambridge during the Civil War*, 79-82; *Calendar of State Papers (Compounding)* 895. The quotation is from *Querela Cantabrigiensis* (1646), 7.

P. 82: Almost the only authority for Cromwell's part in Edgehill is N. Fiennes: *A Most True and Exact Relation* (1642); cf., however, D. Holles, *Memoirs* (1649), 17. The relevant passages from Fiennes are cited in C. Firth: 'Raising of the Ironsides' (*Transactions of the Royal Historical Society*, XIII, p. 19, note 3). Dr. Gardiner relies on Clarendon for the presence of Lord St. John's regiment at Edgehill; but although Lord St. John was certainly there in person his regiment was not, see the specific contemporary statement as to its presence at Worcester in *Eight Speeches Spoken in Guildhall upon Thursday night October* 27, 1642 (1642), 5.

P. 84: The Nottinghamshire lady is Mrs. Lucy Hutchinson, *Memoirs of Colonel Hutchinson* (ed. Firth), I, 211.

Pp. 93-5: For the early history of Congregationalism, see R. W. Dale, *History of English Congregationalism*, esp. 265-7. Cromwell is called the great Independent by R. Baillie in April 1644 (*Letters and Journals*, I, 153).

Pp. 95-6: The Presbyterian officer is anonymous; his narrative is in *The Quarrel between Manchester and Cromwell* (Camden Society, 1875), 72.

Chapter V, p. 97: For the Isle of Ely see *Ibid.*, 73-4.

P. 98-99: For Dr. Ward, see *Querela Cantabrigiensis*, 9, 17.

P. 108: The quotation about 'old almanacs' is from D. Holles, 30, as is also that on Fairfax on page 109 (*Ibid.*, 34).

Chapter VI, p. 126: For Cromwell and Cornet Joyce, see W. Waller, *Vindication*, 136-8.

P. 131: Charles I's remarks on dissembling and Cromwell's two questions to Berkeley are from Berkeley's *Memoirs* (*Harleian Miscellany*, IX, 477).

Chapter VII, pp. 135-8: For Cromwell's political theories see *Clarke Papers* (ed. Firth), I, esp. 226 *seq.*, and Gooch and Laski, *English Democratic Ideas in the XVII Century*, 192-204.

NOTES AND REFERENCES

P. 137: For the 'ship of state' see 'The Standard of Equality' (1647) (*Harleian Miscellany*, IX, 114), cited by W. Kennedy, *English Taxation*, 90 note.

P. 141: The Scot was Robert Baillie, III, 16.

Pp. 152-3: For Mrs. Poole see *Clarke Papers*, II, 150-4.

Pp. 154-5: For the trial of Charles I, I have followed J. B. Muddiman, *Trial of Charles I*, esp. pp. 106, 153.

Chapter VIII, p. 160: The Leveller quotation is from *The Hunting of the Foxes* (1649).

Pp. 160-1: For the Diggers see *inter alia* L. H. Berens: *The Digger Movement*, esp. Chapter IV.

P. 162: For Cromwell's sermon see Whitelocke, *Memorials*, 398; the pamphlet of 1647 is called *The Simple Cobbler of Aggavan in America*, cit. Father Denis Murphy, *Cromwell in Ireland*, 45.

P. 164: For Sir Arthur Aston's leg see Ludlow's *Memoirs* (ed. Firth), I, 234. For Cromwell's Irish campaigns in general I have followed Father Denis Murphy, a Jesuit who is the modern clerical historian referred to on page 167. Lord Morley's comments in his *Cromwell*, Book IV, Chapter I are very wise.

P. 172: Fairfax's defence of his conduct is in his *Short Memorial* (*Somers Tracts*, V, 396). For Cromwell's Scottish campaigns I have followed W. S. Douglas: *Cromwell's Scotch Campaigns*; J. Nicoll's *Diary*; J. Hodgson's *Autobiography*.

Pp. 175-6: Capt. John Hodgson's *Autobiography* (ed. 1822), 44-5, is the sole authority for Cromwell's flank attack. For an important discussion of this flank attack see Gardiner's 1903 edition of his *Commonwealth and Protectorate*, p. 294, note 1, who altered his own account after a discussion with Sir Charles Firth. Firth: *Cromwell*, 283, gives what seems to me the most probable explanation of this flank attack, namely that of the three regiments in reserve, Cromwell's, Pride's and Lambert's, only Lambert's (to which Hodgson was attached) was actually employed in support of Cromwell's regiment of horse and then only after the cavalry charge. Although Mr. Buchan: *Cromwell*, 378, appears to accept Gardiner's older version in which all three foot regiments were used against the Scottish horse, the movement seems so inconsistent with the rest of the military history of the civil war in which foot soldiers were never used to attack cavalry that I feel Dr. Gardiner's second version and Sir Charles Firth's version of what happened must be correct.

P. 178: The quotation about inactivity is given by Douglas from 'Mercurius Politicus' of June 10th.

Pp. 183-4: For Cromwell and Dunkirk see an article by Dr. Gardiner in the *English Historical Review*, XI, 1896.

P. 187: For the locked-door story and some interesting observations about Cromwell at this time see *Calendar of State Papers (Venetian)*, 1653-4, 63-5, also *English Historical Review*, 1893, 526.

P. 187: The Royalist newsletter is in *Calendar of State Papers, (Clarendon)* II, 200.

P. 188: For London after the dissolution of the Long Parliament see especially F. Guizot, *Oliver Cromwell and the Commonwealth* (English trans.) II, 11, etc., and other letters of Bordeaux, the French ambassador (e.g. on June 2nd, August 7th) in Record Office Transcripts 3/93-4.

Chapter IX: I owe a number of my quotations in this chapter to Mr. R. W. Ramsey's books on *Cromwell's Family Circle, Richard Cromwell and Henry Cromwell*. There is a description of Cromwell in 1656 by Sagredo the Venetian ambassador in *Calendar of State Papers (Venetian)*, 1655-6, 312, and in E. Momigliano, *Cromwell*, 264.

Pp. 194-5: The Maidstone quotation is in *Thurloe State Papers*, I, 766.

P. 196: The Duchess of Marlborough at any rate suspected her husband's faithfulness, see the letters in W. S. Churchill, *Marlborough*, II, 294-5.

P.197: Richard Cromwell's letter on his dislike of letter-writing is in the British Museum Lansdowne MSS. 821.

P. 198: The French ambassador's view of Richard and Henry Cromwell is in his report of October 12th, 1656 (Record Office Transcripts 3/100).

P. 201: For Henry Vane and the 'Heron' see J. Willcock, *Life of Henry Vane*.

P. 202: For Thurloe see Appendix A. It is Guizot who observed that 'Cromwell had no friends but his agents'.

P. 203: For Whitehall see E. Sheppard, *The Old Palace of Whitehall*, Chapter XVI.

P. 204: The Jeremy White story derives originally from J. Oldmixon: *History of England*, who said he had it confirmed by Mrs. White.

P. 206: The sack posset story is quoted by R. W. Ramsey: *Cromwell's Family Circle*, 179, from Harleian MSS. 991. The story is supposed to have come indirectly from one who was present.

Chapter X, p. 211: The merchant's quotation is from *The Merchant's Remonstrance* (1644).

Pp. 212-3: The Royalist quotations are from *Calendar of State Papers (Clarendon)*, 11,323, *seq*. 314.

P. 213: For Edmund Waller and his mother see G. Gilfillan: *Life of Edmund Waller*, VII.

P. 221: For Cromwell's foreign policy: S. Bischoffshausen: *Die Politik des Protectors Oliver Cromwell* who prints three versions of Thurloe's survey of foreign affairs; a fourth in the Record Office under State Papers (France) is identical with the version printed by Bischoffshausen from Stowe MSS.; J. Bowman: *The Protestant Interest in Cromwell's Foreign Relations*; G. Beer: 'Cromwell's Policy in its Economic Aspects', *Political Science Quarterly*, 1901-2; G. Jones: *The Diplomatic Relations between Cromwell and Charles X of Sweden*; W. Michael: *Cromwell*; H. Oncken: *Cromwell*. J. Bowman is the historian referred to on p. 245.

P. 225: For the West Indian expedition see Ashley: 133-7; F. Strong: 'Causes of Cromwell's West Indian Expedition' in the *American Historical Review* for 1898-9; A. P. Watts: *Les Colonies anglaises aux Antilles* (1924).

P. 227: The quotation from Cowley is in 'A Discourse by Way of a Vision' in *Essays and Plays* (ed. Waller), 367.

Chapter XI, pp. 233-39: My survey of Cromwell's financial policy and difficulties is based mainly upon my *Financial and Commercial Policy under the Cromwellian Protectorate*, Chapters IV-X. Since I wrote this I have found from the *Calendar of State Papers (Venetian)* that the exact sum Cromwell offered to present to the Exchequer in 1653 was £6000.

P. 240: For agriculture under the Protectorate see especially M. James: *Social Policy during the Puritan Revolution*, Chapter III, to which I owe the quotation of the Master of the Rolls (Burton's *Diary*, I, 175-6); E. C. K. Gonner: 'The Progress of Enclosure in the XVII Century' (*English Historical Review*, XXIII).

P. 241: For Cromwell and industry, see Ashley: 129. Mr. G. D. Ramsay of Merton College, Oxford, has had the courtesy to put his B.Litt. thesis on 'Government and Industry during the Protectorate of Oliver Cromwell' at my disposal. I owe to him the Matthew Hale quotation (T. Hardres: *Reports*, 53-5) and the reference to the Bible monopoly (H. R. Plomer: *A Short History of English Printing*, 74, 180-1, etc.).

P. 241-2: The 1655 sermon was published as *The Vanity and Mischief of Making Earthly Treasures our Chief Treasure, cit.* James, 18; *Short Notes on the Decay of Trade* (1662). For poverty during the Protectorate see E. M. Leonard: *English Poor Relief*, Chapter XIII; M. James: 271, 293, 295, 302; E. Lipson: *Economic History*, III, 254-5. Mr. Ramsay does not accept Miss James's view of 'the changed attitude to poverty which developed during the Interregnum' and stresses the provision of municipal workhouses and 'stocks'. I have given my reasons elsewhere for doubting the common view that there was much un-employment during the Protectorate (Ashley: 171, note 6).

P. 243: For the trading companies during the Protectorate see Ashley: Chapter XI.

P. 243-4: For law reform see W. S. Holdsworth: *History of English Law*, I, Chapters V and VI *passim*.

P. 244: The quotation is from D. Neal: *History of the Puritans*, II, 638, etc.

P. 246: For the controversy about the 1655 rising see articles by Sir R. Palgrave and Sir C. Firth in the *English Historical Review* of 1888 and 1889.

P. 250: For some interesting remarks about the alternatives before Cromwell in 1656 see *Calendar of State Papers (Venetian)*, 1655-6, 224-54.

P. 251: For Cromwell and the charters see the important article by B. L. K. Henderson in *Transactions of the Royal Historical Society* (1912), esp. page 142 from which I have taken the quotation about the Major-Generals.

Chapter XII: This chapter is based largely on W. K. Jordan: *The Development of Religious Toleration in England*, 1603-1640; W. A. Shaw: *A History of the English Church*; J. Tulloch: *Rational Theology*.

P. 265: The French ambassador's view of the English Catholics is taken from his report to Brienne of September 14th, 1656 (Record Office Transcripts 3/100).

P. 266: For the Quakers see especially W. Sewell: *History of the Quakers* (1711), who gives Thomas Aldan's remark to Cromwell; G. Fox: *Journal*; the 'fighting Quakers' are mentioned in *State Trials*, VI, 234.

P. 268: For the Jews in England see A. M. Hyamson: *The History of the Jews in England*; various articles by Lucien Wolf; Ashley: 2-3.

P. 269: For Hane and Blondeau, etc., see Ashley: 151-2 and references there cited.

P. 270: The quotation from Mun is in his *England's Treasure by Foreign Trade*, Chapter III.

P. 275: The letter to Henry Cromwell from Dr. Worth is in W. A. Shaw, II, 168.

Chapter XIII, p. 280: For the origins of the monarchy proposals see Firth: 'Cromwell and the Crown', *English Historical Review*, XVII and XVIII.

P. 283: For the Venetian ambassador's view of Cromwell's motives see his report of February 2, 1657, *Calendar* 1657-9, 12-13.

Pp. 283-4: For the Sindercombe conspiracy see *State Trials*, V, 842 *seq.*, and also *Calendar of State Papers (Venetian)*, 1657-9, 8-9.

P. 289: The quotation is from Whitelocke, *Memorials*, 647.

P. 290: For Cromwell's dinner with Desborough and Fleetwood see Ludlow, *Memoirs*, II, 24.

Chapter XIV, p. 295: For the description of Cromwell as careworn in January 1654 see *Calendar of State Papers (Venetian)* 1653-4, 177, and in 1656, E. Momigliano, *loc. cit.*

NOTES AND REFERENCES

P. 299: Thurloe's paper on the Dutch is in *English Historical Review*, XXI.

Pp. 300-1: The conversation with Broghill is in Morrice's 'Life of Orrery' (*Orrery State Letters*, I, 41-3).

P. 304: For Thurloe's letters see Appendix A.

P. 309: Captain Baynes's speech is in Burton's *Diary*, III, 147-8.

P. 310: Professor Laski's observation is in his *Grammar of Politics*, 49.

Chapter XV, p. 312: For Cromwell's financial difficulties in 1658 see Ashley, Chapter X, *Historical MSS. Commission*, 5th Report, 166.

P. 313: For Parliament see *Calendar of State Papers (Venetian)*, 1657-9, 172, etc. *Thurloe State Papers*, VII, 39, 99, etc.

P. 314, Bordeaux's statement was made on March 25th, 1658 (Record Office Transcripts, 3/102). For the evidence as to exaggeration see R. Palgrave: *Cromwell*, Chapter XIV.

P. 315: For Sir F. Russell's letter see Appendix A.

P. 317 *seq.*: For Cromwell and the empire see C. M. Andrews: *British Committees, Commissioners and Councils of Trade*; G. Beer: *Origins of British Colonial Policy*; Ashley: Chapter XII and works there cited.

P. 317: For Cromwell and the Board of Trade see Whitelocke: 630.

P. 319: There are detailed accounts of the Canadian negotiations in the French ambassador's dispatches; for India see Sir W. Hunter: *History of British India*; Sir W. Foster: *Court Minutes of the East India Company*; Ashley, *passim*.

P. 320: For Cromwell's reputation under Charles II, see S. Pepys: *Diary* (ed. Wheatley), II, 203, VII, 18; G. Burnet: *History of My Own Time* (ed. Airy), I, 139.

P. 322: Elizabeth Claypole's letter is in *Thurloe State Papers*, VII, 171.

Pp. 323-4: For the death of Cromwell see, *inter alia, Calendar of State Papers (Venetian)* 1657-9, 237-240; *Thurloe*, VII, 321, 355, 361, 364-5; *Clarke Papers*, III, 161; *A Collection of Several Passages* (1659); Culpepper to Hyde, September 20, 1658 (British Museum, Stowe MSS. 185, f. 133).

Pp. 325-6: For Cromwell's funeral and what happened to his head see K. Pearson and G. M. Morant, *Portraiture of Oliver Cromwell*; A. Cowley, 'A Discourse' *loc. cit.*; Ashley: 105. The Monk story is in *Historical MSS. Commission*, 5th Report, 166. For a discussion as to whether it was Cromwell's body that was buried in the Abbey see an article by W. W. Cooper in *Dublin Quarterly Journal of Medical Science*, V. 339.

INDEX

INDEX

INDEX

INDEX

Hane, Capt. Joachim, 269
Hanseatic League, 223
Harley, Sir Robert, 31-2
Harrington, James, 198
Harrison, Major-General Thomas, 178, 179, 184-5, 189, 210, 307; quoted, 210
Hartford, parsonage house at, 24
Haselrig, Sir Arthur, 62, 104, 173, 302, 303, 305, 331; quoted, 302.
'Heads of the Proposals' (1647), 129, 131, 134, 136, 138, 150, 160, 307, 308
Healing Question, The (1656), 252
Heligoland, Treaty of, 171
Henrietta Maria, Queen of England, 51, 54-5, 64, 142; attempt to impeach, 72
Henry V, King of England, 317
—— VII, King of England, 222
—— VIII, King of England, 13, 14, 28, 36, 131
Hertfordshire, 84
Hewitt, Dr. John, 315-6
Hewson, Capt., 188
High Churchmen, see Anglo-Catholics
—— Court of Justice, under Cromwell, 314-6, 321
Highlands, Scottish, 111
Hilsden House, 196
Hinchinbrooke nunnery and manor, 14, 16, 17, 18, 27, 38, 44, 57, 75
Hispaniola, see San Domingo
Hitler, Adolf, 7-8
Hobbes, Thomas, 310
Hodder Bridge, 147
Hodgson, Capt., quoted, 176, 205
Holborn, 141
Holborne, Robert, 69
Holdsworth, Dr., 70
Holland, 51, 94, 157, 158, 182, 183, 184, 186, 187, 190, 210, 212, 215, 221, 222, 223, 228, 229, 230, 231, 261, 269, 298, 299-301, 304, 313, 318, 319; war with England, 184, 211, 221, 222, 233
Holles, Denzil, 42-3; in Parliament of 1629, 66, 82; in Long Parliament, 104, 118, 124; Memoirs, quoted, 82
Holmby House, 121, 126, 127, 139
Hopton, Sir Ralph, 87, 115
Hounslow, 130, 271
House of Commons, see Commons
—— of Lords, see Lords
Howlett, Richard, 19
Huguenots, The, 39, 224, 228, 229, 254
Hull, 88
Humber, River, 88
'Humble Petition and Advice' (1657), 274, 286, 291, 292, 301, 302, 306, 307, 311
Huntingdon, charter, 43-4
—— Free or Grammar School, 16, 17, 18

Huntingdon, High Street, 17
—— Mayor of, 43-4, 65
—— Town, 14, 15, 24, 27, 34, 38, 42, 43, 44, 45, 46, 57, 58, 78, 88, 92
Huntingdonshire, 16, 25, 26, 84, 86, 111
Hurst Castle, 152
Hyde, Edward, later Earl of Clarendon, a Royalist leader, 66, 68-9; quoted 52, 53, 64, 66, 249, 314
—— Park, 217, 283

IMPEACHMENT, 27
Independents, 30, 94, 95, 115, 116, 119, 128, 130, 131, 132, 133, 139, 140, 143, 149, 151, 255, 258, 263, 271, 274, 275, 282; see also Congregationalism
India, see East India Company
Infantry, Roundhead, 91
Industry, 251, 270
'Instrument of Government' (1654), 208, 209, 210, 214, 216, 219, 232, 233, 234, 272, 273, 274, 278, 280, 287, 289, 307, 308
Ireland, rebellion of 1641, 69-70; Cromwell's campaign of 1649-50, 162-9; mentioned, 49, 50, 60, 69, 72, 121, 124, 125, 158, 171, 172, 177, 189, 198, 200, 210, 229, 232, 233, 240, 264, 300, 309, 320
Ireton, Major-General Henry, negotiates with King, 126-31; as a political thinker, 129, 136-8; draws up 'Remonstrance', 150-1; death, 184; marriage, 199; quoted, 136, 137; mentioned, 111, 113, 119, 124, 141-2, 143, 152, 160, 164, 197, 202, 307, 308
Ironsides, organization of, 89-92; mentioned, 109, 119, 292
Isle of Wight, 139, 140, 144, 150
Israel, Manasseh Ben, 268

JACOB, HENRY, 30, 93
Jamaica, 227, 268, 314
James I, reign of, 29, 31, 317; quoted, 37; mentioned, 15, 17, 20, 21, 37, 56, 209, 233, 238, 257, 261
Jephson, Major, 280, 282
Jersey, 169
Jews, under Cromwell, The, 268, 269, 270
Jones, Colonel Micheal, 162, 164, 168
Jordan, Dr. W. K., quoted, 257, 258
Joyce, Cornet, 126, 127

KILKENNY, TREATY OF, 163, 170; capture, 167, 168, 264, 265
Killing No Murder (1657), 300
Kineton, 79, 82; see also Edgehill
King's College, Cambridge, 77, 98
—— Lynn, 85, 88

346

INDEX

INDEX

349

INDEX

INDEX

William III, King of England, 210
Williams, Dr. John, Bishop of Lincoln, 46, 47
—— Katherine, great-great-grandmother of Oliver Cromwell, 14
—— Morgan, great-great-grandfather of Oliver Cromwell, 14
—— Richard, *see sub* Cromwell, Sir Richard
—— Roger, 226
Willoughby of Parham, Lord, 99
Wiltshire, 246
Winceby, Battle of, 88, 89
Winchester, 115
Windebank, Sir Francis, 54
Windsor, 86, 142, 152

Winnick, battle of, 148
Wither, George, quoted, 261
Wolfe, General, 90
Wolseley, Sir Charles, 290
Wolsey, Cardinal, 13-4
Wool, prices, 25
Worcester, 79, 82; battle, 179-181, 184, 324
Worthington, John, 259

YARRANTON, Andrew, 271
Yarmouth, 85
York, 49, 60, 83, 101; siege of, 100, 109
Yorkshire, 86, 87, 145, 147, 179
Youghal, 168